De-Introducing the New Testament

De-Introducing
the New Testament

Texts, Worlds, Methods, Stories

Todd Penner and Davina C. Lopez

WILEY Blackwell

Library of Congress Cataloging-in-Publication Data applied for

Hardback 9781405187688

A catalogue record for this book is available from the British Library.

Cover image: Exterior of the Bronx Borough Courthouse (built 1905–14). Architecture attributed to both Michael John Garvin and Oscar Florianus Bluemner; sculpture by Jules Edouard Roiné. Photo by Davina C. Lopez.

Set in 10/12pt Palatino by SPi Publisher Services, Pondicherry, India
Printed and bound in Malaysia by Vivar Printing Sdn Bhd

1   2015

"The world isn't made of atoms, it's made of stories."
Russell Brand

For
Niro
and Nicole

Contents

Contents

Acknowledgments

This is a book that raises critical questions about the stories we tell in the field of New Testament studies: stories about who we are as New Testament scholars, what it is we think we do in the discipline, on what terms, and to what ends. It is not an articulation of a "new" method for "introducing" the New Testament. Rather, we use the term "de-introducing" to denote a practice of excavating and unmasking the most basic categories and operative frameworks in the field so that we might better understand and appraise what discourses and relations of power are at work in the ways New Testament scholars do what they do, as well as how our material conditions shape those power relationships and discourses.

This project is a fully collaborative and co-authored endeavor that has its genesis in questions concerning methodology, as well as the history of New Testament studies on both sides of the Atlantic, to which we had each turned in our own individual work. We are each grateful for the opportunity to have thought through some of the seminal impulses of the present book in different contexts. Todd particularly appreciates memorable engagements at the International Society of Biblical Literature annual meetings, an invited session on Christian origins at the 2006 Westar Institute annual meeting, and invitations to deliver papers for the Redescribing Early Christianity seminar at the Society of Biblical Literature annual meetings (2008 and 2009). Davina highlights invitations to discuss methodological questions in the field at the Institute for History, Archaeology, and Education (2006), in the Teaching Religion section of the American Academy of Religion (2008 and 2009), and in the Nag Hammadi and Gnosticism (2008), Rhetoric and New Testament (2009), and *Journal of Feminist Studies in Religion* (2010) sections of the Society of Biblical Literature. Having the chance to work together at the 2008

Acknowledgments

"Empire: Resistance and Reimagination" conference at Union Theological Seminary in New York allowed us the time, and a timely topic, through which we could explore the ways in which our teaching and research agendas intersected. The decision to co-author a volume with a methodological orientation brought the many threads and trajectories in which we had each already been interested into critical conversation with one another. The "synthesis" offered here is the result of a truly dialectical and dialogical process.

As with the New Testament, portions of this book started life as "oral tradition," in the form of academic presentations. We thank the following individuals and program units of the Society of Biblical Literature for providing a scholarly venue through which to discuss and deliberate various methodological issues and questions related to (de-)introducing the New Testament: Edmondo Lupieri and the Construction of Christian Identities seminar (2010), Colleen Conway and the Jesus, Gospels, and Negotiating the Roman Imperial World section (2012), and Greg Carey and the Rhetoric and New Testament section (2011 and 2013). We are also fortunate to have presented this work, in much earlier iterations, at various public forums. These include an installment of the Friends of the Burke Library lecture series at Union Theological Seminary (2011), and we thank the Friends, especially Mim Warden, for their hospitality. We are also grateful to Whitney Bauman for the invitation to present our work as part of the Religion and International Affairs lecture series at Florida International University (2011). We additionally had an opportunity to explore and discuss some of the ideas and themes in this book as part of the Burchenal lecture series at Eckerd College (2012) and the Class of 1956 Chair in New Testament lecture series at the College of the Holy Cross (2013). Our interactions with the audiences on each of these occasions have assisted in the production of this book in its current form.

Exceptional thanks are due to the staff at Columbia University's Burke Library at Union Theological Seminary, where we had the distinct pleasure of serving as scholars-in-residence during the summers of 2010 and 2011, and where we have continued to conduct research for this and other projects since then. During our first stay at the Burke, then-students Lauren Bridge and Megan Freda (Eckerd College) and Genny Richard (Austin College) provided research assistance, and notably helped us to reflect on the interconnectedness of teaching and research in New Testament studies. John Weaver, then at the Burke and now Dean of Library Services and Educational Technology at Abilene Christian University, enthusiastically encouraged our investigations into the history of New Testament scholarship in the United States, and provided significant support so that we could do so with the Burke's extensive holdings. We are also grateful for John's informal interactions with us during the summer of 2010 on diverse topics related to our research, as we learned a great deal from his insights. Betty Bolden assisted us with our every request over multiple visits. Ruth Tonkiss Cameron provided guidance with at times difficult archival finding aids and subject guides. Beth Bidlack, now the Director of the Burke Library and Professor of Theological Librarianship at Union Theological Seminary, has been most welcoming and accommodating of both our love of libraries and our commitment to old books (and old biblical scholars).

Eckerd College and Austin College have shaped us as biblical scholars and teachers in the liberal arts tradition, and we trust that one of the core values of the liberal arts – to capacity to make connections – comes through in these chapters. Our guest-teaching and co-teaching in each other's class-rooms over the past few years have nurtured the collaborative spirit that we practice throughout this volume. Davina is grateful to the Lloyd W. Chapin Faculty Development Program at Eckerd, which provided generous funding toward archival research on New Testament introductory textbooks for this project during the summer of 2011. The Ford Apprentice Scholarship Program also provided research funding and support in 2010 and 2013, as well as enabled work with capable students who have felt something of a call to academia. We give thanks to President Donald R. Eastman III, Vice President for Academic Affairs and Dean of Faculty Suzan Harrison, Associate Dean for Faculty Development Kathy Watson, and Dean Betty H. Stewart, now of Midwestern State University. Doug McMahon, Director of Eckerd's Center for Spiritual Life and Chaplain, has nurtured critical space and jovial conversation about this project and about matters related to teaching the Bible across vocational affiliations, and has been a good friend and a warm host to us. Todd is grateful for the generous support that Austin College provided over the course of this project. Funding for summer research was invaluable, and came through both the Sid Richardson Fund and a W. M. Keck Foundation grant, the latter of which was for the project "Scientific Method and the Rise of Modern Biblical Criticism." A generous sabbatical travel fellowship for the spring of 2013 was instrumental, as was funding from Austin College's Lemuel Scarborough, Jr., Summer Research Program in the Humanities and Social Sciences, which supported collabora-tive faculty-undergraduate research in the Burke Library during the summer of 2010. Generous travel support for the summer of 2014 was also provided by the Mellon Course Partnerships Program. Special thanks are due to Vice President for Academic Affairs Michael Imhoff, Humanities Dean Patrick Duffey, and Mellon Program Director Bernice Melvin for their support.

We are most privileged to have enjoyed conversations over the contours and controversies in biblical scholarship, and the study of religion more broadly, with the following esteemed colleagues, each of whom has con-tributed in their own way to this project: Eugene Gallagher, Neil Elliott,

Acknowledgments

Bill Arnal, Jacques Berlinerblau, James Crossley, Milton Moreland, Susanne Scholz, Benny Liew, Joseph Marchal, Ward Blanton, Caroline Vander Stichele, Anders Runesson, René Falkenberg, Halvor Moxnes, Elizabeth Clark, Dale Martin, Hal Taussig, Tom Olbricht, David Carr, Colleen Conway, Bart Ehrman, Julia O'Brien, Steed Davidson, James Aitken, Daniele Pevarello, Lillian Larsen, Barry Matlock, Juan Hernández Jr., Patricia O'Connell Killen, Suzanne Watts Henderson, Cass Fisher, Mark Given, Bradley Herling, Sean Adams, Laura Brenneman, Ruth Cape, Bill Felice, Heather Vincent, Jared Stark, and David Bryant. Todd would also like to express his appreciation to Jacqueline Klassen for her support over the years. Davina recognizes the companionship of her "old lady," Blossom the Boston terrier, who is a model of diligence and tenacity. Special thanks to Al Germann, whose hands appear in this work in unexpected ways. Moreover, we are deeply grateful for the friendship of Helmar Nielsen, whose enthusiasm for our field's work is inspiring and most reassuring, and who always prods us to know more about, and do better by, the transformative potential of biblical scholarship in the context of the high (perhaps even higher) calling of liberal arts education.

Andrew Humphries was the initial Blackwell editor for this volume, and was incredibly enthusiastic when the project first took flight. Our first conversation about this book took place in 2006. We are grateful to the five anonymous reviewers of the original proposal who provided substantive feedback that helped shape the final form of the project. Rebecca Harkin assumed oversight and spurred us on. Isobel Bainton, Bridget Jennings, and Sally Cooper were also on board over the course of time. Georgina Coleby, our editorial contact in the final drafting stages of this project, was supremely supportive and encouraging. We cannot thank Georgina enough for her persistence and patience, which ultimately were formative in seeing this book through to completion. She responded to our every inquiry with efficiency and grace until the "last days" of this project, and we wish her well in her new publishing (ad)venture. Ben Thatcher and Lisa Sharp ensured a smooth production process. We are indebted to Sandeep Kumar and the capable staff at SPi Global, and we are especially grateful to Janet Moth for her keen editorial eye. And thanks are due to Beth White, Eckerd College Class of 2015, who helped compile the index.

Niro Lopez and Nicole Penner-Horodyski, our younger siblings, have taught us much over the course of our lives together. Stories have their roots in human relationships and interactions, and there are many stories here that could be told, some inspiring and others less so. There is no doubt, however, that all have been learning occasions and opportunities for growth, all of which continue into the future. It is out of our immense appreciation for all we have learned over the years in interacting with our younger siblings that we have come to dedicate this book to them. May we reflect back on the older stories as we look forward to creating new ones in the years ahead.

(De-)Introduction

Seeing Old Stones Anew

The woman in stone pictured on the cover of this book occupies an important spatial and temporal intersection in the Bronx borough of New York City. The image is that of a large statue of Lady Justice that adorns the front of an imposing neoclassical building. This building, the former Bronx Borough Courthouse, is an icon of the South Bronx and sits on a plaza where several main thoroughfares converge. During the early 20th century, following the consolidation of five boroughs into the City of New York, there was a push to build municipal structures that would reflect the grandeur and cosmopolitanism of this most "civilized" of American cities. Completed in 1914 amidst bickering between architects, corruption charges, and construction delays, the Bronx Borough Courthouse was at the time the most majestic structure in that borough, and yet it was not the courthouse for long. As the largely immigrant population in the Bronx swelled to more than a million people, the demand for "law" was more than this particular Lady Justice could handle and a new courthouse was erected nearby in 1934. The Bronx Borough Courthouse continued to serve as "auxiliary" chambers until 1977, when it was boarded up by the City. Since then, this building has been sold to a private real-estate investor who apparently has long refused to either tear it down (which would be a challenge since the building is landmarked) or render it usable to the residents of the South Bronx again. For the

De-Introducing the New Testament: Texts, Worlds, Methods, Stories, First Edition.
Todd Penner and Davina C. Lopez.
© 2015 Todd Penner and Davina C. Lopez. Published 2015 by John Wiley & Sons, Ltd.

moment, Lady Justice is enthroned atop a fenced-in façade. Adorned with her usual attributes, as well as with graffiti and pigeon roosts, she watches over one of the poorest neighborhoods in the United States.

To some, this image is just of an old building in disrepair, and nothing more. If we look at little closer, though (Figure I.1), we might notice something else, we might ask some larger questions, and we might make some connections between this particular image and others in our culture. The figure of Justice as depicted here is part of a long history of representing personifications of virtues as female bodies, and sometimes goddesses, a tradition that goes all the way back to the ancient world, including the world of the New Testament. Lady Justice has been used to signify a particular kind of project in humanity and the humanities: she stands for morality, order, and righteousness. This image of Lady Justice is very much contextualized. Like the New Testament in terms of Western culture, the figure of Justice is a classic icon that has appeared over a long period of time. She is everywhere on courthouses, in the night sky (as the constellation Virgo), and in popular culture, and yet it is easy to overlook her or to relegate her importance to law alone. Indeed, Justice carries the weight of tradition, which is historical and value-laden.

Figure I.1 Detail of Lady Justice, exterior of the Bronx Borough Courthouse (built 1905–14), Bronx, New York. Architecture attributed to both Michael John Garvin and Oscar Florianus Bluemner; sculpture Jules Edouard Roiné. Photo by Davina C. Lopez.

And yet we are compelled to look twice at this particular image in the Bronx, for Justice here is deconstructed by what seems to be a real invasion – the graffiti. But the graffiti is also now part of the image: who is to say it does not belong? It would not be a stretch to speculate that many people would be horrified at the desecration of this statue. But what would that say about the viewers' assumptions? The building has been empty for nearly 40 years – could we reasonably expect it to remain pristine? Likewise, it would be easy to suggest that the markings actually mar the image of Justice, implying that people desecrated the statue, not knowing or respecting her or that for which she stands. However, such a view would also ignore the machinery and conditions – poverty, abandonment, municipal and bureaucratic negligence – that helped nurture the physical space that made the graffiti possible in the first place. The artists might be called "vandals" and "criminals" – but in some way the street drawings bring Justice "home" and welcome her to the realities of the neighborhood. There would be some resistance to this particular reading since Justice still holds weight – or she should – as a guarantor of what is good and right and lawful. But we find ourselves wondering, as we dwell on this image: is Justice *betrayed* by these marks, or is she *liberated*?

The presence of graffiti, which is thought to be lawless and thoughtless, creates a tension in this image of lawful, thoughtful Lady Justice. What are we to make of such a venerable figure being both desecrated and appropriated at the same time? Is this a dismissal of something old or the creation of a new image altogether? How would we know the difference? Certainly the tension created between the revered image and its more recent appropriation generates a space for critical reflection on a host of issues related to the intersection of the past and the present, and the assumptions and expectations we hold with respect to both. As with Lady Justice, so also with the study of the New Testament. In this book we aim to "tag" and decenter several current methodological claims made about, and trajectories followed in, the discipline of New Testament studies, itself a venerable icon of sorts. We are calling our exploration "de-introducing" the New Testament, which acknowledges the ancient texts and modern disciplinary formation as important sites for the articulation of identity, power relationships, and questions about the connections we want to cultivate with the past. The stories we tell about our field, particularly in the context of explaining it via "introducing" the New Testament, also provide occasion for reflection on what we take for granted in terms of categories and methods. In so doing, we will look again at what we think we know, and articulate some themes and questions about the study of the New Testament that we hope will provide an occasion for further consideration and conversation, particularly with respect to methodology in the study of early Christian history

3

and literature. In our view, thinking about not just *what* we do as New Testament scholars, but *how* and *why* we do it, and what difference it makes, matters a great deal, and these sentiments undergird this book. If the New Testament and the study thereof stand on the side of Lady Justice in this configuration, our current book is something akin to the graffiti. However, by this we intend no disrespect, but hope, rather, to open up a space for examining the intersection between the past and present, and particularly the deeply rooted interconnectedness of the two. In so doing, we understand that the venerable tradition might well gain renewed vitality, imagining a different kind of future in the process.

Introducing the New Testament as Introducing Traditional New Testament Scholarship

In order to articulate more fully what exactly it is we mean by "de-introducing" the New Testament, and why we think it might help us gain renewed vitality in the field, we will attend briefly to what could readily be conceived of as its semantic opposite: that is, "introducing" the New Testament. Obviously one rather large area to engage here is a genre of introductory materials, namely textbooks, that are put to service in pedagogical contexts claiming to "introduce" students to the New Testament and early Christian literature. This is no small matter, as the most popular (as in, most often taught) undergraduate religion course in the United States is, and has been for some time, the introductory Bible course – either Old Testament, New Testament, or, as is increasingly the case, the one-semester "Introduction to the Bible." Accordingly, there is a substantial niche of the publishing industry devoted to the production of introductory Bible and New Testament textbooks (not to mention "handbooks" and "guides" and other hybrid introductory reference works). These books are thought to make a profit due to their "relevance" for teaching, e.g. their ready-made customer base of students taking courses that use introductory materials. Indeed, the landscape of the field is shaped by the proliferation of such materials in the academic marketplace.

We should note that we both have extensive experience teaching under-graduates at small, private liberal arts colleges in the United States, and as such are quite familiar with the introductory Bible course and its textual apparatuses. We have not had the luxury of working with graduate teaching assistants, so we are subject to a rich array of direct experiences with undergraduate students and their understandings of what it is that is going on in the classroom. We do not object to introductory textbooks as such, and we have used introductory textbooks and see their value inside the class-room. At the same time, as we will discuss in this book, New Testament scholarship – indeed, biblical scholarship as a whole – is likely one of the more opaque and misunderstood disciplines in the higher-educational landscape, especially among undergraduate students. We can say that the majority of our students come to our courses with some measure of familiarity with, and piety, trepidation, and/or skepticism about, the Bible, for they have an idea that it is an "important book" in some way. They might have questions that they cannot yet fully articulate, or they might want to "dive deeper" into the material they hold so dear. For the most part, though, these students certainly do not expect to be introduced to biblical scholarship as an academic discipline when they sign up for a "bible class," and many of our own students would say they had no idea, before taking such courses, that something called a "biblical scholar" exists. And yet the uncritical presentation of biblical scholarship is, for the most part, the predominant direction in which introductory textbooks are slanted. Why that might be the case, and what difference it makes to organize "introducing" in that way, is, to us, an enduring question of our field and the humanities as a whole.

The introductory New Testament textbook serves as a means to introduce to readers not only the texts of the New Testament themselves – although the rhetoric of textbooks might argue otherwise – but also, if not primarily, the academic discipline of New Testament studies. Contemporary introductory textbooks tend to be presented in such a manner that New Testament scholarship is mentioned in a surface-level way throughout the work. Textbooks might attend to the chronology, backgrounds, and sources of the New Testament writings, which will affect how material is organized. While not all introductory textbooks are the same from cover to cover, we do note some structural similarities in terms of how these books reflect the norms of the discipline. An introduction that claims to be "historical," for example, will often start with a discussion of Jewish and Greco-Roman backgrounds as well as the "world" and person of Jesus before the canonical New Testament texts are explored. An argument for organizing the material this way in an introductory textbook is that "context matters," without a discussion of how scholars arrive at decisions as to what to include, and not include, in contextual considerations in the first place. Presenting material in an historical framework, of course, suggests a different orientation than the canonical organization of the New Testament texts themselves.

Similarly, an introductory textbook might include a cursory discussion of the two-source theory concerning the formation of the Gospels, canon formation, or the Pauline epistles, without going into great detail about the live and unsettled debates in scholarship about any of those issues. An introduction to the New Testament could include photos of archaeological objects and sites, suggesting that material culture is important for understanding the texts, without helping readers understand how exactly that came to be the case or what is at stake in working with objects. Although the author of an introductory textbook may provide an introductory essay written in the first person that could explain his or her own interest in and/or ideological positioning vis-à-vis the material, the author's "voice" largely disappears as the textbook progresses, giving the illusion of "objectivity" in the presentation of information. These maneuvers are methodologically significant, they have their own histories as part of larger discourses, and yet they are rarely explained to new initiates beyond statements that ancient contexts are important for understanding how these ancient New Testament texts came to be, and what significance they might have had in the ancient world that produced what we now call "Christianity."

A cursory survey of introductory textbooks in, say, Germany and the United States over the last century will reveal some measure of diversity in terms of organization, orientation, and outlook. In our estimation, a commonality that books in this genre share is that they serve a largely contradictory function in relation to their audiences in their own historical and social contexts. That is, textbooks serve as a means to introduce readers to a collection of texts that in many ways needs no introduction. The Bible is, and long has been, a foundational text, object, and fetish of people across time, appropriated and re-appropriated throughout history and across cultures for various ends. The "religious" or "theological" appropriation of the New Testament is also a popular use. Even as ecclesiastical structures constitute an important piece of the interpretive landscape, those structures do not have a monopoly on meaning-making by any stretch of the imagination. In the United States, some aspect of the New Testament and related literature – be it the characters of Jesus, Paul, or the apostles, the sayings of the Gospels or letters, the "rapturous" events of Revelation, or the "forbidden" texts that did not make it into the canon – is invoked regularly in the media, in public debates, in advertising, literature, and other cultural forms, well beyond church boundaries. The New Testament is, in some respect, a cultural apparatus of its own, deployed both as a catalyst for culture-making and a means of understanding culture itself. The New Testament is the site of much cultural production and argumentation – to be sure, not about the ancients, but about us: who we are, where we came from, and who we ought to be together. And yet introducing the New Testament is an introduction to disciplinary formation through purportedly attending almost exclusively to the ancient world that produced the New Testament texts and canon.

Further, no matter the thematic accent – whether historical, literary, or theological – the rhetoric of the New Testament textbook assumes either a certain kind of previous engagement with texts on the part of the reader or no engagement at all. The problem, of course, is that in the United States it is extremely difficult to find oneself in a situation where one would have had no exposure to the New Testament. People may not have read the texts or be "biblically literate," but they are the heirs to the complex legacies and afterlives of the New Testament – even if unwittingly – through its deployment as Christian scripture. Readers who pick up an introductory textbook or enroll in an introductory course in New Testament are not "blank slates" – at least, not as far as the basic idea that the New Testament is somehow important in culture. Another primary assumption of introducing the New Testament is that the texts, and their ancient contexts, are interesting, relevant, and useful to the reader. Even if the implied audience of an introduction to the New Testament has never read the texts (which actually applies to "believers" and "non-believers" alike), the case can still be made for an introduction: after all, the New Testament is prominent as a foundational text of Western civilization.

That said, introducing the New Testament through introducing the field of New Testament studies serves as a means for readers to unlearn whatever it is that they have "brought" to the material, or at least become aware that their learning does not represent the only available position on the texts. If a reader learned the New Testament in the context of an ecclesial community, then "introducing" the New Testament might involve learning a different, non-faith-based, viewpoint and framework for interpretation. An embedded assumption common to an "historical" introduction to the New Testament is that the student has already been "introduced" to the texts – that such an introduction has occurred, before the introductory course and textbook are encountered, in a setting and framework that are more conducive to theological agendas and patterns of faith-based or spiritual engagement – that is, in explicit relation to a Christian church community or individual religious experience. The implied audience of the introductory New Testament textbook, then, is that which has had a prior relationship with the texts, perhaps in an explicitly "religious" way that is more concerned with faith than facts. Thus, the "historical" agenda in introducing the New Testament is itself a de-introductory project of its own in that it comprises an unlearning of theological ways of reading through an introduction to historical ways of reading. However, the same could be said for any position that a student might bring to the material: "introducing" the New Testament is a signifier for challenging and evaluating one's assumptions through encountering a different view.

What, then, does it mean to "introduce" the New Testament if everyone already has an idea of what that is, but also has no idea? According to the logic of the introductory textbook (and, by extension, the introductory course), it means to orient students to the texts through learning the rather traditional procedures, methods, and conclusions of the field, which are presented without critical reflection as that which is the way to be "introduced" to the texts, contexts, and histories of interpretation. That is to say, scholars who participate in "introducing" the New Testament might be well aware of its enduring status in culture, and yet persist in maintaining that the best way to introduce the New Testament is through extensive attention to the ancient contexts in which the texts and traditions originated, which in the language of the discipline is called a "historical-critical" approach. It is the historical-critical study of the New Testament that is positioned as that which must be learned against the unlearning that students must do so that they might be properly "introduced" to the texts. In this schema, the New Testament must be studied historically if it is to be understood correctly, historical criticism must be consistent with "scientific" and systematic methodology, and engaging the New Testament through historical criticism should precede efforts to make the texts relevant or meaningful in the present. In introducing the New Testament, the field is presented as stable, fixed, and isolated from the history of ideas and the humanities more broadly. Delineating and stabilizing the categories of the field is almost a prerequisite for introducing the New Testament, irrespective of what the audience brings to the material.

Aside from serving as introductions to the study of the New Testament through various issues in the discipline, introductory textbooks also implicitly assist in narrating the field as that which is concerned with the ancient world alone – concerned with authorial intent, for example, or with the sources, occasions, and meanings for the texts in the first century CE. This traditional way that the New Testament is introduced through the classroom and textbooks is not without criticism. As we have already mentioned, there inheres a potent disconnect between contemporary orientations to the New Testament and the focus on the ancient world characteristic of introductory materials. In some way, this apparent contradiction between historical-critical introductory materials and the orientation of the reader and audience is symptomatic of a long-standing tension in New Testament scholarship between historical criticism and newer approaches aligned with literary criticism, social-scientific approaches, or methods that front the social locations and identities of readers and interpreters. While these tensions may not always be addressed in introductory New Testament materials and courses, they are certainly alive in the discipline. Whether the ancient or modern world should be emphasized in the study of the New Testament is a core question with no easy solution or professional consensus. Nevertheless, criticisms of historical criticism persist, and we will sketch below, in broad strokes, the contours of such criticisms as well as the difference they might make for a project that claims to "de-introduce" the New Testament such as this one.

Introducing Criticisms of Traditional New Testament Scholarship

"Historical criticism" enjoys a long and complex history as the foundational orientation of the discipline of New Testament studies. In the broadest possible sense, historical criticism is less a method on its own and more a catch-all term for a range of approaches to biblical interpretation that focus on attempting to understand ancient texts in their original historical, literary, cultural, and political contexts, according to, as far as it is possible to discern, the standards, norms, and values of the time in which those texts were produced. The hallmark of historical criticism, in our view, lies in cultivating an understanding that ancient texts meant something quite different in those worlds than they do and have in other worlds, which points to a basic sentiment that meaning changes across time and cultures. Moreover, reconstructions of ancient worlds and meanings are much more provisional and partial than universal and totalizing. In a best-case scenario, historical criticism should yield important "de-introducing" questions of its own about how meaning and purpose are never fixed, stable, or universal, showing in the process that biblical texts are not the sole property of contemporary apparatuses of power such as the church or state.[1] In much contemporary rhetoric about the field, however, historical criticism serves as an important signifier when discussing the state of methodological development and engagement. Critics of this most basic approach in biblical scholarship tend to characterize it within an oppositional framework. Depending on the position taken with respect to historical criticism, it is deployed as a cipher for what is wrong with the field, or what is right with it – what must be overcome, or what must be preserved – in order for the study of the New Testament, Christian origins, and early Christian literature to proceed.

There are many criticisms of historical criticism that rely on arguing that it represents the dominant and traditional way of doing things that scholars would do well to challenge, resist, and overcome. Let us be clearer about the contours of these conversations through thinking about some contemporary characterizations of biblical studies by its professional practitioners. We will note here that the contemporary landscape of biblical studies is rhetorically configured in such a way as to consist of a tension and dichotomy between "historical criticism" and "everything else." We find ourselves interested in the discursive configuration of the complex of approaches to biblical studies called "historical criticism" by both proponents and detractors, although here we focus on the latter. We highlight here two main and interrelated tropes in such discussions: the assumed consolidation and control of meaning by biblical scholars who use historical criticism, and historical

9

criticism's purported denial of the contours of identity and social location among readers and interpreters.

A central trope of narratives about the history of biblical scholarship that seek to engage the "status quo" is that the discipline can be divided into a universalizing, monolithic, "traditional" historical-critical past and a particularizing, pluralistic, less traditional present and future. As John Collins has noted, "it is not unusual to narrate the history of biblical scholarship as a succession of methods, each of which initially exhibited its anxiety of influence by attempting to kill its father, and whose fathers sometimes disowned the offspring."[2] One major shift that is often noted is due to the so-called linguistic turn in the humanities and social sciences, the effects of which saw a tension between "historical" and "literary" approaches to biblical texts and traditions.[3] Proponents of newer, less "traditional" approaches accuse historical criticism and its proponents, in the past and in the present, of being overly concerned with the text at the expense of the reader, and empirically and imperially inclined by way of being scientistic, objective, falsely value-neutral, and so on. By great contrast to the singularity of historical criticism, a plurality of approaches that privilege other matters than those of the ancients is positioned as "making progress" or that which breaks from "traditional" ways of doing things by attending to the plurality of meanings, the "real readers" of texts, and the subjectivity of scholarship.

A chief complaint about historical criticism claims that by focusing on the origins and orientations of biblical texts in the ancient world the range of possible meanings in the present is limited. The expert biblical scholar then becomes the sole mediator and guarantor of meaning, as opposed to churches, other institutions, scholars who might want to use different (e.g. literary) approaches, or ordinary people who read biblical texts in non-scholarly circumstances. Indeed, we note that a primary anxiety about historical-critical discourse among its contemporary critics is that it represents the promotion of a singularity of meaning that can only be produced, controlled, and disseminated by biblical scholars. As Stephen Moore and Yvonne Sherwood have put it,

> the emergent science of biblical criticism was designed precisely to ward off a plurality of meaning, and hence a plurality of readers, by identifying the true meaning, and making specialist scholars its official guardians ... [p]rofessionalized philological method emerged as the touchstone and guarantor of valid biblical meaning. Biblical scholarship became a discipline that was narrowly specific in terms of the meaning that could legitimately be attributed to the biblical text, but diffuse in terms of the methods that could legitimately be utilized to mine and refine that meaning.[4]

For Moore and Sherwood, the issue seems to be that the increased specialization of biblical scholarship and its emergence as a disciplinary formation served to foreclose on who could access and read biblical texts as well as what they could say about those texts. With the invention of "the biblical scholar" as an interpretive entity and subject position, an elite class of readers and meaning-makers was established. To some, this has functioned as a means to produce a univocal, authoritative, "true" scholarly reading and meaning that prevents the proliferation of multiple readings and meanings. Of course, the rhetoric of "identifying the true meaning" has a history grounded in the articulation of biblical criticism as an epistemological framework separate from, and resistant to, ecclesiastical authority in the specific context of Enlightenment-era Europe, and particularly Germany. The meaning that historical analysis yielded was "true" as opposed to the "true" meaning that church tradition, especially through dogmatics and doctrine, had long maintained to the exclusion of other meanings.

Thus, while doing history in other disciplines might take for granted the contextualization of texts and traditions, the history of historical criticism as a means of examining biblical texts has always been in tension with ecclesiastical hierarchies and mechanisms of authority and control, which in Europe were bound up with the nation-state. These debates were not without consequences. In the United States, early historical critics who trained in Germany and argued for biblical interpretation that was free from ecclesiastical control could lose their academic posts and, in some cases, be tried for heresy by denominational bodies. The tension between scholarly and ecclesiastical authorities persists. In some cases this tension precipitates the charge that biblical scholars "control" meaning – which hurts the church in the end, since the biblical texts are, as Roy Harrisville and Walter Sundberg claim,

> remote from the concerns of contemporary life. In this perspective, biblical interpretation tends to be treated as a forbiddingly difficult attempt to find a way to leap across the great chasm of time that separates the present from the biblical era. The enormous effort thought to be required for this dampens the traditional Christian habit of reading the Bible spontaneously and experiencing one's life directly mirrored in its pages.[5]

We note that Harrisville and Sundberg come to biblical scholarship from different ideological orientations and inclinations than Moore and Sherwood, and the latter duo may not claim that historical criticism has caused a "serious and recurring problem" for theology and an "intellectual and spiritual agony" for the life of the church.[6] Yet both sets of scholars have characterized historical criticism in similar terms: it is a tool that biblical scholars use to "control" meaning and to remove biblical texts from ordinary, contemporary (Christian) readers by fronting a concern with history, and with the ancient world in particular. In both cases, the predominant concern appears to be that historical criticism is a means by which biblical texts are "taken" from the hands of non-specialists – importantly, theologians – and placed under the "exclusive" care of a new class of expert.

Closely related to the claim that historical criticism is a method that is used to help biblical scholars exact exclusive control over biblical texts and their meanings is the claim that historical criticism, as "objective" scholarship, fosters and encourages a "hegemonic" view that reifies its position as value-free. Further, in this schema historical criticism becomes a "colonial" tool that denies the possibilities for non-dominant-culture identification and meaning-making. According to some critics, biblical scholarship in its traditional forms lacks self-reflexivity on its own positionality and participates in the "silencing" of minority voices. Elisabeth Schüssler Fiorenza, for example, has long argued that biblical studies must attend to its "margins," rather than its "center," in order to become relevant, stating that

> only if biblical studies relinquishes its posture of value neutrality and claims of scientific status, will it be able to turn into full-fledged critical rhetorical studies. Only if it moves out of its academic ivory tower and becomes a publicly responsible discourse, will biblical scholarship be able to recognize the voices from the margins and those submerged by the kyriocentric records of biblical and contemporary hegemonic texts.[7]

For Schüssler Fiorenza, a "full-fledged critical rhetorical studies," as opposed to traditional biblical studies, is part of a "rhetorical-emancipatory" paradigm that is necessarily informed by critical feminist theory and praxis.[8] Such a paradigm attends to the rhetorical effects and ideological contours of biblical discourses, as well as the discourses of biblical scholarship. Unlike historical criticism, which is positioned as hiding its own rhetorical dimensions and not being all that interested in liberation or justice, critical rhetorical studies is invested in the well-being of all people, and as such attempts to cultivate all voices in struggles against domination.

One antidote to the traditionalism that historical criticism is thought to represent lies in the proliferation of different identity-based criticisms – feminist, queer, postcolonial, African American, "cultural," and so on. Proponents of these criticisms tend to characterize the field in a linear, developmental manner, moving from "old" value-neutrality and dominant identity formation to "new" paradigms that privilege the social locatedness of interpreters as driving the meaning-making process as far as biblical texts are concerned. Herein biblical scholarship is narrated as proceeding in stages, with each stage across time dismissing and/or improving upon the previous one. Each group that desires to participate in biblical interpretation, then, will propose a reading that takes the identity and experience of the group seriously as a source of knowledge and power, rather than adhere to the Enlightenment-era rationalistic, elitist, positivistic antiquarianism of historical criticism. In fact, reading from a specific social location has become a hallmark of biblical scholarship that seeks to challenge the "hegemony" of historical criticism and its implied universal (male, European, heterosexual) subject. Again, biblical scholars who use historical criticism are the target for the charge of forced singularity and domination, and the use of social location in biblical scholarship serves as a way to suggest that, contrary to how traditional scholarship might be presented, it is not actually without values, perspectives, or ideologies of its own.

As far as some critics are concerned, then, historical criticism is thus positioned as a methodological tool that both hides its own positionality and potentially shapes, even denigrates, the positionalities of others. It is linked to a dominant "center" of biblical scholarship that is opposed to the "margins," both in terms of method and identity. And when "imported" from one social location to another via pedagogies of biblical studies, historical criticism, which developed in the context of European imperial and colonial prowess, can serve as a colonial "civilizing" tool of its own. As R. S. Sugirtharajah has stated,

> The greatest damage that historical-criticism did was … making the contents of the Bible look primitive and uncouth alongside the march of modern progress. In the stages of human development and human thought, biblical narratives came to be seen as the literary product of tribal people and uncivilized times. As seen from the urbane, romantic and humane eighteenth-century Western perspective, the biblical myths and morality looked crude and in need of refinement and civilization.[9]

As the Bible, and then historical-critical biblical scholarship, were brought to theological classrooms in India, Sugirtharajah notes that the colonial assumption that the indigenous population was less civilized was implicitly supported by biblical scholarship that used historical analysis to determine the developmental stages of biblical literature: "[w]hereas in the West [the Bible's] poetic images were seen as a pure and lofty form of spiritual aesthetics, in India the biblical images were seen as a way of exposing the spiritual inadequacies of Indians, and, as such, a vehicle for eventual conversion."[10] Accordingly, the indigenous Indian population, as the orientalized "other," was perceived as in need of education and civilization, on the one hand, and incapable of higher-order thought, on the other.[11] Through colonial (re-)education, those who received theological training absorbed and inhabited an identitarian space defined by expatriate colonizers who were aided by the tools of historical criticism. While the particulars might change, the basic structure – that is, that historical criticism is a tool that helps to position those on the margins as "others" who must learn the dominant ways of (European) knowing and thus assimilate in some way into dominant culture – can be traced throughout narratives of the field as articulated by critics of "dominant" biblical scholarship.

Thus far we have been concerned with a major tension in biblical scholarship that can often be obscured by the ways that "introducing" the New Testament might occur, at least as presented in much introductory material. That tension can perhaps be summarized by the question of whether, and to what ends, we might interpret biblical texts: by starting with the ancient historical context in which the texts were produced, or by starting with our own contemporary situation in which the texts survive and are deployed. We empathize with these difficult methodological issues, and are well aware of the ways in which power has been exerted in the name of the Bible and biblical scholarship. We are also keenly aware that a primary reason to investigate the ancient world of the New Testament is that the texts are of critical importance to understanding many aspects, religious and non-religious, of contemporary culture. We do find that attention to contemporary issues, balanced with attention to the ancient world, works well in our classrooms, even as introductory textbooks may not explicitly "go there" in terms of contemporary questions and concerns.

That said, in terms of the conceptualization and rhetoric of the field itself, we are not convinced that an "either-or" approach works when it comes to introducing the study of the New Testament. We should be clear that we would not deny that there are significant methodological questions and difficulties that historical criticism poses for the present. As is the case in our context, earlier scholars who developed historical criticism were doing so at least partially in response to the world in which they were situated. Nevertheless, the tension we have been describing in the discourse of the field is fraught with a persistent series of conceptual binaries that place historical criticism – the basic mode of conducting biblical scholarship wherein texts are placed in their historical contexts – in a largely negative position. In addressing the question of methodology, historical criticism often serves as the "tradition" out of which the "innovation" of newer approaches is generated; it is "controlling" in contrast to approaches that provide greater "freedom"; it is the "center" that pushes the "margins" down; it is the "objective" stance of "elite specialists" that denies the lived "experience" of "flesh-and-blood readers."

As part of the project of "de-introducing," we are concerned with how we develop, reify, and deploy the categories we do in the study of the New Testament and early Christianity, with the understanding that all of these categories and narratives about the field will necessarily reflect modern, and not ancient, circumstances and questions. In other words, we want to underscore the point that the study of the New Testament is not simply about the texts themselves, but also concerns what people do with texts in different time periods, cultures, and media forms. In some way, texts and what people do with them are intertwined. To this end, we observe that rhetoric in the field that aims to denounce historical criticism in some sense repeats the same structural narrative about the history of the field as is present within historical-critical narratives about Christian origins and the development of early Christianity. Representing historical-critical discourse historically as the "old" against which the "new" is framed creates a linear developmental model for the "stages" in the history of the field, as if there were a single origin point and branches that came off over time, with there now being an emerging panoply of approaches thanks to the diversification of practitioners and methods. This "from the one to the many" narrative functions as a myth of origins of sorts that serves more to justify current social relations and hierarchies than it does to say anything substantive about the actual history of the field.

Some New Testament scholars who are critical of historical criticism might take to theory, and particularly deconstruction, as a means to appraise and destabilize what are thought to be a text's intentions and implications. By identifying and challenging a text's assumptions, or what it might take for granted, a whole host of new readings and questions might be possible beyond those concerned with origins, authorship, and ancient social settings. Aside from "new" readings of "old" texts, though, the deconstructive task also, in a best-case scenario, aims to reveal something of the frameworks and scaffolding that have shaped the ways we think about early Christian texts and phenomena in the first place. Within methodological approaches to the study of the New Testament that are inclined toward deconstruction, though, we observe a tendency to participate in another process of stabilization concerning the "biblical scholar" and "biblical studies" as fixed and singular entities. We wonder whether such a maneuver represents, to some extent, a reluctance to use deconstruction to its full potential as a tool that could reveal the ideological contours of a discipline through appraising the ways texts are created and managed by readers and interpreters, historical critics and deconstructionists included.

Further, representations of historical criticism such as those we have considered above tend to downplay the reality that all historical analysis takes place in political and social contexts, even if not explicitly stated in

15

the writings under discussion. It is certainly the case that earlier incarna-
tions of historical-critical biblical scholarship were largely conducted by,
for example, elite Protestant males of European and American descent.
That the shape of the field has changed dramatically in terms of who can
actually become a New Testament scholar is a critical part of its legacy. We
would also not deny that New Testament studies, as a discipline, has been
implicated in affirmations and perpetuations of oppressive hierarchical
power arrangements. However, to focus on the politics of inclusion and
exclusion, "center" and "margins," without attending to broader discourses,
socio-political and historical circumstances, and power relationships denies
the possibility that for every narrative about the field there is always a
counter-narrative. When we write our narratives of biblical scholarship, we
might do well to consider to what extent have we conflated the proposals of
New Testament scholarship with the identity politics of the scholar(s) making
them. It is critical to talk about who we are in relation to our work, and the
politics of identity has emerged as a critical component of doing that work.
But to focus on identity, who's in and who's out, to the exclusion of broader
issues and structural matters that any power analysis demands is to do what
we might call cultural criticism without critical theoretical engagement. We
do find it curious that so much responsibility, for so many problems in the
field and the world, is mapped onto those who have practiced historical
criticism of biblical texts in the past and the present. For example, to criticize
European biblical scholarship for its orientalizing tendencies without
criticizing the missionaries that brought the Bible to the Third World in
the first place is to leave out an important piece of the puzzle of power
relationships. We would rather argue that sustained attention to power
dynamics is a vital aspect of interacting with the vast and varied history
of the discipline, recognizing that human lives and relationships are
complicated and not, as it were, binarily formed.

   We do not raise these questions and issues to criticize or dismiss important
conversations and controversies in the guild. In our view, biblical scholarship
has long enjoyed status as an intellectually challenging field in the
humanities – one of its strengths lies in its attention to methodological
debates. We also agree that there is no consensus on a way forward in biblical
scholarship as a discipline. However, we are not sure that consensus is
necessary or possible – nor is consensus a goal of ours in this book. We do,
though, want to engage the problem, if we want to call it that, in New
Testament studies – even the current problem that poses historical criticism
as the enemy or opponent – as part of a core issue that has been a part of the
discipline for quite some time. To this end we would underscore that what we
call "historical criticism" and "New Testament studies" constitute fundamentally contested and contestable disciplinary spaces. Contrary to what critics

might contend, the methods and ideologies embodied by historical criticism have contributed to its inhabiting a site where basic dissension over aims, goals, audiences, and assumptions continues.[12] Again, we would not disagree that there are some aspects of historical criticism that may not be worth rehearsing in a contemporary context. That said, there are many different trajectories for historical criticism, including the trajectories embodied by those who would characterize themselves as its most trenchant critics and detractors in this very moment. Our task, then, is not to say historical criticism is "right" or "wrong." Rather, in this book we aim to encourage critical thinking as well as foster more, not less, dialogue about the categories we use and stories we tell about who we are, what we do, and why we do it.

Introducing De-Introducing the New Testament

As scholars of the New Testament, we are interested in thinking about the material conditions that make our field possible as a disciplinary configuration, as well as the modes by which the various categories and methods of the discipline are rendered natural, inevitable, and universal. In other words, we are interested in how the study of the New Testament works on an ideological level. For us, the study of the New Testament, at least in its historical and literary trajectories, might indeed be a gateway to understanding the ancient world. However, in our view the study of the ancient world is best understood as a way to configure and articulate our relationship with that world in the present. The New Testament, then, serves as a particularly rich site for the conceptualization, delineation, and naturalization of discourses of power. Thus, the study of the New Testament affords an opportunity to think through and with such discourses.

The study of the New Testament, like many of the texts themselves, is occasional. By this we mean that it is located in space and time, and as such its procedures and outlook reflect the realities of those moments. It is also the case that the field is rhetorical, that is, it narrates and naturalizes a certain version of reality as well. We are interested in the stories that the field tells, as well as the stories one can tell about the field. There is no unmediated access to these texts, contexts, or histories of interpretation – since reading and interpreting are human activities we cannot ignore the fully human dimensions of biblical scholarship. In so far as the study of the New Testament serves as a mediator of sorts, then, we are interested in exploring what effects that has on the way the field is conceptualized and performed. We contend that we still need to ask historical questions about "our" texts. However, the terms on which we do history writing need to be examined over and over again.

Moreover, introductory courses and textbooks in New Testament studies are primarily pedagogical in nature, that is to say, such environments and practices have embedded in them teaching aims that make specific assumptions about the material, teachers, and students. In our view as professors, education is ultimately about making this world visible through interrogating that which is thought to be natural, universal, and stable. In our estimation, education, broadly conceived, is *not* about helping people think in certain ways or with certain frameworks that we happen to prefer or otherwise find agreeable. We are far less interested in students adopting our, or any other, framework than we are in an acknowledgment that every perspective has a framework, including our own in this book. We are less interested in introducing our discipline than we are in revealing the operating assumptions and questions behind it. Less a "method" on its own and more a set of practices, "de-introducing" as we seek to conduct it herein turns our attention away from the ordinary procedures of introducing the New Testament, which is usually done through introducing the professional study of the canonical texts in their ancient historical contexts with some attention to the history of interpretation, particularly in the form of the texts as Christian scriptures. The "historical" mode of introducing the New Testament is configured as a straightforward, unadulterated, and unmediated encounter that inducts the student into a means of understanding the ancient texts, in their original ancient contexts, as a collection of documents, ordered chronologically or canonically, that do not "mean" the same things in the ancient world as they might in the modern one. The meta-questions about methods and categories are left aside for a more "official" story of the field itself with very little, if any, explanation.

Given the above-mentioned contours of the field as far as "introducing" is concerned, as a part of our "de-introducing" project in this book we intend to look underneath the traditional ways in which the field is "introduced." Our exploration will extend beyond the classroom to critically engage the conceptual framework of the field as a whole. To be sure, introductory textbooks provide a window onto the landscape of the field in a given time and place. *De-Introducing the New Testament* is thus a means of engaging biblical scholarship through identifying and appraising its "order of things." In our view this project has not only scholarly but also educational and pedagogical dimensions. We are concerned with and invested in how, and why, we should study and teach the New Testament, and to what ends. As a modern project, "de-introducing" is about pulling back the proverbial curtain on the field, so far as we are able to do that. We aim to empower our readers to engage the field not through specialization, but through thinking critically about some of the basic categories involved in studying the New Testament – or, frankly, any set of texts or traditions. Much of New Testament scholarship has been invested in narrowing the range of focus and relegating meta-questions to highly specialized conversations among "peers." We contend that one does not have to be a New Testament scholar to think about categories or methodology, nor does one need to be an expert to pose new questions about old material. We aim to help cultivate critical thinking skills by turning to what we feel are some of the live and unsettled issues in our discipline, regardless of how "natural" these issues seem to be in the stories that are often told about the field.

Implicit in the practice of "de-introducing" the New Testament is defamiliarization, or the process of being able to describe, as if for the first time, what it is that we take most for granted in a given situation. Defamiliarization is a dialectical engagement between the strange and the familiar, and includes attempts to bring the strange things closer and seeing whether and how those strange things can become familiar. Such "estrangement," as literary critic Viktor Shklovsky would have it,[13] is done partly through a rereading and redescription of that which seems to be too familiar or cliché, in this case the ordinary way of introducing the study of the New Testament and the basic categories of the field itself. The defamiliarization process is not dependent upon the object as such – it is dependent on what we, as viewers and readers, do with objects, on what, and really how, we are willing to see.

As students of the New Testament, and as teachers in the liberal arts tradition, an integral part of our job is to observe what we have not noticed before, and especially to identify strange things about that which is most familiar to us. It is imperative that we make robust connections between different materials, perspectives, and life-situations. To be a student of the liberal arts is to see what we think we already recognize in renewed ways, to perceive beyond what is assumed or what we think we know. Thus, we must dig wider and deeper than what seems natural or what we take for granted about the study of the New Testament in order to ask more robust questions of these materials and ourselves. To engage in "de-introducing" the New Testament, then, is to attempt to revisit the familiar and see it as if we had never before encountered it.

In this book we will seek to "de-introduce" the New Testament through engagement with four interrelated sites that, in our view, seem "natural" in the field. Our interest in seeing these sites anew, and thus in exploring and problematizing these themes in the discipline, is methodological. We aim to use a defamiliarizing understanding of the field in order to engender sustained reflection on methodological questions. We are interested in doing so not because we are invested in "deconstruction" per se. Rather, we maintain that studying the New Testament might start with the ancient world, but only through modern means. Any engagement of the ancient past is about how we might relate to that past in the service of understanding the present and making a different future.

In Chapter 1, "The Order of New Testament Things: Questioning Methods and Meanings," we lay the groundwork for "de-introducing" the New Testament by setting up larger questions about how the discipline works, articulating some guiding principles that are operative in scholarly work and re-presented in the process of "introducing" the New Testament. To this end we will contend with how we classify, categorize, consolidate, and convey the "order of things" as part of an overarching narrative of the discipline. Herein we will include attention to modern concepts often taken for granted in the study of the New Testament texts and traditions, such as origins and development; consistency and coherence; stability, definability, and simplicity; genetic connections and interrelations; difference, distinctiveness, and identity; and truth, fiction, and reliability. In raising these issues, it is our goal to understand how, methodologically speaking, we might better assess the assumptions and logic of the disciplinary work that shapes our introductory senses.

Having sketched a framework and set of questions about the discipline, in Chapter 2, "Foregrounding New Testament Backgrounds: Contextualizing Interpretation," we turn to using those categories to appraise how we situate the texts of the New Testament in relation to its Jewish and Greco-Roman milieus or backgrounds. The main question we explore in this chapter is why, and to what ends, scholars have long reified a commitment to exploring Christian origins and the development of Christianity through, and against, ancient backgrounds or "worlds." We outline, in broad strokes, the tension between "Jewish" and "Greco-Roman" backgrounds for early Christianity, how some of these trajectories are being followed in modern scholarship, and what difference this primary problem makes in the imagination of the guild as well as its mechanisms of knowledge production.

The imagination of the guild and its mechanisms of knowledge production is also a key theme in Chapter 3, "Objects, Objectives, and Objectivities: Material and Visual Culture and New Testament Studies." Taking up questions posed by the role of archaeology and material culture in the study of the New Testament, Christian origins, and early Christianity, in this chapter we explore the location, examination, and haunting presence of objects and material culture in modern scholarship. We examine particular assumptions mapped onto objects about the ancient world – assumptions that generate its naturalness, stability, coherence, and genealogical link to the present. Material culture is one of the most sensational and least transparent areas in modern biblical scholarship. While objects are hailed as providing "proof" for the historicity of the New Testament, they also reflect modern stories about ancient Christianity and its texts. We also raise questions about how our narratives about the relationships among people, texts, and objects, in the past and in the present, involve several operating presuppositions regarding the relationships between ancient texts and material culture as performed in the field. These are understood in part by deployments of objects as both illustrations for texts and external validation of their veracity and interpretive priority.

We turn our attention from texts and objects to people in Chapter 4, "Brand(ish)ing Biblical Scholars(hip): New Testament Studies and Neoliberal Subjectivity." How people understand what it is that "New Testament scholars" do with texts, contexts, and histories of interpretation is our main concern therein. The persona and performance of scholars matter a great deal, and in this chapter we engage the politics and procedures of constructing ourselves as "brands," as a means of managing and performing individual and social identities under neoliberalism. In our view, this is a critical aspect of New Testament studies as it is construed in our late-capitalist economic context. Branding functions as the means of producing what we call a neoliberal subjectivity, and is an important, if under-recognized, part of the contemporary methodological landscape of the field. While in other chapters we focus on various aspects of methodological predilection, in this chapter we focus on the New Testament scholar him/herself. Ultimately, we would suggest that scholarly persona comprises a critical component of "method" overall.

We extend our analysis of the persona and performance of the New Testament scholar in "Back to the Future: Concluding Observations on History, Method, and Theory in New Testament Studies." In this final chapter, we examine the role of the biblical critic in contemporary discourse, as well as the various issues at stake in that role and what difference it makes to think creatively and expansively about methodological issues. As we emphasize throughout this book, it is our position that any discussion of the New Testament is not innocently about the ancient texts or their contexts, or their histories of interpretation and deployment, but is also, or rather primarily, about the relationships we have with those texts – by inheritance, accident, or choice. We would include relationships we want to overcome as well as those we want to cultivate in that assessment. The New Testament, and indeed the Bible as a whole, is not only about relationships, it also is a site where relationships are negotiated. Method is thus ultimately about us.

The study of the New Testament, which foregrounds the reality that no one is neutral in relation to the texts and traditions under consideration, presents us with the opportunity to make a substantial contribution to history writing, both with respect to the ancient world and religion and also to intellectual history, philosophy, and the humanities as a whole. This kind of broad critical engagement is, in our view, the promise of New Testament

21

scholarship and intellectual activity more broadly. By thinking critically about the human condition and human experience with the material thought to be most sacrosanct, most beyond question, most taken for granted as "the way it was" and "the way it is" and "the way it ought to be," we have the power to interrupt dominant narratives, to question our ways of knowing, and to imagine something else altogether. Put another way, we have the power to both write a "tag" on Lady Justice – and simultaneously honor her as a critical iconic element of the neighborhood landscape. This book, we hope, will contribute to conversations about the field and its potential, and we dearly hope our readers will be empowered to think critically and expansively through de-introducing the New Testament with us.

Notes

1. For a development of this perspective on historical criticism and a tracing of its influence in feminist and gender-critical biblical scholarship, which is often thought to radically oppose the procedures and claims of historical criticism, see Davina C. Lopez and Todd Penner, "Historical-Critical Approaches," in *The Oxford Encyclopedia of the Bible and Gender Studies* (ed. J. M. O'Brien; Oxford Encyclopedias of the Bible; New York: Oxford University Press, 2014), 327–336.
2. John J. Collins, *The Bible After Babel: Historical Criticism in a Postmodern Age* (Grand Rapids, Mich.: Eerdmans, 2005), 4.
3. For a summary of the tension between historical and literary approaches to the New Testament, see Lynn M. Poland, *Literary Criticism and Biblical Hermeneutics: A Critique of Formalist Approaches* (American Academy of Religion Academy Series 48; Chico, Calif.: Scholars Press, 1985); Stephen D. Moore, *Literary Criticism and the Gospels: The Theoretical Challenge* (New Haven: Yale University Press, 1985); Moore, *The Bible In Theory: Critical and Post-Critical Essays* (Resources for Biblical Study 57; Atlanta, Ga.: Society of Biblical Literature, 2010); and Anna Runesson, *Exegesis in the Making: Postcolonialism and New Testament Studies* (Biblical Interpretation Series 103; Leiden: Brill, 2011), especially 56–59.
4. Stephen D. Moore and Yvonne Sherwood, *The Invention of the Biblical Scholar: A Critical Manifesto* (Minneapolis: Fortress Press, 2011), 102–103.
5. Roy Harrisville and Walter Sundberg, *The Bible in Modern Culture: Theology and Historical-Critical Method from Spinoza to Käsemann* (Grand Rapids, Mich.: Eerdmans, 1995), 11. The tensions between "historical" and "theological" readings of the New Testament, and the Bible as a whole, are long-standing, particularly in the United States where the legacy of the fundamentalist-modernist debates endures and the rise of evangelicalism has had an impact on scholarship. For a contemporary "middle way" between what is perceived as the two oppositional "poles" of historical criticism and faith-based interpretation, see Christopher M. Hays and Christopher B. Ansberry, eds., *Evangelical Faith and the Challenge of Historical Criticism* (Grand Rapids, Mich.: Baker Academic Press, 2013).

6. Harrisville and Sundberg, *Bible in Modern Culture*, 13–14.
7. Elisabeth Schüssler Fiorenza, *Rhetoric and Ethic: The Politics of Biblical Studies* (Minneapolis: Fortress Press, 1999), 12. This argument is developed more fully, and recently, in Schüssler Fiorenza, *Democratizing Biblical Studies: Toward an Emancipatory Educational Space* (Louisville, Ky.: Westminster/John Knox Press, 2009).
8. Schüssler Fiorenza, *Democratizing Biblical Studies*, 90–91.
9. Rasiah S. Sugirtharajah, "Catching the Post or How I Became an Accidental Theorist," in *Shaping a Global Theological Mind* (ed. D. C. Marks; Abingdon, Oxon.: Ashgate, 2008), 176–185: 168.
10. Sugirtharajah, "Catching the Post," 169.
11. Rasiah S. Sugirtharajah, *Postcolonial Criticism and Biblical Interpretation* (New York: Oxford University Press, 2002), 74–78.
12. For a reflection on this point, see Mary Ann Tolbert, "Writing History, Writing Culture, Writing Ourselves," in *Soundings in Cultural Criticism: Perspectives on Culture, Power, and Identity in the New Testament* (ed. F. Lozada, Jr., and G. Carey; Soundings Series; Minneapolis: Fortress Press, 2013), 17–30.
13. Viktor Shklovsky, "Art as Device (1925)," in *Theory of Prose* (trans. B. Sher; Champaign, Il.: Dalkey Archive Press, 1990), 1–14.

1

The Order of New Testament Things
Questioning Methods and Meanings

The Bone-Box of James, "the Brother of Jesus"

Both the scholarly and larger lay communities were set abuzz in early October 2002, when an announcement was made that an ossuary – a Jewish "bone-box" used for the "second burial" of Jewish remains in antiquity – had recently surfaced with an Aramaic inscription that stated: "James, son of Joseph, broth(er) of Jesus." The Washington press conference was co-hosted by the Discovery Channel and the Biblical Archaeological Society. The latter entity would publish the more detailed epigraphic evidence suggesting that the inscription was authentic and thus quite likely represented the earliest material evidence for the existence of Jesus, whose name is attested on the box. Ironically, although the bone-box had purportedly once housed the bones of James, he was less of a focus, as his brother was much more famous! André Lemaire, a professor of Hebrew and Aramaic philology and epigraphy at the Sorbonne University, was the person who stumbled upon the James ossuary, and he was instrumental in vigorously arguing for its authenticity.[1] As the story goes, Lemaire, while in Jerusalem, was approached by a collector of antiquities who mentioned that he had several artifacts that he would like Lemaire to examine. The collector, Oded Golan, had a fairly extensive assemblage of ancient objects, including an inscription designated as the "Jehoash Tablet," which was claimed to be an artifact connected to the first Temple, built by Solomon. This particular ossuary was one of many in Golan's collection.

De-Introducing the New Testament: Texts, Worlds, Methods, Stories, First Edition.
Todd Penner and Davina C. Lopez.
© 2015 Todd Penner and Davina C. Lopez. Published 2015 by John Wiley & Sons, Ltd.

The ossuary attributed to James, the son of Joseph, the brother of Jesus, generated greater attention than Golan's other objects, in part because of its presumed ramifications for authenticating a critical component of Christian history. Some scholars were interested in the figure of James himself, whose bones were to have been at one time placed in this ossuary for burial. When examined by Lemaire, the box was empty of bones, although Golan later claimed he had a small bag of fragments that he had preserved. James is an important character in the history of early Christianity as narrated in the Acts of the Apostles. It is believed that this James, either the half-brother of Jesus (by Joseph) or a cousin, took over leadership of the Jerusalem church in its early stages. A similar James is referred to in the apostle Paul's letter to the Galatians, where Paul acknowledges him as one of the "pillars" of the Jerusalem church, alongside Peter and John (Gal. 2:9). Paul also explicitly refers to a James in Galatians 1:19 whom he calls "James, the brother of the Lord." Although often obscure in previous Protestant scholarship, in the decade or so just prior to the announcement of this discovery the figure of James had become an important character for New Testament scholars, not least because of the link he provided between Judaism and Christianity, which is significant also for contemporary Jewish-Christian interreligious dialogue. In other words, here was a venerable early Christian leader who evidently followed Jewish law, including the purity rituals. Indeed, in Galatians Paul refers to "men from James" (2:9), who arrive from Jerusalem in Antioch, and who appear to have some influence on Peter when he withdraws from eating at the same table with Gentiles, who were according to Jewish law considered to be unclean. Acts 15 details some of the broader issues involved in the initial challenges and controversies instigated by the inclusion of Gentiles in the emergent Jewish movement that acknowledged Jesus to be the Messiah and risen Lord. Thus, the James ossuary could provide material evidence that would further knit these early Christian texts together into a cohesive narrative.

Of course, the major hype was generated over the fact that the James ossuary mentioned the name of "Jesus." Aside from the obvious public interest in "proof" for the historicity of Jesus, in the scholarly world this matter is of major significance, since there are relatively few references to the figure of Jesus outside of the New Testament that remain from the ancient world in which he lived. There are some ancient literary references to a figure of "Jesus" or "Christ,"[2] but none of them fully achieve the result of affirming the existence of an individual named "Jesus" who did and said the things that are attributed to him in the Gospels of the New Testament. And to be sure, there is no artifact from the ancient world that attests to the existence of Jesus – no written graffiti, e.g., that states, "Jesus of Nazareth, son of God (and Mary), Savior of humankind, brother of James, was here." The bone-box of James proved to be a major excitement for this reason. For many scholars the James ossuary became something like the Rosetta Stone, providing an anchor of sorts in terms of historical orientation – that is, providing both an assurance that Jesus of Nazareth really did exist and a key to "translating" the terms of that existence. Frankly, while a few critics – mostly those who do not study the New Testament and early Christian literature professionally – have from time to time doubted that Jesus existed historically, the vast majority of scholars believe he quite likely did. Thus, the James ossuary really tells us nothing new. It does have much more significance for putting us in touch with James of Jerusalem, the brother of Jesus. And, for sure, there were calls for doing DNA analysis, to see what we might learn about the genetics of the lineage of Joseph.

The James ossuary was brought to the Royal Ontario Museum in Canada about one month after its existence had been rolled out publicly with great fanfare. In November 2002, an exhibition of the ossuary went on display, exactly around the same time that the Society of Biblical Literature and the American Academy of Religion held its annual meetings in that city. Obviously the fact that the largest professional gathering of biblical scholars and scholars of religion took place at exactly the same time as the exhibit made for the possibility of a large audience of critical scholars who would not just want to see the exciting artifact for themselves, but who also would be quite willing to comment, blog, and discuss the James ossuary at length in any media format that would be made available. As we recall, there was a definite stir at that conference, with one of the first questions asked of fellow participants being whether or not they had gone out to see the ossuary yet. Some biblical scholars took pride in declaring that they were not going to see the exhibit, that they were not going to give in to the hype and media frenzy. Wherever particular scholars stood, most were aware of the controversy surrounding the James ossuary – and that it was considered by many scholars to be a forgery. The specter of forgery was in fact a major facet of the early conversation, right after the announcement of the ossuary's existence. Scholars were skeptical – it was a bit "too easy" that a bone-box with the three names "James," "Joseph," and "Jesus" surfaced; it was a little too convenient. Indeed, the fact that details regarding the origins of the find were somewhat murky, and remain so, added to the skepticism around the James ossuary's authenticity.

Golan claimed he had been sold the ossuary many decades earlier by an antiquities dealer whose name he could not recall. Given that it was bought off the open market, and not properly excavated, one can reasonably presume that the object had been acquired illegally and most likely looted from its site of origin. The bone-box was in Golan's possession for a long while before he approached Lemaire and asked him to examine the object. It did seem a little too good to be true, that this Israeli collector happened to have this potentially shocking artifact that somehow lay in obscurity for so long. If Golan had thought to ask someone to look at it years later, why not earlier? Or was the inscription not on the bone-box earlier? Was it in fact a forged inscription, added by someone in order to make an otherwise ordinary ancient ossuary (which is not all that rare a find) into something quite extraordinary – and for sure also incredibly valuable from a monetary standpoint. The James ossuary itself is estimated to be worth several million U.S. dollars, but only because of its inscription and attribution. Any ordinary ossuary or one with the inscription of an unrecognizable figure from the past, which is almost always the case, would be worth much less. This is as close to the "Holy Grail" that collectors and scholars get, and so the value is raised significantly as a result.

Scholars of the New Testament, Christian origins, and early Christianity were, and are, split on the issue of the James ossuary. Many wanted to believe, and still do believe, that the ossuary was the authentic bone-box of James, the brother of Jesus. Others are quite convinced that the inscription of an ossuary dating to the first century CE had been added or altered later, in the much more recent past. There was some evidence for this conclusion in terms of analysis of the lettering. The first part, "James, son of Joseph," seemed to be done in a different cursive script than that of "brother of Jesus." Of course, that could still mean the first part was genuine, which would perhaps not undermine its value all that much. The patina that had developed around the inscription was analyzed as well, and the results of analysis were mixed. Some of these results suggest that the patina could have been added later, others insist that the patina was uneven throughout the inscription, and still others attest to its antiquity and thus proof of the authenticity of the inscription. It did not help that the inscription was partially damaged in the transit of the James ossuary to the Royal Museum of Ontario, when a crack developed in its façade, a fact which only served to heighten the media spectacle surrounding the object. Not only had this sacred relic from the past been at long last revealed, but now it was also damaged!

The Israel Antiquities Authority (IAA), which is the main arm of the Israeli government in charge of overseeing archaeological projects and remains, believed the James ossuary was a fake. More specifically, the agency believed that Golan or someone else came across an ancient and authentic ossuary, which was initially uninscribed. According to the IAA's reconstruction of events, someone then added the inscription as a means to create the potential for selling it on the open market at an exorbitant price. Within the year of the announcement of its discovery, the ossuary was confiscated by the IAA and Golan was investigated for forgery and attempt to commit fraud. The forging of artifacts is a widespread phenomenon and has become increasingly sophisticated, and certainly when it comes to "Holy Land" objects it is all the rage as there is a considerable consumer base for such items. As it turns out, in the investigation of Golan the authorities uncovered a facility that had evidence of a group invested in reproducing replicas of ancient artifacts, with all the tools necessary to create the various elements to indicate "antiquity," such as patinas and inscriptions. Golan was charged, and so began an intricate ten-year long struggle with the Israeli state regarding his alleged involvement in a forgery ring, along with the fraudulent nature of the James ossuary and the Jehoash Tablet. After a long legal process, utilizing an array of experts of all types examining all possible aspects related to the authenticity of the ossuary, the court finally ruled in Golan's favor. No one claimed him "innocent" by any standard. However, it was deemed impossible to prove beyond a reasonable doubt that the ossuary, or the inscription on it, was fake. The IAA then waged a legal battle to keep the ossuary in its custody. Golan, however, finally won the privilege to have the ossuary returned to his collection in the spring of 2014. In a somewhat ironic, if circular, twist of events, the James ossuary will now – some twelve years after it was first put on display at the Royal Ontario Museum in Toronto, only to be seized shortly thereafter – go back on display in a museum, once again as the famous find that attests to "James, the son of Joseph, the broth[er] of Jesus."

While it is quite likely that we will never know with certainty whether or not the inscription on the ossuary signaling this individual "James" from antiquity is genuine, we ourselves are nevertheless highly skeptical of its authenticity. That said, many scholars, particularly those committed to the relative historical accuracy of the accounts of early Christian history that we find in the New Testament, continue to be adamantly committed to the genuineness of the inscription and, more importantly, to its significance as an assurance that events described in the New Testament have a factual, historical, and material basis. In other words, rather than simply pointing us in the direction of a historical curiosity – "look at the way that Jews in the ancient world buried their dead, and isn't it interesting that we find in this instance a reference to an ancient figure who might be James of Jerusalem and also the brother of Jesus" – we find, rather, an opening for a fairly heated public debate regarding the broader historicity of the New Testament materials more generally. In other words, the James ossuary has come to signify a much larger issue regarding our own certainty about the events described in the New Testament and the significance they might have. The James ossuary is thus a site for thinking about some of the most basic methodological issues and questions in the study of the New Testament, Christian origins, and early Christianity.

We raise the matter of the James ossuary at the opening of this book not because we are interested or invested in the outcome of the debates and controversies that swirled around the bone-box of the brother of Jesus, but because, in our estimation, it provides a helpful heuristic framework in which to think about the larger questions that guide New Testament interpretation and that shape the categories and issues that scholars of early Christianity might use to ask such questions about the material. For instance, that the first major issue became one of "authenticity" versus "inauthenticity" related to the inscription on the James ossuary reveals something important about how scholars have come, over a long period of time in the development of New Testament studies as a discipline, to conceptualize the past. The James ossuary clearly has struck a visceral nerve with scholars and the public, as it appears to be a tangible object that could place one directly in touch with an ancient sacred past. Like the relics of the Middle Ages, which would lure Christian pilgrims from all over to this shrine or that one to see this bone of Saint Peter or that bone of Saint Paul or Mary Magdalene's tooth, so also today we see the power of the object to transport the viewer back in time, to a period of "holy beginnings," allowing us to nearly touch this past, becoming a part of it in an unmediated manner.

One cannot discount the powerfully emotional and mental feature that something like the James ossuary can provide. For us, though, the use of such objects by scholars is most interesting, and we are particularly struck by the deployment of the language of "beginnings" and "origins" to facilitate for a larger lay population the link to the past that is already partly in motion. Scholars do not invest their energies in those emotions, however. They are more concerned about situating the object in question within a larger "order of things," a greater structure of meaning in which the ossuary both invokes and answers questions that New Testament scholarship considers vital for assessing this past. And to be sure, whether the James ossuary is considered to be "authentic" or not is beside the point. Both sides in this debate are still invested in the same fundamental set of questions regarding the New Testament, along with how our investigative efforts should proceed and how they should be framed. The James ossuary controversy thus reveals a great deal about how scholars focus on the past, how we conceptualize history, and how we structure the knowledge that is gleaned from the materials we study.

The James ossuary affair, alongside all of its attendant intrigues, identifies for us that scholarly analysis of early Christian material occurs at the highly contentious crossroads of personal and institutional faith orientations, articulations of individual and collective identities, political ideologies and social imaginaries, and multiple operative scholarly discourses. As in all fields of inquiry, our analysis of biblical literature is ultimately about intersecting power relationships, which becomes even more complex at precisely those moments when no one comes to the table neutral about the material at hand.

The questions we ask of ancient materials play a large role in configuring the answers we get to those questions. To be clear, it is not a matter of who is asking the better or worse questions. As with the James ossuary, for us it is not about right or wrong on this score. Rather, at heart, we are invested in exploring what kinds of questions are asked, how those questions shape the subject matter under discussion, and, finally, what those questions say about us. It is an awareness of the larger questions, what we would call "meta-questions," that ultimately is most illuminating for the study of the New Testament, as it is through those that we begin to learn how it is that we come to learn the way we do regarding the material at hand. In other words, underlying all of the scholarly work and the introductory presentations of early Christian texts, practices, beliefs, and social histories is a basic structure of assumptions and values that guide the manner in which much of this work proceeds, which in turn shapes the books, articles, presentations, and such that are produced and consumed. It is a commitment to explore and unmask these assumptions and the implications thereof that frames not only the first chapter of this book, but also in many respects the book in its entirety.

Ways of Knowing a Subject of Study

The primary theme of this book, which we explore in a variety of ways in its different chapters, is that knowledge and information related to the New Testament, as in any other field of human inquiry, are organized in ways that are not in some universal and natural form or the product of necessity. Rather, these structures of knowledge and knowing, the methodologies employed for arriving at the conclusions we do within larger epistemological structures, and even our means of acting and being within these same bodies of reference, all have a root in a vast array of historical, social, political, economic, and cultural factors that help shape how we see and experience the world. Michel Foucault is most often associated with the more fully articulated version of this viewpoint on knowledge and knowing, and *The Order of Things* is his signal work that details a larger historical and epistemological framework to bolster his view that we order the world in specific ways that are unique to particular people groups and individuals in particular time periods and regions of the world. There is no absolute, uniform, timeless way of ordering what we see and experience in the world. Rather, through time, across cultures, and throughout geographical divides people have ordered the world in differing ways, sometimes coming up with drastically divergent means by which to understand and interpret the world than how we might do in our Western context.

To be sure, Foucault does not deny that there is an external "world" that we all experience. Whether one lives in China in the 15th century, or in India in the 6th century, or in the United States in the 19th century, many people in these cultures have come into contact with, say, a cow, a horse, a dog, a rat, or a bird. Certainly, all people in these cultures have encountered some kind of species of animal or reptile. The issue is not that we do not observe, touch, feel, and, in some cases at least, taste these external biological organisms. All humans, to varying degrees, have some form of physical interactions – indeed, entanglements – with animals. The main issue that Foucault and others in his wake have raised is that we categorize our experiences of and observations on these animals in divergent and sometimes contradictory ways depending on how we order knowledge more broadly.[3] And the way we do so is largely a result of historical trajectories of interconnected facets of society that shape the way we synthesize, categorize, and classify our data. It is in precisely the categorization and classification, moreover, that meaning evolves. In other words, things do not order themselves, and do not mean anything in and of themselves. They need to be situated within a larger framework of knowledge – an epistemic system that orders and arranges the thing within the whole – in order to signify meaning in relation to other elements within the configuration of that same system. Admittedly, Foucault's system is more expansive than this, and in some respects the version presented here in rather bare form departs from his original articulation. However, we concur with his basic statement that "the fundamental codes of culture – those governing its language, its schemas of perception, its exchanges, its techniques, its values, the hierarchy of its practices – establish for every man, from the first, the empirical orders with which he will be dealing and within which he will be at home."[4] In this book we are concerned with the codes within which New Testament scholarship is "at home." Overall, then, the framework within which we proceed to analyze the "Order of New Testament Things" is very much a Foucauldian approach.

One way to illustrate the analytic framework we are delineating herein is to draw on an example offered by Wilfred Cantwell Smith,[5] a scholar of religion who was particularly invested in the meaning of religious traditions and the methods by which we study them. In an effort to describe the complexities of the comparative study of religion, Smith raises the question: What is the functional equivalent of Jesus Christ (known from the Christian tradition) in the Islamic faith? Most people would proffer "Muhammad" as the response. This makes somewhat intuitive sense, since both of these historical personages are founding figures of major "Western" religious traditions. Moreover, both of these figures are venerated in their respective traditions. Smith, however, suggested that a better functional equivalent would be the Qur'an, even as many people would suggest that "the New Testament" or "the Bible" is the proper corollary of the Qur'an. Now, the key element here is the way in which the information "Jesus," "Muhammad," and "Qur'an" are ordered within a larger system of signification. In other words, if the primary means of organizing data is on appearance, wherein one classifies the information based on whether something is a biological organism or not, then Jesus and Muhammad would seem to be parallels. However, if one is thinking in terms of functionality within a larger system of religious meaning, then the question is not what Jesus Christ is as a biological entity, which would be a scientific categorization, but what Jesus Christ is as a religious signifier. And, while some might suggest that the figure of Jesus is a "prophet," like Muhammad, it is also the case that in principle, within the broader scope of the Christian religious tradition, Jesus Christ functions as "revelation." Certainly the "historical Jesus" may have been a prophet, but, according to Christian interpretation, in the New Testament John the Baptist is the prophet who witnesses to the final revelation of God embodied in Christ. The New Testament in this configuration is not actually revelation per se. Rather, it bears witness to the revelation that is in Christ Jesus. Thus, the equivalent to Jesus Christ in the Islamic religious tradition is the Qur'an, which is the final revelation of God, written down by Muhammad as communicated to him by an angel. In functional terms, Jesus Christ and the Qur'an are the closest corollaries to one another in a comparative framework.

Obviously the example of aligning Jesus with the Qur'an according to functionality leads us into the field of comparative religions as well as fairly heavy-laden theological territory. Jesus Christ, understood as revelation, is a developed concept in Christian theological and religious traditions, although there are bases for this view scattered throughout the New Testament, such as in the Gospel of John and in Paul's letters. That said, our interest here is not to get involved in a discussion of the theological meaning of Jesus Christ. Rather, we want to illustrate that there are a variety of ways to order and classify information, and the guiding framework into which data is placed will ultimately determine how meaning is derived, reified, and contested. It is the pre-existing framework through which information is perceived, processed, analyzed, interpreted, and arranged that makes the fundamental difference in the ways that we receive this information and in what we can do with it, how we will deploy it in the future, and how we will subsequently use it to help us frame other related observations.

For Foucault, broadly speaking, the "order of things" is precisely this phenomenon: our knowledge, although often seemingly self-evident and natural, is in fact based on a highly complex, ever-evolving contingent system that classifies and categorizes information in a way that makes sense based on the terms and conditions *of that contingent system of knowledge*. This is not to say that perception is then all relative and arbitrary. No one denies the existence of the "thing" that is being ordered or suggests that there is an entirely random manner in which that "thing" is taken up within the ordering process. Looking back at Smith's question, then, one would acknowledge that depending on how the operative system of ordering data is structured, Jesus Christ and Muhammad could be parallels, which would indicate an arrangement based on classifying these "things" in terms of their being biological entities and the significance that holds within Christianity and Islam. Alternatively, Jesus Christ and the Qur'an could be parallels, which would represent a configuration premised on categorizing these "things" in terms of their religious functionality, which exists in relation to other "things" within those larger religious systems.

The upshot of the approach to understanding the ordering of knowledge we have been exploring thus far is that the specific categories and methods we use, as well as the questions we ask, in studying the New Testament are in some sense already predetermined by a long history of development of a modern, Western ordering process. In other words, we investigate the New Testament and interpret it the way we do as part of a modern disciplinary configuration, but it could be otherwise, and elsewhere in other times and/ or places it is, and has been, otherwise. We should make clear at this juncture that we are not at all invested in dismantling the "New Testament order of things," that is, in deconstructing the system of ordering entirely. This project is, rather, committed to highlighting and exposing some of the fundamental premises that lie behind how we classify and categorize the information we glean from early Christian sources. That is, when we are presented with information either in a scholarly or more popular/introductory format, it is important to note that the material has already been arranged for us. The basic assumptions that underlie the arrangement are almost never revealed and, frankly, most interpreters proceed without realizing that their investigative endeavors have been negotiated and framed within a larger episteme. Our goal in what follows, then, is to examine more closely some of the fundamental assumptions that undergird the "order of things" as that relates to New Testament scholarship. Our hope is that through detailing some of the ordering principles that shape the ways we examine the New Testament, the questions we ask of that material, and the results we produce for scholarly and lay consumption, we will be able to open a space for exploring more expansive ways in which to think about this ancient material. In other words, the categories, while still relevant in New Testament studies, are, in our estimation, frequently deployed in rather rigid ways that undercut some of the vitality and complexity of human historical phenomena. The problem in this respect does not necessarily lie with the larger epistemic ordering structure, but with particular internal arrangements that are made based on a variety of other ideological, religious, and/or theological commitments.

Sometimes the "order of things" is impeded not by the system itself, but by the inability to see the potentiality of the larger episteme at work. In the introduction to this book we suggested that feminist and postmodern criticisms and dismissals of historical criticism as a relevant interpretive enterprise were a bit misguided. The historical-critical method of investigating the New Testament arises out of fundamental principles within a larger modern historical-scientific episteme, which is intricately and intimately interconnected with every facet of everyday life, from economic markets and political principles to medical science and the means of social interaction to the role of technology and spirituality in our daily lives. Thus, historical criticism is not something that can simply be dispensed with in favor of greener, perhaps more personal pastures. However, at the same time, if we conceptualize perception and experience within contingent systems of knowledge, then we understand that (a) we could order and arrange the system differently and divergently, and (b) we can also creatively engage, push, and interrogate some of the existing ordering principles to see if they might make better sense out of the information we find, in this case, in the New Testament. It is precisely in this way that we can also talk about our study of the ancient world impacting our assessment of our own, as the two are intertwined through the classificatory system that arranges knowledge and produces meaning. That is, our approach to the ancient materials reveals something fundamental about how we also conceptualize our own world, as the ordering structure invoked in the former is that which structures the latter as well. It is in this way that we can say that the past, as we perceive it through our own ordering episteme, shares the same structure of knowing as our perception of and experience in the present. Therefore the past and the present share in the same system in which things have meaning and make sense – *to us*. As we venture forward into the next section, then, we are ever attentive to the potential for liberative hermeneutics that historical criticism can provide, even as we are fully aware of the limitations and narrowness of its methods based, not in small part, on fairly flat, sterile, and impotent deployments of the ordering principles of knowledge in our world.

Ordering Principles in the Study of the New Testament

In the following discussion we highlight several complexes of categories that we consider to be essential in modern study of the New Testament: origins and linear development; stability, definability, and simplicity; consistency and coherence; and difference, distinctiveness, and identity. These complexes are not the only ones that could be pulled out and highlighted, nor are they innate principles of ordering themselves, since we ourselves have framed this analysis and commentary in light of a particular understanding and interpretation of history and method of historical criticism as that relates to a larger modern episteme. These categories, then, might be considered epistemological principles or structural coordinates that shape in fairly significant ways the manner in which we generally approach the New Testament, as well as the kinds of questions we raise in our course of study. Moreover, with these categories, sometimes overtly invoked and at other times unwittingly so, the interpreter orders the material in a particular configuration that appears to be natural and obvious – and it is so according to the system of ordering that has been followed. However, we are aware that with the same data another interpreter can rearrange and realign the information and create a substantively alternate constellation that signifies a different set of meanings and purposes. The question that guides us at present is not the differences between two arrangements, or whether they are competing or contradictory, but rather an assessment of the main ordering principles as they are generally and traditionally used by New Testament scholars. Innovative and imaginative readings of the New Testament are ultimately products of rearrangement and reordering. Our purpose in this chapter is to open the door for the latter (innovation) by exploring some of the limitations of the former (the generally and traditionally used ordering principles of interpretation).

There is, in our view, one additional element that is important to the discussion that follows. The discipline of study of the New Testament, and of biblical scholarship as a whole for that matter, was forged in a period of high intellectual activity centered in major universities in Europe. From the 18th century onwards the university concept took on more of the shape we know today, and the study of philology, philosophy, history, and theology were central disciplines during this time of this heightened intellectual engagement. At the same time, we see a spurt of growth and expansion of the scientific disciplines, such as biology and chemistry. None of these areas of study are unique to the modern era, of course, but certainly major scientific advances were being made during that time. Not the least of these, in the 19th century, was the rise of evolutionary theory, most closely associated with Charles Darwin (1809–1882). The theory of development and evolution across time and according to environmental circumstances was already part of a rich intellectual heritage of Western philosophy – seen, for example, in the philosophical history of the development of human institutions outlined in G. W. F. Hegel's (1770–1831) work. The further application of developmental themes to humans and human social organization was a natural step to take. The study of the New Testament was forged in this environment, wherein scientific discourses had a significant influence on the human sciences in philology, philosophy, history, and theology.

At the same time, the universities in Europe, along with the various disciplines, and certainly the study of the Bible in particular, were seeking to create distance between the investigation of the physical and historical world and the control of ecclesiastical authorities. At one level, most disciplines in the university setting were conscious of the importance of this divide. Certainly, the controversies of the past, such as the trial of Galileo Galilei (1633), had made clear that the advancement of knowledge should not be subject to any limitations set by religious authority. The loss of the vast and exclusive claims of the Catholic Church on political and social conditions, as well as the spread of Protestantism, also aided significantly in the growing influence of the "secular" state, where rational principles separate from church dogma would guide law, societal organization, national interests, education (including universities), and so forth. Combined with the cross-fertilization between the natural and human sciences, the ground was rich for the planting of a substantively new approach to the study of the Bible, evolving into a complex of methods we now call "historical criticism." Early proponents and practitioners of historical criticism consciously deployed the term "scientific" for their approach to biblical texts and traditions, utilizing the term *Wissenschaft*, which in German means something akin to "scientific investigation." This term signified in particular the need and desire for the study of the Bible to be separated from church interference and the control of ecclesial dogma, as well as a claim that the Bible must be investigated like any other humanly produced text. According to early historical critics, such study was to be accomplished particularly through the scientific method of collection of data, observation and analysis of the material, and then placing the results of inquiry within a framework that made sense of the discrete bits of data presented to the researcher. It was understood that the investigation of the past would have to be somewhat reconstructive, and that it would not be possible to achieve the exactitude that many felt the sciences provided – but neither were such reconstructions meant to be aligned with the unbroken lines of religious and social tradition that had for so long served to justify the present. That said, these scholars of the 18th and 19th centuries were clear that such an approach to the biblical material resulted in some radically new ways of understanding those texts and the ancient world that produced them, from how we thought about the composition of the documents to the manner in which we conceptualized the development of the Jewish and Christian religions. Most of the historical work done today on the New Testament has its methodological grounding in the approaches and results of this earlier period of historical-critical scholarship.

Going one step further, however, we should emphasize one important feature of this period of the "birth" of modern New Testament studies that is often downplayed or overlooked by scholars examining the meta-questions related to the field we are engaging in this book. Namely, the study of early Christianity by the historical critics of this time was heavily influenced by conceptions generated elsewhere in the broader intellectual milieu. Such influence was not something that happened mechanistically, but rather it was a product of the convergence and confluence of ideas that were taking shape in the rich environment of the universities and among the interactions of the social elite. It was also rather commonplace, moreover, for scholars of, say, the biological sciences to reflect on the larger philosophical and theological questions raised by their work. Darwin himself is known to have contemplated the implications of his own research on natural selection for thinking about the place of God in the schema of the universe, leaning at one time toward a theistic approach to the evolutionary process: the idea that there might be a divine "hand" operative in the natural selection process. In any case, as a result of this rich and varied interaction among the natural and human sciences, and also the burgeoning of fields like anthropology and sociology, and the turn to the origins of religion in both of these areas of inquiry, the study of the New Testament was infused with concepts drawn from the scientific "order of things."

In an intellectual environment so focused on the natural world, it was *natural* for Bible critics, immersed in this larger ethos, to deploy various concepts that are most closely connected to a "scientific worldview." So, from questions related to origins and beginnings, to development and stability, to genetic relations, all of these were notions taken over from a larger scientific discursive world. To be sure, of course, it was not simple borrowing without thought or attribution. Currents in philosophy and the science of philology were also influencing the other manifestations of scientific investigation of human phenomena, as well as the study of the New Testament. That is, the model we have inherited and in many cases prefer is one of cross-fertilization rather than simply a mechanical framework for the process. In a best-case scenario, we might consider this to be an environment of free-flowing and mutual movement of ideas, language, and structures of knowing. All of that said, however, we also need to keep in mind that these dynamics profoundly shaped the New Testament "order of things."

It is not coincidental that many of the ordering principles that continue to shape historical study of early Christianity are deeply rooted in a kind of language and epistemological structure that we now would most closely associate with disciplines such as biology, chemistry, and physics, as well the related discourses and methods of the Social Sciences. As disciplines have become more differentiated and isolated in the contemporary intellectual landscape, it has become less apparent that the earlier polymathic and integrative environment of intellectual activity in the 18th and 19th centuries, and even earlier to be sure, made it possible for the modern study of the New Testament and its continuing use and development of the ordering principles of this earlier period to think and look a lot like what we would now call the natural sciences. Even as many New Testament scholars who investigate the historical and social contexts of those writings would insist that they do not assume an atheist or agnostic stance toward their subject matter, and that they believe that God really did work in history to initiate and be involved in the experiences of the early Christians, the methods used to derive the results of study are consistent with the ordering principles used in the natural sciences. Indeed, if it were not for that deep historical connection and legacy, the modern study of the New Testament would look and feel remarkably different than it does. It is only because the field participates in the epistemological foundations of the sciences that it proceeds the way it does in terms of analysis and interpretation. Of course, the study of history in the 18th and 19th centuries, alongside the development of the discipline of philology, had a significant impact on the manner in which New Testament studies proceeded, and these two disciplines more than any other were intimately connected with the origins of modern biblical scholarship. However, it should be noted that those disciplines were already participating in the cross-fertilization we have described above, so influences from history and philology only served to bolster and reinforce the embeddedness of the scholarly episteme in early Christian studies within the larger scientific paradigm. It is to the exploration of this episteme that we now turn.

Origins and linear development

To some of our readers, it probably goes without saying that one of the major impulses in the study of the New Testament has been a quest for origins and beginnings, whether it be a search for the historical Jesus, the earlier or earliest church or emergent Christian community, the earliest Gospels or sayings or traditions, the beginning point of theological reflection on Christ or ecclesiology, the various early Christian rituals such as baptism or the Lord's Supper, the mission to the Gentiles, or any other number of original and originary moments in the first decades of early Christianity.[6] Frequently, the underlying premise of such engagements is as follows: that which is chronologically more original, prior, or earlier is also thought to be that which is more historically grounded. That is, the earlier the better, for what is earlier is in some way more "real" or authentic. For example, that which is closer in chronological period to the lives of Jesus or Paul carries the implied stamp of being more historically accurate and reliable, bringing with it a certain epistemological primacy in terms of configuring those principles that are determinative for assessing the truth-validity of what comes after that which is earlier. Interest in origins leads to a question such as whether, for instance, the Gospel source Q, or the Gospel of Matthew, or the Gospel of Mark, the Epistle to the Galatians, or the Gospel of Thomas, or the Didache represents the "real" point of entry into the development of the Christian tradition as known today. Naturally, the trajectories that we observe in early Christianity will vary depending on where one begins. So the origin point is critical in almost all historical studies conducted on the New Testament.

Within the New Testament "order of things," an origin point provides the initial coordinate by which everything else can be traced, the single point from which all things flow. In some sense, much of what we do in the historical arena of study related to the ancient world is predicated first and foremost on having a place to start from and with. This may seem like a relatively basic point to make; it is also one that is all too infrequently the subject of critical reflection. It is, as one would expect in terms of ordering principles, an assumption that guides the basic framing of our evidence. Everything has a beginning point – the Earth, humans, the universe. It has become natural to think of historical phenomena in the same way – as "things" that have a beginning and a teleology, a moving toward some end. Interestingly, within this framework, there is an implied order to how things unfold. Although we may frequently speak of a random world, the natural order is in fact, according to modern conception at least, anything but random. It operates according to rules and laws – and rules of law. The universe expands according to fixed rules, even if those rules are not always obvious to us. And even when one raises the matter of relativity one still knows how to plot the coordinates to engage in alternative configurations of the physical universe. The ability to predict is critical in this respect. And while scholars of the New Testament, Christian origins, and early Christianity have not been involved in the predictive process in usually such a deliberative way, the basic historical methodologies act according to the same rules. In order to reflect on where things come from, how they began, and how they developed, and to be able to describe those facets in comprehensible ways, one has to assume that there are originary moments and that whatever emerges from that beginning point develops and evolves in some fashion. To be sure, even as linear movement forward is the assumed principle, scholars still acknowledge there will be messy elements along the way. We thus understand "linearity" to denote the basic principle that the phenomena that emerge at a beginning have a forward movement of sorts. Like the universe, it expands, after the "big bang," according to a certain logic.

Now, we should be clear that the notion of a beginning point and a linear development of some kind for a historical religion or people group is not simply a modern conception. Ancient writers had long conceived of their pasts as having moments of beginning and also development and change over time. Thus, the concept of origins, as an ordering principle, is not purely the product of the development of the modern "order of things." One could point to any number of ancient Greek or Roman writers of history or epic and easily trace out the commitment to origins and linear movement as key ordering principles. Indeed, Rome itself has its moment of origins with the rape of a virgin by a war god and the resultant brothers suckling at a she-wolf – it does not get any more fixed than that! The ancient Jewish writer Josephus (c. 37–100) seeks to demonstrate for the Roman world that Judaism has a particular point of origin, that it is an ancient ethnic, religious, and political entity with a distinct heritage. Moreover, in his linear developmental history Josephus is able to show that any problematic aspects of Judaism with respect to Roman rule arise from elements that are not representative of the "core" of Judaism itself. Thus, both deviation and normativity can be traced fairly clearly. The early Christian ecclesial authority and historian Eusebius of Caesarea (c. 265–340) extensively detailed the origins of Christianity in his *Ecclesiastical History*. He was adept at showing the clear line of the Christian faith moving from Jesus through the authoritative apostles of the early Christian community to their disciples and so on, with a demonstrable lineage extending into the time of Eusebius. Were there deviations and "heresies"? Absolutely! But those could readily be explained by examining the offshoots from the main line that culminates in orthodoxy. Heresy, for Eusebius, is an evident deviation from the truth of the Gospel that was passed on through a single chain of early Christian leaders.

It would thus be inaccurate and misleading to suggest that somehow only moderns are interested in origins and beginnings, and in the perceptible linearity of development and evolution. At the same time, there are some key differences that should not go unnoticed, not least that an entire technology of historical study has evolved to support the modern quest for origins as a major ordering principle of the discipline. When someone picks up the multi-volume works of James Dunn (*Christianity in the Making*) or N. T. Wright (*Christian Origins and the Question of God*), one does not get the impression that they are in the same historical territory as ancient writers like Josephus and Eusebius. In the latter we are in a rather obvious arena of tendentious, ideologically inclined historical narrativizing that pays little attention to the weighing of evidence or close historical assessment. True, modern scholarly quests for origins are without a doubt similarly invested in the ideological commitments that result from their treatment of origins and development. What is different, however, is the presumed objective and neutral operative framework, just like science – indeed, it is a "historical science." This is the major shift, and accounts, at least in part, for the prodigious amount of scholarship on the matter of Christian origins. No contemporary scholar would pick up Josephus or Eusebius, for example, and simply move forward with an assessment of Jewish or Christian origins and development based on these sources. One will use these ancient sources, but critically evaluate them *based on other kinds of evidence*, the latter of which represents the more sophisticated historical technologies of the modern critic. Hence, while origins as a principle of historical investigation is not new in and of itself, the manner in which it is configured within the modern New Testament "order of things" is. And within that modern framework, the possibilities for configuring origins are multiple and varied – the only universal commitment among New Testament scholars seems to be that there is a beginning and there is linear development.

For instance, earlier scholars like Ernst Troeltsch (1865–1923) utilized the theory of evolution more explicitly, understanding the development of the phenomenon of early Christianity as moving from a simple to a complex organism.[7] Drawing more generally on the work done in the anthropology of religion such as that of Edward Burnett Tylor (1832–1917) and James George Frazer (1854–1941), historians such as Troeltsch saw development as an obvious way in which to articulate the structure of Christian institutional growth.[8] Therein the Jesus movement moves to another stage, from charismatic leadership in gatherings of believers to a fairly rigid structure of ecclesiastical hierarchies wherein dogma and authority rather than experience become the major foci. This basic movement from simple (charismatic leadership and experience) to complex (highly structured church hierarchies) represented one earlier model for understanding early Christian development.

The linear accent of the developmental model focuses on the movement from simple to intricate, which proceeds according to a natural progressive order observable in many other comparable institutions and religious movements, and of course also nature itself. Earlier, Ferdinand Christian Baur (1792–1860) detailed his Hegelian dialectical understanding of the development of early Christianity in similar terms, in his case being invested in the "thesis-antithesis" model, wherein conflict between the two was resolved in a "synthesis." For Baur, in what is one of the most oft-cited examples of this modality of thinking, the more conservative, law-bound movement of Peter (associated with early Christian communities in Jerusalem) came into conflict with the relatively law-free program of Paul (associated with non-Jerusalem, Gentile communities). This conflict resulted in a synthesis propagated by the writer of the book of Acts, who sought to resolve it by mediating between the two polar positions. This resolution of the conflict, whether it was historically factual or simply a product of literary fiction, in the end becomes the basis for the further development of the ancient church, which in some sense incorporated aspects of "law" (even if not "Jewish" per se) and "freedom." Again, one can readily see here a set of rules that are operative that explain how the evolution of the church took place. We note, moreover, that both Troeltsch and Baur had a preference for the earlier period of Christianity, prior to the rise of the structured ecclesial hierarchies, which, for these two Protestant interpreters, was readily associated with the Catholic Church, a definite negative in their view.[9]

Generally speaking, in terms of where New Testament scholarship has evolved from scholars of Christian origins in the 19th century, we see a similar pattern of thinking about origins and development, even as many critics have also wanted to challenge the dominant narrative offered by ancient writers like Eusebius or even the New Testament itself. Indeed, on the current and persistent methodological scene, critics frequently disagree on the beginning point or the movement therefrom, and the fixing of the origin point is frequently used in debates regarding the "true" nature of early Christianity. Was early Christianity at its core what later became touted as orthodox Christian faith? Was it something different and perhaps more radical? Scholars who posit different points of origin or who emphasize different texts or documents as more primary over others frequently are engaging in larger ideological and theological debates about the fundamental core of Christianity as a religious phenomenon. For instance, notable "popular" New Testament scholars, such as Bart Ehrman and N. T. Wright, are highly invested in their own theological/ideological commitments when they perform in public. Ehrman, for example, is insistent that the Gospels are not documents that can be utilized for the grounding of personal faith, as the fundamental core of the "gospel" is based on relatively non-trustworthy accounts of Jesus. Wright, by contrast, is adamant that the Gospels offer a portrait of Jesus that is relatively reliable, and certainly something that can (and should!) ground Christian faith. The issue for us is not who is right or wrong, but that both Ehrman and Wright have profound personal investment in the outcomes of their research, which obviously dictates how they utilize the principles of ordering in New Testament scholarship to come up with the results that they do. The ways in which they investigate the original documents are similar, based on the same principles of analysis and interpretation. However, their characterizations of those same *original* documents dictate how origins are, in turn, constructed or deconstructed. In other words, the nature of the origins as assessed and interpreted by scholars determines the implications of the development that follows. In our view, there is no escaping this particular scenario, and any reader and consumer of New Testament scholarship, whether advanced or introductory, would do well to bear this in mind.

Ultimately, the ordering principle of origins and linear development has a profound impact on the entire field of New Testament studies. It would be difficult to find a particular area in the discipline that has been untouched by commitments to beginnings and evolution. One only need to look at the subfield of textual criticism to see precisely the manner in which the origin and linear development principle operates. We know, for example, that we do not possess the original manuscripts of the New Testament texts – or any early Christian texts for that matter. Moreover, we know, based on the manuscripts we do possess, that there was tremendous textual diversity and pluriformity in the various manuscript trajectories and traditions that arose in the early centuries in which Christian movements were taking shape. That being a given, we still observe a fairly strong commitment by text critics to affirming original textual trajectories over others that deviate and become desecrated, polluted, or deformative in some way. The most recent turn in text-critical studies is to embrace these "deviations" as offering important insights into the world of the early Christians in their own right, and so there has been a movement, at least in part, to embrace the multiformity of early New Testament textual traditions. Now, it may no longer make sense to speak of "original texts," since texts frequently are composed over longer periods of time, with additions and deletions made in the process of composition. At the same time, the notion of there being a "beginning text" is still vital for many scholars, even if they can only refer to an originary text in a relative sense. And this should give us pause. It is in the textual discussion in particular that we see most clearly the invocation of the rhetoric of biology and evolution, with the designation of species of texts, derivations, branches, and such.[10] The biological metaphor may well be the primary conceptual metaphor operative in textual transmission assessments, but that same model is active beyond just textual traditions. Fundamentally, we almost always conceive of Christian origins in terms of an implicit biological organism: a "thing" that originates, grows, and evolves, with offshoots sprouting in a variety of directions. It is true that few scholars consider the earliest iterations, those nearest the origin point, to be the "monkeys" whilst the latter developments are more evolved, even as there might be quite a few "missing links" between the earlier species and our own. In this respect, the judgment, as noted earlier, is the opposite: the point of origin is the point of definition for that which follows, and it allows the scholar to determine what is "true" to the beginning and what is a derivation.

Especially helpful at this juncture are the comments by Edward Said, who, in his discussion of the renowned New Testament text critic A. E. Housman, notes that since there can be no absolutely correct and "original" text firmly anchoring subsequent transcriptions in reality, all texts exist in a constantly moving tangle of imagination and error. The job of the textual critic is, by fixing one text securely on the page, to arrange all other versions of that text in some sort of linear sequence with it … [D]iscursive prose about a text only makes explicit the implicit filiation which the cumulative emendations and restorations of the edited text have established.[11]

In this formulation it becomes evident just how fundamental it is to establish the beginning point so as to be able to coordinate all that follows. Furthermore, without a firm commitment to a linear (and stable – on that more below) development, there is no way to confidently affirm the lineage and true character of that which originates at the founding or beginning moment. Obviously, without a certain measure of faith in linearity there would also be no purpose in referring to an originating point. The developmental lines may be messy and blurry, and they may be obscured at points, but the commitment to an originary moment entails the ability to reasonably predict the broad contours of the "tradition" and to allow it to be identified, quantified, described, analyzed, and interpreted.

From the perspective of de-introducing the New Testament we would raise the question as to what is lost in such formulations of early Christianity, its texts, and its communities and practices. That is, we would inquire as to what extent the obsession with origins and development is a product of our modern episteme, deeply rooted in a scientific configuration that necessarily hinges on beginnings and some traceable form of linear development. Further, it is important to consider whether this ordering principle adequately captures the complex vicissitudes that would seem to constitute the historical "process." In other words, it is worth deliberating whether we are doing more of a disservice to our study of the ancient past by consistently constructing our subject – be it texts, people, communities, or practices – as having a single moment of beginning at a fixed point in time. Foucault's comments on "tradition" and how it operates for us within our modern framework are quite helpful on this score:

Take the notion of tradition: it is intended to give a special temporal status to a group of phenomena that are both successive and identical (or at least similar); it makes it possible to rethink the dispersion of history in the form of the same; it allows a reduction of the difference proper to every beginning, in order to pursue without discontinuity the endless search for the origin; tradition enables us to isolate the new against a background of permanence, and to transfer its merit to originality, to genius, to the decisions proper to individuals.[12]

45

For Foucault, there is in some respects no "origin" point for historical phenomena. Rather, the ordering concept of "origin" serves our modern interests quite well, as it allows us to reify unity at the expense of historical differences, creating a stable context and background against which our historical tasks and modern investments can effectively operate. Without a fixed origin point we would have a most difficult time tracing out with certainty historical, conceptual, and theological lineages, which in our epistemological framework are central not only for understanding history, but indeed for doing history in the first place. As Foucault notes in his essay on Nietzsche and genealogy, "the true historical sense confirms our existence among countless lost *identities*, without a landmark or a point of reference."[13] In this respect, the focus on beginnings, and the movement that proceeds, functions to anchor our own world and its episteme. As Foucault states, "an entire historical tradition (theological or rationalistic) aims at dissolving the singular event into an ideal continuity – as a theological movement or a natural process."[14] Herein lies a more sublimated feature of the modern "order of things," since, irrespective of one's own belief in divine or supernatural reality, the ordering principles presuppose in many respects a teleological movement that embeds the deeply rooted Western belief in a supra-human purposeful force that drives history forward.[15]

Nearly a century ago, some scholars were already raising such questions about linearity and origins. Walter Bauer, in his often overlooked and frequently misunderstood study entitled *Orthodoxy and Heresy in Earliest Christianity*,[16] noted that the Eusebian paradigm of a steady movement from the orthodox origin of the Christian faith in the earliest Christian communities outwards to increasing heretical splintering off from the "true" character of that faith did not cohere with the ancient evidence – even as orthodoxy can clearly be traced, in Eusebius's view, down to his own present time. Bauer's analysis focused on regional developments in early Christianity. He ascertained that different locales and regions throughout the Roman Empire had diverse versions of Christianity, some of which seemed to start with more "orthodox" (as that came to be defined later) beliefs and in time turned more "heterodox," while others seemed to start off with the reverse, with "heterodox" (as defined by a later standpoint in church history) beliefs being the earliest expressions of the Christian faith. Upon reading Bauer's erudite treatment, one does not come away with ready answers or an easily attained framework in which to understand origins and development. Rather, one becomes all the more aware of how complex, and story-driven, the emergence of any particular movement, belief, or practice in fact is – and likely always has been.

46

In the end, we would argue that rather than talking of "origins" and "linearity" one should conceive of early Christian phenomena as *emergent*. That is, there is no true moment of beginning – there is no "big bang" for a particular Gospel tradition, manuscript, New Testament concept, or early Christian practice. Rather, there inheres a confluence of streams, both synchronic and diachronic, that swirl together, in the process generating all kinds of innovative and inspired emergent phenomena. Historical investigative efforts, and the concomitant interpretive results, may be better spent examining the broader confluence of ideas, practices, personages, circumstances, experiences, and such that created the context for the emergence of phenomena which we may never be able to pinpoint or to fully define with exactitude. That is not to suggest that ancient writers did not present us with narratives and stories and frameworks that do often compel us to think of an originary moment and subsequent linear development. Our sources for early Christianity do seek to elucidate the definitions of the movement. However, for the historian of the New Testament, it would be better to see these definitions as a matter of identity formation (see below) rather than as precise historical fixed points of reference. We do definitely capture glimpses and even more powerful images of the emergent character of what we call the New Testament and early Christianity, but we submit that the desire to firmly coordinate the phenomena ends up oversimplifying much more complicated historical processes.

In our view, there is no precise origin of Christianity, just as there is no particular person such as Jesus or Paul who is the singular "founder" of the movement. And yet, to be sure, what we now call early Christianity did emerge within a particular region and time period; it did not disappear from the scene, even as it was constantly reconfigured; and it did feature major figures who were seminal or remembered as such for the emergence of the movement(s). In our minds, however, this comprises a different understanding than that which is engendered by fixating on the precision of origins and development. Indeed, we would argue that the heterogeneous framework we are articulating here elucidates differences in the emergent period of early Christianity, and encourages multiplicity, complexity, and also contradiction in our understandings of the New Testament.[17] There is no easy story – no readily transparent narrative for us to grasp. And questioning the manner in which the modern "order of things" shapes our apprehension of the past is a good place to begin in terms of rethinking the whole enterprise of New Testament study and interpretation. In the ordering principles that follow, one will see the continuous replaying of these same themes in the modern New Testament "order of things," similarly indebted to the epistemic scientific structures of thinking and being.

Stability, definability, and simplicity

From the above discussion it should be clear that if precision and exactitude are at least goals in historical investigation, then it will follow that other ordering principles, alongside origins and linear development, will undergird sustained efforts to coordinate and affix points of interpretive relevance. As we use them here, the categories of "stability," "definability," and "simplicity" are interrelated, and more or less signify the same general principle that is operative in the New Testament "order of things": the need for creating a constant and unchanging subject for investigation. Postmodern considerations have for some time focused on the instability of the subject – that people are not entities that can be solely defined by a rigid set of rules and laws governing how subjects think about themselves, experience the world, and interact with others. The theme of many postmodern methodologies is in fact the fundamental instability of the subject, and much is owed therein to both Freudian and particularly Lacanian psychoanalytic applications. In our exploration here, however, we are less interested and invested in rehashing and rehearsing postmodern configurations, although no doubt our argument in this chapter as a whole is somewhat in conversation with such notions. Rather, we are consciously reflecting here on the idea of constants as those are conceived of in historical analysis and conceptualized and manifested in the study of the New Testament. In so doing, we aim to question the possibility and indeed usefulness of this ordering principle. Our own stance, in contrast to some of the positions outlined in the Introduction, is based on the premise that historical investigation is not only possible, but also an engaging, necessary, and potentially transformative project. It is a matter, rather, of how we proceed in such investigation that is at issue.

As anyone who has undertaken even a rudimentary science experiment in high school knows, in order to test a hypothesis one must set a series of limitations on the process of inquiry and investigation. This must be done in order to create a controlled environment so as not to interfere with the end result. Now, contemporary scientists might well question why pursuing hypotheses, and seeking to refute them, is the best way to actually come up with advances in science. Following what many historians would suggest with respect to investigating the New Testament, many scientists would claim, in fact, that the better way to proceed is to ask a series of good questions with a view to providing responses to those queries.[18] That said, regardless of the particular method by which one works, there is a direct need for affixing the constants or "control group" by which one can conduct historical exploration. Even in cases where the results are predetermined and actually configure the way in which the coordinates are arranged – which happens in our field more often than New Testament scholars would like to admit – the "experiment" only works if the interpreter can count on there being stable, fixed, and definable elements that provide limitations and boundaries for the historical work. That is, the absolute requirement of restrictions and confinements for historical work is one of the key components that reinforce the categories of stability and definability. In short, we cannot, it is presumed, move forward in the interpretation of the New Testament data without a sure footing and a firm foundation that guarantee that the ground will not shift as we are busy mining for the "truth" regarding Christian origins, beliefs, and practices.

And this is where the concept of "simplicity" comes into play, as any attempt at regulating boundaries and imposing limitations will necessarily streamline and simplify the incalculable and often inscrutable complexity that is at work in every historical moment. Most scholars may not necessarily be conscious of, or willfully employ, an approach that is committed to simplifying the data. Indeed, the illusion is quite the opposite: scholars are working with and sifting through a myriad of multifaceted traditions and historical circumstances reflected in the New Testament writings, deciphering the nuances in order to provide a relatively objective assessment of the discrete bits of data that lie before them. The "story" of what it is that New Testament scholars do often stands in contrast to what actually happens in practice. And in this respect, the need for constancy is a key factor, and one that overlaps with the other categories discussed below. Overall, then, we seem not to move forward in the interpretive task without a strong orientation to stability, and without data that is firmly fixed. Through the category of stability, meaning can be rendered in a clear and patent manner, which can in turn be delineated and defined, and that, finally, can be quantified for scholarly and popular consumption.

There are innumerable ways in which the category of stability works itself out in the study of the New Testament. Whether at the more advanced level of scholarly research production or the level of the introductory textbook, one is regularly exposed to this ordering principle. If one opens up an introduction to the New Testament, for instance, almost everything presented therein has been manufactured based on the premise of constants, even as the scholar responsible for writing that book may be relatively unware of the operation of this ordering principle. One speaks with confidence of early Christian texts as fixed entities, the content of which we can be relatively certain is as we have it now before us in our Bibles. We are also introduced to communities of believers in different cities and regions of the Roman Empire, assessing their theological beliefs as a unified pattern, even as we might also suggest that there were "opponents" whose opposition is similarly traceable and definable. Similarly, we will need to know something about the conceptual backgrounds in Judaism, Hellenism, and

Romanism that influenced the theological developments evident in early Christian belief. It is ubiquitous in New Testament introductions, for example, to refer to "Jewish Beliefs and Practices in the Diaspora and Palestine" and "Greek and Roman Beliefs and Practices." We additionally encounter the constitution of early Christian communities, composed of either or both constituents of Jews and Gentiles, with a firm "faith" that we know what "Jew" and "Gentile" mean when we deploy these categories as signifiers of ancient identity. And so on.

Without a strong guarantee of carefully regulated boundaries and borders, it is much more difficult to make specific and relatively certain statements about ancient Christian materials. Indeed, we might consider this a situation not unlike receiving a coloring book, where there are traced-out shapes of identifiable objects defined by firm black lines on a white or newsprint background. The task of the one using such a tool is to provide the shades of color that help give the black and white lines more depth and bring the image to life. While there might be variations on the coloring activity – some might choose to color a figure of a bear brown, others purple, most often dependent on their level of commitment to presenting the *realia* of the object – most consider the *lines* that outline the colorless figure to be hard and fast guidelines, as without those the figure would lose shape, and perhaps not even be recognizable as a figure in the first place. So we are called upon – culturally, socially, and perhaps even with an underlying moral imperative – to "color inside the lines." And such is also the case in the field of New Testament studies, in so far as failing to color within the lines results in a distorted and unreliable figure, which becomes functionally problematic in aiding the coordination of other bits of data that we are seeking to pull together in order to create a recognizable and consumable constellation of information. It should be pointed out, of course, that even if there is coloring outside the lines, we are always aware of the fact that there are lines to begin with. That is, even those interpreters who seek to bend the rules, who push the limitations of analysis beyond the merely obvious shades and patterns, still understand that there are borders and boundaries and lines. To color outside of a line is to already recognize there is a line. And therein lies the rub of much New Testament scholarship: the lines are in place before we even begin our historical interpretive tasks. It is these lines in fact that need to be challenged (and erased!) if historical work is to reflect more accurately the booming, buzzing confusion that is human historical experience.

Our contention is that stability, definability, and simplicity are potent theoretical concepts that help establish constancy in coordinates for plotting out interpretive results for New Testament analysis, but they do not necessarily reflect well the more incarnate realities of early Christianity. We can refer to

"Pauline communities," and by that signify a consistent, demarcated, boundaried, and stable gathering of people in Galatia, Corinth, Rome, or elsewhere whom we understand to read and think in similar ways. Yet this kind of historical homogeneity is also highly improbable. The fact is that every member of a community experiences the enunciative language of (Paul's) letters differently, configured in a highly complex set of networks of meaning, some shared with other members of the group, and others not.[19] There is no unified perspective, audience, or reception of a letter from Paul. There may be a discourse that arises that is accessible and readily apprehended, but that discourse represents something supra-human and not the particularities and contingencies of historical personages in concrete periodic moments that converge to generate the emergent discourse.[20]

Yet, when modern New Testament scholars describe the "Pauline communities" or "Pauline assemblies," there is a decided focus on "coloring within the lines." Even when a feminist scholar like Antoinette Clark Wire famously argues that behind the Corinthian correspondence lies an oppositional movement of female prophets that Paul seeks to oppose, we cannot assume that the female prophets, who are at once addressed and erased in Paul's discourse about veiling (1 Cor. 11), are a unified, boundaried, and stable *counter*-group.[21] It is understandable, of course, that it is tempting to utilize these categories that assure constancy. Many scholars would, in fact, consider these categories necessary. Herein, then, Paul becomes a stable entity, the Corinthian community to which he writes is similarly constant, and the opposition group to whom Paul responds in at least a portion of the letter is also firmly delineated as a distinct segment of the community that is challenging Paul's authority or at the minimum asserting its own in contradistinction to his. The picture that is offered in scholarly analysis is simple and straightforward, and as a result there is broader approximation of what conflicts might have existed in Corinth, based on an abstracted, distilled, and highly diluted representation of a more concretely messy configuration of human experience.

Whether we are examining Pauline communities and the reception of his letters or the development of the oral and textual history of the sayings of Jesus and the composition of the New Testament (and other) Gospels, we consistently rely on the principle of stability in our defining of the parameters of our study, making sure that we know where the lines are for our historical work and then that we "draw" within them. Some will argue that there is no other way to go about historical work than to do precisely this. And, to be sure, any presentation of information necessarily requires a framework in which it is assessed and interpreted. In the model of historical work we are affirming as part of de-introducing the New Testament, we do not believe one can necessarily escape this particular reality. It is, in the end, a result of what Fredric Jameson refers to as the "prison house of language."[22] That said, at the same time we need to be aware that the presentation and maintenance of the information within the "lines" is also a distortion of the fluidity and instability that are inherent in all historical experiences and products, inherent in all human beings and human communities.

Consistency and coherence

Stemming from the focus on stability, definability, and simplicity, the categories of consistency and coherence arise quite naturally. If one is to think of stability as the "lines" within which we must draw, then in consistency and coherence we are dealing with the colors with which we choose to detail the subject. In other words, bears are a variety of colors – white, black, brown – but they are not purple or pink or orange, and if we see colored bears like this, often drawn outside of the lines as well, we may very well assume they have been done by children with imagination and a carefree attitude about the bears rather than an "adult" with a view to precision and accuracy in representation. And herein lies the focus on patternization and flattening in the study of historical data. Very much like our contemporary scientific foci (that is, outside of the realm of quantum physics), in order to study a particular subject one has to presume, within reasonable parameters, that not only is the entity stable in its basic orientation, but that it also has consistency and coherence in terms of its overall structure. In other words, as a corollary to stability (the "lines") one also has to imagine the presence of coherence (the "coloring"). The basic element in view here is that enunciative statements are presented and sketched out in a way that we recognize as functionally intelligible, understandable, and reliable.

There are numerous points of entry through which we might draw out some of the ways in which these ordering principles are manifest in the study of the New Testament. In general terms, one could look to any of the New Testament texts, say the Gospel of John or Paul's letter to the Romans as examples. Scholars are adept at tracing out every possible bit of data from these texts that can be used for interpreting those same texts. First and foremost, one of the main presuppositions is that an "original" author (and usually only one author – for some reason we do not imagine New Testament texts to be co-written) has a particular message that he or she wishes to communicate, and that the text is shaped with this communicative end in view. In principle, such an assumption is largely true. However, the focus on coherence and consistency suggests that an author will also communicate clearly and convincingly, and that every phrase is constructed with a high level of intentionality. With coherence in mind, interpreting a text presumes that every word "counts" and is meant to be exactly where it is in relation to other words. Perhaps there are texts that meet these high standards – certainly modern scientific papers seek to communicate in text and symbol as accurately as possible the point that is to be made. The question for our ancient literature, however, is that we are dealing with a complex intersection of communicative strategies and interests, where literary artistry may be as important as the straightforward communication of a propositional statement. And certainly we cannot and should not assume that every New Testament text offers us a clear and coherent, or even completely rational and articulate, "message." There are tropes and themes, to be sure. However, it is the modern scholar, and not the ancient author, who seeks to connect these themes together into a much larger whole – often, in our view, making more of a text than is actually in that text.[23]

Historical critics tend to have the view that our ancient authors approached the task of writing a narrative and/or communicating complicated theological themes or nuanced instruction on community practice with a superior rhetorical awareness about the capacity of their specific audiences to understand coupled with an almost superhuman ability by these authors to transcend their own mental limitations and human fragilities when it came to composing texts. It is as if there is a commitment to an incarnational framework for the high-minded theological concepts of the New Testament (such as "Jesus became human"), but when it comes to thinking of the New Testament itself as a product of human enfleshment, we quickly can lose sight of the implications of such a view of humanity. It is in this way that our ancient writers are often conceived in somewhat cardboard-cutout fashion, almost lifeless, and devoid of what it is that makes us human, not least *making mistakes*, or at the minimum reflecting inconsistency, incoherence, and failure in the art and act of communication, the latter being comprised of the use of the wrong words to signify an idea, poorly phrased sentences, grammatically improper sentences, and so on. In the quest for coherence it is often overlooked that, aside from all of the other social and cultural facets that played out in the process of textual transmission in early Christianity, scribes also corrected grammar and clarified ideas, and often outright added their own content to texts – which we would say renders texts more, and not less, unstable and incoherent.

This is not to say that we cannot perceive, as noted above, various themes that emerge as we read the Gospel of John or the letter to the Romans. However, at the same time, in making meaning with biblical texts we are also *looking for* patterns and themes, and it need not be the case that just because we find something emerging throughout a particular text that the author in fact intended as much. Moreover, we frequently assume that all the twists and turns of intertextuality, including references to other biblical texts, and especially Hebrew Bible/Old Testament materials, is deliberate.

That is, our premise is that of consistency of intention to utilize pre-existing scriptures, when in fact all kinds of extra-textual materials might end up in a text without any particular purpose. Of course, early Christian writers did "cite" Hebrew Bible texts, such as the Psalms, Isaiah, the Pentateuch, and much more. It may be the case that they cited such texts from having access to scrolls or books, it could be that they had the material memorized, or it could be some other means of "knowing" such texts entirely. Further, despite the presence of explanation and interpretation at times, we cannot always readily decipher the connection of the pre-existing to the context or the logic and rationality of its deployment. And in order to make things work out in terms of coherence, scholars will frequently engage in extensive exegetical contortions to make sense of the pre-existing text or tradition, often depending upon a fairly sophisticated understanding of Hebrew, Aramaic, and Greek grammar, an understanding which is itself based on modern, and not ancient, philological study and codification. In other words, what is presented as apparent and clear in modern scholarship is frequently not the case when one looks more closely at the ancient materials themselves.[24] We assume intentionality when there might well be randomness, we assume rational progression in argumentation when we might find inconsistency and contradiction, and we assume an overall coherent structure in terms of content of a text when there might well be disarray and even confusion.

Some three decades ago, Heikki Räisänen wrote a book on Paul's view of the law that provides a particularly cogent example of a challenge to coherence and consistency as categories in New Testament study.[25] The topic of Paul's position on the Jewish law in both Romans and Galatians has been one of the most heated and controversial discussions in the history of the discipline, with scholars seeking to grapple with what seems to be at times an opposition to, and at other times an appreciation for, the Jewish law. Earlier German Protestant scholarship had proposed a fairly sharp break with the law in Paul's understanding of the new community founded "in Christ," and this view has been challenged by much anglophone scholarship in the past half-century or so, as we will discuss in Chapter 2. A significant portion of New Testament scholarly energy has been placed in service of attempting to resolve the puzzle of the law in Paul's thought, using everything from Jewish and Greek background traditions to complicated exegetical configurations in order to ascertain the correct interpretation of Paul's relationship to the law.

Räisänen's proposal went against the grain in that he quite simply argued that Paul was inconsistent in his rhetoric, and thus was possibly, if not likely, inconsistent regarding his views on the law. Ultimately, Räisänen argued, it becomes very difficult to put together a fully coherent theological position on the law based on Paul's writings as the primary source for such a position. To be sure, in the letters we get broad threads and themes, and certainly one can discern therein a sense of the spirit of Paul's relationship to the Jewish law and its place in his broader theological view. However, any attempt to make sense of all of Paul's statements as (a) stable and coherent in their own right, and (b) connecting together into a larger theological framework that stands above the letters themselves, simply involves too many contortions and loopholes to fully work. In fact, we might not even know whether Paul was anti-law or pro-law – or, even if he were one or the other, what precisely that would entail in his ancient context as opposed to how it would look in our own. We simply know that in his writings the (Jewish) law has a complicated and convoluted, if not also contradictory, positioning. Needless to say, Räisänen's view has not gained widespread scholarly acceptance in large part because his framework does not provide for a fully coherent, stable, and abstracted Pauline position on the law. That said, it should be noted that Räisänen arrives at his position on inconsistency using the exact same scientific categories of analysis that other historical critics do. It is only that he uses the principles of coherence and consistency to show that Paul is neither coherent nor consistent – he disproves the hypothesis, if you will.

Broadly speaking, not only do we have the larger issue that authors are not necessarily, if ever, fully consistent in their presentation of subject matter, but their approaches to writing may not be particularly useful in terms of providing overarching patterns of cohesion of theological and narrative themes in the New Testament. For instance, letters are frequently written for specific contexts, and the content is contingent, especially regarding the rhetorical strategies that are employed. It is possible, for that reason, that the law in the letter to the Romans functions differently than in Galatians or Philippians, since the writer(s) of those letters may well have had different rhetorical interests, and the subject matter thus is shaped and molded to be persuasive in that context, without any intention to reflect a broader personal theological perspective on the law. Paul's discussions of Christ and his significance for communities can be viewed similarly, that is, as highly contextualized configurations that seek to persuade an audience to act in a particular manner, which is seemingly the goal of most of Paul's letters.[26] Thus, even Paul's view of Christ, at least as written in the letters, is quite likely inconsistent. That does not mean he did not have some broad ideas of who Christ was and his significance for early Christian life and community. However, even in that respect, views change over time, and there is no reason to assume that even if Paul had some relative consistency in his views that he himself did not "grow in understanding." Another similar example is that of the literary activity in the Acts of the Apostles. If we assume that the sole purpose of the speeches in Acts is to provide a historically accurate presentation of what was actually said on a particular occasion that will read very differently than if we understand the writer of Acts to be creating "speech-in-character," which serves to curtail the thought and expression to how the writer of Acts assumed particular characters would speak. Thus, it is very possible that much of the so-called theological content in the speeches of Acts only generally represents the author's own views, and, rather, reflects his (or her) narrative artistry. Thus, the notions we have of how ancient people think reflect a view in which there is only static individualism, with no sense of development or of changing one's mind or an ever-expanding conceptual world in which new connections are made, articulated, and elaborated.

Through the examples we have briefly discussed above, it should hopefully become apparent that throughout the discipline of New Testament studies scholars seek to shore up the data, ensuring that, in this instance, it is "colored" appropriately so that it is recognizable, easily grasped and quantified, and readily available for interpretive consumption. One could add a variety of other subsidiary ordering principles that would also aid to bolster these overarching ones. For instance, genetic connections and interrelations offer a means by which we link a variety of discrete material in either a particular text or across a variety of texts. It is the strategy of interconnecting materials that helps us further draw the lines that generate the image of the larger stable structure of the New Testament. There is a clear sense of "cause and effect" in these epistemic ordering principles, even as it should be noted that just because there is a genetic connection does not mean that there is necessarily a positive development, as that connection is generally assessed from the vantage point of a particular value judgment. Connections and interrelations are assumed throughout the New Testament materials, and scholars are adept at creating them when they often seem absent, helping provide the "missing links" that conveniently knit together the threads that are being traced. And to be sure scholars also find mutations and deformities and perversions, although, again, the latter is a particularly pejorative term often reflecting the value judgment of interpreters. Thus, the issue here in terms of the New Testament "order of things" is not necessarily the manner in which the genetic relationships are formed and shaped – be they conceptual, textual, or social – but that they exist in the first place. Their existence allows the critic to tease out the lines of the larger picture, at times carefully brushing away the dust of the centuries that can occlude from full view the presumed inner dynamics that were operative in early Christianity.[27]

Difference, distinctiveness, and identity

Difference, distinctiveness, and identity comprise three interrelated categories that in many respects readily evolve out of the principles that we have delineated above. In order to fully identify a phenomenon that we can call "early Christianity," and a set of texts that we can label as the "New Testament," we require stable coordinates and categories that will allow our subject matter to rise above and out of its historical context and fully reveal itself to the modern critic. That is to say, early Christianity and the New Testament have to be grasped as actual entities in order to be interpreted as such. If they cannot be separated out clearly and consistently and coherently from the larger environment, then we cannot actually talk about these subjects – they have to be distinctive, different, and in many respects have a separate (even if "but equal") identity that frames the "self-awareness" of the subject. In other words, if early Christians of, say, the late first century CE could be in a position to not actually recognize themselves as "Christian," since belief in Jesus as the "risen Messiah," for example, need not on its own lead to a distinctive category of identity, then we are left with a quandary: what makes these people different from someone who might be Jewish or Greek or Roman – and how would we even know what "Jewish," "Greek," or "Roman" might mean within a larger network of contingent identity markers? Thus, within the broader ordering structure of the episteme of New Testament studies, identity is both *stabilized* as an actual thing to be quantified by particular identifiable features, and also *differentiated* from the identity of "others" who are not considered to be "early Christian."[28] And it is in this distinction that we can also begin to develop and refer to *innovation* by these identified groups/subjects.

Similarly, we may well ask: even if we could identify early Christians as a distinct group in antiquity, how would we know that we have identified a "religious," a "political," or a "social" movement? It seems very obvious to us today, in a world that appears to be sharply categorized into discrete domains of religious and secular or private and public (regardless of whether that reflects "reality"), that early Christianity is a religious movement. However, it is not at all the case that the historical contours of the ancient world support that particular modern assumption. Here is a very good point at which to examine how our own ordering of the world affects the ways in which we arrange and assess the data related to the ancient world. A very strong case can be made that when the Roman Empire came to oppose early Christians it was on the basis of political, and not religious, interests, since religious investments, as we would see them, were "political" from the Roman perspective, even as a recent scholarly cottage industry concerning "Roman religion" might insist otherwise. Moreover, we might well see, as some scholars of early Christianity invested in modern social-scientific approaches would have us do, that early Christians actually functioned as a social movement. The increasing emphasis on ancient guilds and associations as the location of early Christian gatherings would imply that early Christians may have been more of a social organization than a strictly religious phenomenon, at least as the latter is seen by modern eyes. That said, most scholars of ancient Christianity might also argue the case both ways: early Christians constituted a religious social movement or a politically motivated religious group. However, the lines are very difficult to draw, and it may well be that the majority of early Christians were very much unlike how we perceive them today, including the notion that many may have been polytheists despite the clear impression in the "authoritative" documents that they were not of that orientation. We actually do not know the answers to most of these questions even if our categories and methods suggest that we do.

Some of these facets of ordering can be observed in the tremendous amount of recent work that has gone into studying the Roman Empire as the backdrop for the emergence of early Christianity. We will address this trend in more detail in Chapter 2; for the moment we note simply that the broader focus on empire and imperialism, by which we largely mean the Roman institutions and their diverse machineries of implementation, helps to contextualize the New Testament, not unlike the way in which Judaism has often done as well. In some sense, related to the above point about making the distinction between politics and religion, the contrast between Roman Empire (as a political entity) and Judaism (as a religious entity) provides an excellent example of how distinction and differentiation serve to formulate how the identity of early Christianity is presented and interpreted. What is drawn into the conversation creates, to a large extent, the identity of the New Testament texts, concepts, and early Christian practices.

"Empire," then, has had the inadvertent effect of creating a unifying principle for reading the New Testament as the textual product of a single occasion. Granted, there is a diversity of viewpoints among scholars about, for instance, the precise relationship of the Gospel of Matthew versus John's Gospel versus Paul with respect to the Roman Empire. However, the growing consensus in New Testament scholarship is that the Roman Empire is the objective reality that provides the context for interpretation, irrespective of internal differences between the New Testament texts. "Empire" is thus stabilized as a mechanism that controls the terms on which the New Testament is written, produced, transmitted, and consumed. Further, imperial prowess and processes are located as that which must be violent and oppressive in contradistinction to the early Christian message, even if the latter is viewed by some scholars as compromised in many respects. Doubtless it is the case that the Roman mechanism of government and intervention differed substantially depending on locale and context – classicists and ancient historians have made much of the differences in governmentality and cultural orientation between the Roman "center" and the "provinces," for example.

Yet empire, and perhaps especially imperial images, provide the broad universal link across local differences, since the Romans deposited these potent displays of Roman claims to power throughout the empire and imposed them on the territories it controlled. Regardless of regional particularities, then, Roman visual representation is often stabilized as that which knits the territories together into the "fatherland." Herein the modern turn to Roman visual images in New Testament studies, which we will discuss further in Chapter 3, proves particularly useful, since the image can be said to provide the representation of the local operative ideologies, rather than, say, the more seemingly speculative work of archaeology and textual analysis. The Roman imperial thread serves to make sense of Christian community identity and theological claims. Scholarly disagreement with respect to the specifics does not change the stable entity that forms the backdrop against which early Christian responses can be measured and engaged. Differences in interpretive orientation and outcome[29] do not detract, for most scholars at least, from the notion that behind these divergences lies a common thread of major importance that underpins, in unison, the background against which Christian responses to the world can be coordinated and, therefore, something of the common ground from which a construction of meaningful difference and identity originates.

Indeed, it is one thing to accept Vincent Wimbush's proposition that all biblical texts are responses to the world in which they are situated, and therefore are rhetorical constructions in which those responses are embedded, and that in those responses we detect traces of negotiation, and possibly of rhetorical and social formation.[30] It is quite another to suggest that there is a universal series of such contexts and processes in the ambient sphere of early Christian textual production and identity formation that in some sense predetermines particular kinds of realities and experiences in stabilized and normative ways. Even if one could somehow position the various writers on some kind of "response to the Roman Empire" grid, one would still need to contend with the mass of self-identified early Christians themselves – however such identifications functioned in practice – who are not represented or may not identify with the so-called "authorial" perspective we tease out of the New Testament texts. Where is a Philemon or a Phoebe to be positioned in such configurations? And what basic set of criteria is used for measuring the nature of the response? This further goes to show that we actually know relatively little about early Christians in general – or about the ancient writers and readers of the New Testament – and that our views of ancient Christian phenomena are largely shaped by the perspectives of the texts themselves, perspectives which only exist for the modern scholar dependent on the assumptions we have just denoted.

Although the use of the Roman Empire and especially its visual imagery is only one small example, its attraction to modern scholars is palpable, as these vivify an objective apparatus constructed through texts and archaeology, with the major accent falling on the former. We can *see* the empire in action, and pictures do not lie! These images make things real – or make them appear so. In this way, the various entities (armies, emperors, cities, battles, etc.) that they invoke also take on the appearance of the real in the process. So whether we are talking about early Christian groups or particular theological concepts that need an objectifiably traceable "background" in order to bring them into existence and imbue them with meaning, in all cases, when these differentiated elements are deployed it is with the aim of producing such an immutable background over against which early Christianity can stand out, in whatever shape the particular configuration of data we have arranged allows.

The question of what makes someone "Christian" in antiquity provides an excellent foray into the basic issues raised in this chapter. How is it that we order and arrange our data in order to produce ancient Christians? At one level, it would appear that there are traces of evidence in the ancient materials that offer us a basic outline of what someone who might have identified as a Christian could have looked like. However, upon closer inspection one has to raise the question of whether or not we have not simply created the category of "early Christian" as a result of our own ordering principles for framing the New Testament data. To a large extent, we have to decide on the features that we will use to differentiate early Christians from their larger context before we actually begin our investigation. How else would we know what it is we are seeing unless we have some preconceived notion about the data for which we are looking? This is, in fact, the great unspoken problem regarding the study of the New Testament. Here, more than in any of the other categories we have discussed above, we have to fall back on the ordering principles that undergird our study of the ancient materials.

To be sure, inevitably we need to utilize the New Testament and other early Christian texts to formulate what it is that constitutes the distinctive identity and also the innovative contribution of early Christianity *in relation to* other movements, identities, and religions. That said, a potent question is how we might move from the texts to the realities behind those texts, to the historical personages and communities to which the texts do not give us direct access. This is probably one of the more difficult principles to grasp, since the automatic assumption is that all early Christians in the ancient world knew and believed what the New Testament texts set forth (as a coherent and consistent whole!), just like all ancient Jews knew and believed what is present in the Torah and Mishnah and Talmud. The fact of the matter is, however, we simply have no idea what it is that the people "on the ground" thought or believed, and from what evidence we glean from the ancient sources the best guess is that some people likely "fit" the description that we construct from the New Testament, but many others quite possibly did not. And "not fitting in" did not preclude them from being "Christians."

The natural question will be, then, from where does the concept of "Christian" originate? Functionally speaking, it is only with the emergence of the structural hierarchy of the church that we begin to observe the emergence of Christianity, which is an *institutional representation*. In the final analysis, it is actually institutions, and not people on the ground, that help to solidify tradition and stabilize concepts. Somewhere along the way some people – but by no means all people – decided that "this" and not "that" represents what Christianity is – and the "this" and "that" changes based on individual authorities and over time and across cultures as well. We can only guess as to what degree the institutionalized forms represent the general mass of people left out of the structural hierarchies. However, we can also assume with some degree of confidence that the overarching determinations of councils and those in significant positions of power are relatively unreflective of what the "others" thought. That said, we have only the institutionalized forms with which to work. Indeed, it is this same framework by which we know that something is "Roman": it is only through the institutional structures, in their multitudinous expressions, that we can frame what it means to be "Roman." Yet what it meant to be "Roman" in general, even if one were a small cog in the larger wheel of the institutionalized form such as a solider in the Roman legion, is much more complicated. One often had multiple loyalties and affiliations, and a vast array of other factors that combined to shape the identity of the individual over the course of a lifetime. Being "Roman," at its most basic form, signifies someone who lived during the period of "Roman history" and participated in that arena in some way.

In a similar way, being "Christian" means, in the ancient context, in some way being related to the materials that we sift out as being "Christian-related." But that is not saying much! And to be sure, in so far as we only identify "Christian" materials by key words and concepts (e.g. "Christ Jesus"), we likely miss a variety of texts that may be Christian*ish* and affiliated in some way with our structure of identification but which do not fit the categories we have set out to create difference and distinction. And lest we forget, the production of individual texts and the collection of such into an authoritative canon such as the New Testament do not occur at the grassroots level. Rather, it is institutional investment and initiation that bring about interests in solidifying the boundaries of what counts as "Christian," what emphatically does not count, and what is simply left by the wayside. To that extent, our modern attention to identity and distinction is not original – in every time period people in institutional contexts have sought to draw the lines and patrol the boundaries. The difference is, however, that many modern scholars understand themselves to be doing something different – they are discovering the lines and uncovering the boundaries that have always existed.

In this respect we, as modern scholars, are frequently unaware of our own positioning within institutional settings that similarly function to dictate the terms and conditions of "discovery," which is what often opens up the space for critique of the historical-critical task. We are not seeking to undermine this task. However, we note that a lack of reflection on the larger framing issues of historical study – some of them quite basic – has not helped in making a strong case for the relevance or importance of historical study of the New Testament. In short, then, a great deal of reflection is required on the ways in which we create early Christian identity through distinction and difference. It may well be that the New Testament is, in the end, much less distinctive and innovative than scholars suggest. And, to be sure, in what other ways can we rethink the boundaries of identity in order to reshape the landscape of what it means to be "Christian" in the ancient world? Such imaginative exercises are not mere language games, but critical components of a larger historical enterprise that seeks to use the current categories in ways that open up other historical possibilities and configurations for discussion and analysis.

Ways of Knowing New Testament "Things"

As we have moved through this opening chapter, we have sought to develop a larger framework that contours the chapters that follow. In particular, we have focused on the modern epistemic "order of things" that shapes the order of New Testament "things." That is, we have argued that the modern framework for viewing and interpreting the world is the major factor in organizing the historical data for the ancient world, how we classify and analyze that data, and, finally, the results we produce for both academic and popular consumption in our world. Most scholars would agree that there is the inevitable problem of the "two horizons," where we, as modern readers, have to negotiate our own assumptions about the way the world operates along with those of the ancient materials.[31] The "two horizons" framework refers to the meeting of the two interpretive spheres – the ancient world's and our own. The essence of this approach highlights the intersection and convergence of the two perspectives, and accents the need to negotiate that meeting in order to better arrive at a more accurate interpretation and representation of the ancient materials. It is not our world – and we are in a position to be able to work around that particular quandary and still access ancient meanings.

Our standpoint in this chapter is fundamentally juxtaposed to the "two horizons" approach. Making critical use of Foucault's work, we have contended that there is in fact no way to negotiate the "two horizons." In fact, we have gone one step further to suggest there is only one horizon – and that is the horizon of the present, which is ever present, even as we most often do not perceive it as such. Again, as we have emphasized above, this focus on the modern episteme and its powerful ordering function does not mean that the ancient world does not exist. For us, the ancient world most certainly exists, as surely as this book does. And further, we want to be clear in our claim that the task of historical work is by no means devalued in this framework. Rather, we understand historical work on the New Testament, conducted in the tradition of historical criticism, to be of immense value and of paramount importance. Where our approach differs from many others is that we are committed to the understanding that there is no escape from the ways in which our modern, science-infused, "order of things" shape how we view the world. Now, that is not to say there is no possibility for the use of imagination and creativity in terms of expanding upon the operative ordering principles, making them work at a higher level than they are often deployed. We do believe in invigorating historical-critical work with an inspired deployment of ordering principles, in some sense using its logic against itself in order to explore the contradictions and embrace them, therein also moving into a realm that challenges our own "order of things" on its own terms.

Foucault was, in many respects, seeking to engage long-held issues and problems in epistemology that can be traced back to one of the forefathers of such thinking, namely Immanuel Kant (1724–1804). The basic issue that Kant, among many others, sought to address is how we perceive and order the world in a way that allows us to have access to some *objective* reality. Is that even possible? Kant's system is highly formalistic and involves a great deal of speculative reasoning. Foucault, who wrote his dissertation on Kant under the noted Marxist scholar Louis Althusser, sought to think about epistemology in materialist terms, with a healthy infusion of other philosophical traditions that moved beyond a strictly Marxist tenet that economics – and the relationship to the means of production in particular – was the sole cause of the epistemic structure of perceiving, knowing, and experience. Ultimately, for Foucault, the system of knowing and perceiving is arbitrary at one level, but also conditioned by a variety of historical and social intellectual processes that have gone into shaping the overarching system of knowledge. The episteme out of which we order the world does not simply arrive on the current scene of any time period as something descended from the "heavens" or given by God. On the other hand, neither it is entirely a momentary, impressionistic product that arises from sensory apprehension. It is, rather, a fairly complex configuration of the intersection of the temporal moment at hand and the history of intellectual development.

Within this schema, once the episteme is in place, even as it may shift and morph over time, it is also fairly stringent in the application of its principles. So there is a very clear sense and apprehension of objectivity from within the system – and there is a patent logic and an evident set of congruencies and principles of verifiability and veracity that shore up the core of the ordering system. "Things" thus appear as they naturally are to the episteme, but not as they would necessarily be within an entirely different ordering system. Hence, there is a measure of objectivity in an explicit system propelled by contingency, which means that objectivity itself is highly contingent.[32] The epistemological framework rests on the notion that objectivity is always relatively so, but there is no specific relative position to be held apart from the episteme either, and any principle of relativity only exists in so far as it is objectively ordered as such within the larger episteme. In short, there is no magic "red pill" that reveals the reality behind the Matrix, but neither, at the same time, is there a "blue pill" that necessitates a state of harmony with status quo ignorance. For Foucault, there is something in between these two options, and historical work can and should take place with the full knowledge of the relativity of the objectivity that arises out of our diverse analytic projects.

Given that we are focused in this chapter, and in this book as a whole, on the epistemic framing of the discipline dedicated to the study of the New Testament and early Christianity in a variety of formats and functions, our aim is to elucidate the broader context of interpretation – to denaturalize, if you will, via the process of de-introducting the manner in which information about the "facts" of the New Testament appears before us. In this respect, then, knowing that the modern episteme is deeply rooted in a scientific framework, and that the ordering principles of this structure of knowledge play out in historical study of the New Testament, helps us understand how it is that the New Testament "historical science" is so adamantly committed to "getting it right," to revealing the coherent principles and stable outlines of the emergent organism known as "early Christianity."[33] Again, we see revealed here the broader stabilizing work of the New Testament "order of things," an epistemological framework that is thoroughly grounded, as we have repeatedly noted, in a firm commitment to identifying and positioning the coordinates that allow the modern interpreter to firmly fix the data points in order to allow for precise and accurate evaluation and interpretation.

We should make it clear that over the last two centuries there have been numerous scholars who have been hermeneutically self-aware and reflective on the rich tradition of historiographical reflection and who would agree that there is no direct access to historical facts as such. The German tradition of New Testament scholarship is surprisingly rich in such reflection, wherein the *science* of New Testament study and historical analysis more generally does not construct a system in which we have direct access to a historical moment that is uninterpreted or unmediated. It is, in fact, the recognition that everything we read in the New Testament is fully mediated to us by "witnesses" and "interpreters" in the early period of the emergence of Christianity that gives us pause in our attempt to construct a fully objective history that we can directly access.[34] In this respect, then, the historical study of the New Testament can seem different than studying contemporary subjects in a science lab. However, to the degree that both of those participate in the same episteme, and construct their subject and its apprehension through language, they are actually not all that different. Yet for the moment we posit a particular fictive distance between the New Testament and the lab bench. We also recognize that attempting to appear to enter into an interpretive world that acknowledges the role of human meaning-making, and proceeds as if that role can be negotiated in a way that provides substantive grounding for current theological commitments, in some sense represents a docetic view of history. In this view, there is the appearance of "incarnation" that ultimately represents a rather limited understanding of such. In this kind of historical understanding there is a strong commitment to the objective principles of science along with an acknowledgment that objectivity is not at all attainable in the historical sciences.

In our understanding that lies behind the questions and queries posed in this chapter, we are positioned in a framework that in some sense is more akin to the study of quantum physics, where randomness and chance are prominent, where there is discontinuity and contradiction, where the more we learn about one facet of an element the less we know about another, where disorder and chaos seem to be the order of things. In terms of how we proceed in our daily lives, we consider the quantum level of physics to be radically different from our own world, and in some sense it exists as a theory that is completely unrelated to our actual experience of reality, or at least our apprehension and framing of that experience. In our estimation, however, we would do well to consider historical study of the New Testament in a similar light, as producing results that are fundamentally unstable and incoherent. Such effects are not simply a result of deploying differing "witnesses" or variant hermeneutic prisms that arrange data for us, and which we in turn evaluate and interpret and then render accessible in alternative narrative forms. Rather, we understand that, without our epistemic system and its principles of ordering the ancient world, the New Testament would appear as a "booming, buzzing confusion." And while we appreciate the vibrant complexity and contradiction that lurk beneath the surface at the "quantum level" of history, we are also committed to a kind of "this-worldly" apprehension of the early Christian past. The two need not stand as options between which one must choose, but there definitely is a distinct tension that exists as a result. There are the "things" that our episteme orders and interprets relatively well, and then there are the "other things" that challenge the principles of ordering that seem so natural and universal. We live in both worlds simultaneously, and in some sense being aware of the latter helps us better assess the limitations of the former.

Further, in our view it is knowing how the order of New Testament "things" functions to categorize and classify data and to produce results for analysis that allows one to be a *critical* reader of New Testament scholarship, from introductory materials to specialized studies. Understanding how the system works allows one to appreciate the results that arise out of historical work, to assess those results, and finally to interrogate the results of all research, with the express purpose of engaging the larger meta-issues of the epistemic framework that is implicitly working behind the scenes. We would argue, further, that it is the task of the critic to provide historical counter-readings, not only as a means to test the hypotheses of New Testament research but to actually expose the hypothetical nature of all research in the first place. This orientation does not mean, as we have repeatedly emphasized, that one abandons the epistemic framework and its ordering principles. This is functionally impossible. Rather, in our estimation we could use the larger "order of things" in creative and imaginative ways. That is, we could utilize the ordering principles as a means to expand beyond the often facile deployment of those same principles, even in scholarly work on the New Testament that utilizes the language of "distance," "interpretation," and "narrative" as code words to signify something of the relative nature of human meaning-making activity but that ultimately ends up reifying the more superficial deployment it has the appearance of avoiding.

Ultimately, we contend that historical work can be more complex than it currently is. Such complexity entails a willingness to embrace contradiction and unknowing as constitutive features of historical analysis. In this respect, we would argue that scholarship on the New Testament should by no means abandon the operative ordering principles, but that scholarly analysis requires more critical complexity in both its historical work and in its presentation to scholars and students. There is no reason, for instance, that introductions to the New Testament could not be much more complicated and multi-layered in the exhibition of the products of New Testament scholarship. In fact, a more multi-faceted presentation might even encourage critical thinking in students and scholars, challenging all to reflect on and to evaluate the episteme in which they live, move, and have their being. In our assessment this is the task and potential of historical-critical work on the New Testament.

Notes

1. André Lemaire, "Burial Box of James the Brother of Jesus," *Biblical Archaeology Review* 28.6 (2002), 24–33. For further discussion of the various issues we raise here concerning the James ossuary, see R. Byrne and B. McNary-Zak, eds., *Resurrecting the Brother of Jesus: The James Ossuary Controversy and the Quest for Religious Relics* (Durham: University of North Carolina Press, 2009); Craig Evans, *Jesus and the Ossuaries: What Jewish Burial Practices Reveal about the Beginning of Christianity* (Waco, Tex.: Baylor University Press, 2003); and James Tabor, *The Jesus Dynasty: The Hidden History of Jesus, His Royal Family, and the Birth of Christianity* (New York: Simon & Schuster, 2007).

2. Among ancient literary sources, there are only a few "famous" passages that mention the Jesus of the New Testament. Josephus refers to more than 20 individuals named Jesus in his writings, and the Jesus of the New Testament is thought to be mentioned in the famous, if "inauthentic," *Testimonium Flavianum* (*Antiquities of the Jews*, 18.3.3). Josephus also refers to the stoning of "James, the brother of Jesus" (*Antiquities of the Jews*, 20.9.1). The Roman historian Tacitus refers to Nero blaming the Christians, who had followed "Christus" who had been executed under Pontius Pilate, for the Great Fire of Rome (*Annals*, 15.44). And Suetonius mentions that Claudius expelled Jews "who constantly made disturbances at the instigation of Chrestus" (*Claudius*, 25.4).

3. Michel Foucault, *The Order of Things: An Archaeology of the Human Sciences* (New York: Vintage Books, 1970), 128–129.

4. Foucault, *The Order of Things*, xx.

5. Wilfred Cantwell Smith, *Islam in Modern History* (Princeton: Princeton University Press, 1957), 17–18.

6. For a discussion of the issues at stake in this area of investigation, see Todd Penner, "'In the Beginning': Post-Critical Reflections on Early Christian Textual Transmission and Modern Textual Transgression," *Perspectives in Religious Studies* 33 (2006): 415–434.

7. See Ernst Troeltsch, *Religion in History* (trans. J. L. Adams and W. E. Bense; Fortress Texts in Modern Theology; Minneapolis: Fortress Press, 1991).

8. For an analysis of how history and historiography worked on both sides of the Atlantic during the 19th-century development of "Early Church History" as a discipline, see Elizabeth A. Clark, *Founding the Fathers: Early Church History and Protestant Professors in Nineteenth-Century America* (Divinations: Rereading Late Ancient Religion; Philadelphia: University of Pennsylvania Press, 2011), 97–204.

9. Unlike in nature, it is not always the "higher" form that is most prized in the study of history, and this is particularly the case in the study of the Bible, where the conflicts between Protestant and Catholic interpretation frequently played a role in the assessment of the ancient data. That is, Protestants in some sense saw themselves as circumventing the ecclesial hierarchies and going back to the "source" in the scriptures themselves. For a methodological analysis of this shift and its implications for the study of religion see Jonathan Z. Smith, *Drudgery Divine: On the Comparison of Early Christianities and the Religions of Late Antiquity* (Chicago Studies in the History of Judaism; Chicago: University of Chicago Press, 1994).

10. For a discussion of the intersection of the discipline of textual criticism with the rhetoric of science, see Yii-Jan Lin, "The Erotic Life of Manuscripts: A History of New Testament Textual Criticism and the Biological Sciences" (Ph.D. diss., Yale University, 2014).
11. Edward Said, *Beginnings: Intention and Method* (Morningside edition; New York: Columbia University Press, 1985), 206.
12. Michel Foucault, *The Archaeology of Knowledge and the Discourse on Language* (trans. A. M. Sheridan Smith; New York: Pantheon, 1972), 21.
13. Michel Foucault, "Nietzsche, Genealogy, History," in *Language, Counter-memory, Practice: Selected Essays and Interviews* (ed. D. Bouchard; Ithaca, N.Y.: Cornell University Press, 1977), 139–164; 150–151. The use of italics here signals our change to the plural.
14. Foucault, "Nietzsche, Genealogy, History," 150.
15. One sees this clearly in Hegel's dialectics, and in Kantian epistemology as well. In more recent times the work of Michel de Certeau has been especially critical for historiography. De Certeau notes that the ordering principles behind the Western theological tradition were transferred into the configuration of the modern nation-state, which assumes the structure, authority, and function of the former church. As a result, progress becomes a key concept (particularly in ethics and culture), reflected, one can infer, in the discourses of historiography, which in some sense became an alternative way of doing, and implicitly affirming, although for the most part unconsciously, theology in a secular, de-sacralized, emergent modern world episteme. See De Certeau, *The Writing of History* (trans. T. Conley; European Perspectives; New York: Columbia University Press, 1988), 178–179.
16. The German appeared in 1964. See Walter Bauer, *Orthodoxy and Heresy in Earliest Christianity* (trans. Philadelphia Seminar on Christian Origins; ed. R. A. Kraft and G. Krodel; Philadelphia: Fortress Press, 1971).
17. In Foucault's framework, which we are following here to a certain extent, there is no linguistic product (a statement, concept, etc.) that does not "presuppose others … that is not surrounded by a field of coexistences, effects of series and succession, a distribution of functions and roles" (*Archaeology of Knowledge*, 98). In other words, there is no specific originating statement – there is only one that is tied to innumerable and often untraceable nexuses of meaning of which the statement that stands out for our observation and analysis is a moment – a fragment – of an extended series of significations that flow in and out of the statement in "our hands." In other words, there is never a precise moment of origin and never a clear path of development.
18. See the argument made by David J. Glass and Ned Hall, "A Brief History of the Hypothesis," *Cell* 134 (2008): 378–381.
19. As Christopher Stanley has proposed in his work on the use of scripture in Paul, it is quite possible that Paul's audiences had a range of responses to his rhetorical efforts, including not "getting it" at all. That there would be multiple responses to Paul's argumentative strategies is just one example of how much more complex the situation on the ground is than has been supposed and imagined by much New Testament scholarship. See Stanley, *Arguing with Scripture: The Rhetoric of Quotations in the Letters of Paul* (New York: T & T Clark, 2004).

20. It is for this reason that Foucault focuses on discourses rather than historical moments – they generate a particular set of rules by which they can be engaged, but there is a fiction that is also in play as a result, of which Foucault is also well aware. See Foucault, *Archaeology of Knowledge*, 138–140.

21. See Antoinette Clark Wire, *The Corinthian Women Prophets: A Reconstruction through Paul's Rhetoric* (Minneapolis: Fortress Press, 1990).

22. See Fredric Jameson, *The Prison House of Language: A Critical Account of Structuralism and Russian Formalism* (Princeton: Princeton University Press, 1972).

23. There is a long and venerable hermeneutical tradition that argues for this particular approach to interpretation, wherein making more of a text in the act of interpretation is what pushes interpretation into the realm of "art." See the modern classic articulation of such an approach in Hans-Georg Gadamer, *Truth and Method* (trans. G. Barden and J. Cumming; New York: Seabury Press, 1975). However, historical critics, by and large, do not see themselves as seeking to create art in their interpretations, but rather reflecting things as they actually are in the text.

24. For a development of this approach with respect to the Hebrew Bible, see Jacques Berlinberlau, *The Secular Bible: Why Nonbelievers Must Take Religion Seriously* (New York: Cambridge University Press, 2005).

25. Heikki Räisänen, *Paul and the Law* (Wissenschaftliche Untersuchungen zum Neuen Testament 29; Tübingen: Mohr Siebeck, 1983).

26. For an overview of how Paul's use of the art of persuasion, along with our own use of rhetoric, can be understood in differing and even contradictory ways, see Todd Penner and Davina C. Lopez, "Rhetorical Approaches: Introducing the Art of Persuasion in Paul and Pauline Studies," in *Studying Paul's Letters: Contemporary Perspectives and Methods* (ed. J. Marchal; Minneapolis: Fortress Press, 2012), 33–52.

27. A good example of this principle of ordering in action is found in Jens Schröter, "Beginnings of the Jesus Tradition: Tradition-Historical Observations on an Area of the History of Early Christian Theology," in *From Jesus to the New Testament: Early Christian Theology and the Origin of the New Testament Canon* (trans. W. Coppins; Waco, Tex.: Baylor University Press, 2013), 73–94. Also see Francis Watson, *Gospel Writing: A Canonical Perspective* (Grand Rapids, Mich.: Eerdmans, 2013). The main aim in this scholarship is to generate extensive networks of genetic connections that serve to create a definable and stable Gospel tradition. The linear development, albeit complicated, confirms the veracity of the material contained in the tradition, testifying to the historical truth that lies behind contemporary theological and church commitments. The genetic tracings by scholars create this absolute certainty, and without that interconnection the New Testament looks more like an American university fraternity party (wild and out of control, with arrests to follow later in the evening and stories to tell the next day) than one of the Oxford college's literary clubs (disciplined, ordered, and regal, with only minor infractions along the way).

28. In terms of historical understanding, scholars may acknowledge "hybrid" identities, such as "Jewish-Christian" and "Gentile-Christian," that are more difficult to draw out and delineate than "Jewish" and "Gentile" and "Christian."

Aside from these particular examples, however, the notion of hybridity is somewhat under-discussed in modern New Testament research aside from scholarly trajectories that take seriously the notion of "hybridity" as it has been developed in postcolonial discourses. For an array of such approaches as they are applied to the full range of New Testament writings, see F. S. Segovia and R. S. Sugirtharajah, eds., *A Postcolonial Commentary on the New Testament Writings* (Bible and Postcolonialism 13; London: T & T Clark, 2009).

29. Even when scholarly differences seem to be as thoroughgoing as that between Richard Horsley, who reads Paul as "anti-imperial," and J. Albert Harrill, who reads Paul as an example of *Romanitas*, the common thread is that the Roman Empire is that which provides the means by which early Christians and the New Testament can be "measured" and to which it can be compared. See, for example, Horsley, *1 Corinthians* (Abingdon New Testament Commentaries 1; Nashville, Tenn.: Abingdon Press, 1998), and Harrill, *Paul the Apostle: His Life and Legacy in Their Roman Context* (New York: Cambridge University Press, 2012).

30. While we are aware that Wimbush's framework has itself evolved considerably, we find ourselves returning to his classic formulation in Vincent L. Wimbush, "... Not of This World ...": Early Christianities as Rhetorical and Social Formation," in *Reimagining Christian Origins: A Colloquium Honoring Burton L. Mack* (ed. H. Taussig and E. A. Castelli; Philadelphia: Trinity Press International, 1996), 23–36.

31. This particular framing can be found in Gadamer's *Truth and Method*, which offers something of a classic formulation of the "two horizons" interpretive situation. For a fairly extensive discussion, see Anthony C. Thiselton, *The Two Horizons: New Testament Hermeneutics and Philosophical Description* (Grand Rapids, Mich.: Eerdmans, 1980).

32. For an exploration of how objectivity has a history, see Lorraine J. Datson and Peter Galison, *Objectivity* (Brooklyn, N.Y.: Zone Books, 2010).

33. For a well-articulated statement of how historical assessment of the New Testament might directly rely on knowledge from the sciences, and natural science in particular, see Frederik Wisse, "The Origin of the Christian Species: Lessons from the Study of Natural History for the Reconstruction of the History of Earliest Christianity," *Canadian Society of Biblical Studies Bulletin* 63 (2003–2004): 5–23.

34. See the discussion in Schröter, "New Testament Science beyond Historicism: Recent Developments in the Theory of History and Their Significant for the Exegesis of Early Christian Writings," in *From Jesus to the New Testament*, 9–20.

2

Foregrounding New Testament Backgrounds
Contextualizing Interpretation

"Jew" or "Judean"? The Present Confronts the Past

In an online essay for *Marginalia*, a review of books, entitled "The Vanishing Jew of Antiquity,"[1] Canadian biblical scholar Adele Reinhartz engages in a forceful critique of the modern scholarly trend to translate the word *ioudaios* as "Judean" rather than "Jew."[2] Now, the novice approaching this particular debate – sometimes quite heated in nature – might not see the stakes at play in this translation problem, at least not on the surface. In a nutshell, the contentious issue represented by what seems like a simple translation problem hinges on whether "Judaism" existed as an identifiable religion in antiquity – or whether we have simply constructed it as such given modern constructions of "religion" as an identifiable category of analysis.[3] In other words, the question concerns whether the Greek term *ioudaios* designates Judaism as a "religion" with "Jews" as adherents, or whether it identifies, rather, a group of peoples who occupied a particular geographic region in the ancient Mediterranean world known as "Judea." In this sense, in the broadest possible terms, the various references to "Jews" in the New Testament could be better translated, according to a certain group of scholars, as "Judean." The result would be, of course, that our modern associations that identify "Judaism" and "Jews" with a particular set of religious practices, doctrines, and beliefs would not necessarily find a correlation in the New Testament texts when they refer to "Judeans" in a negative manner.

De-Introducing the New Testament: Texts, Worlds, Methods, Stories, First Edition.
Todd Penner and Davina C. Lopez.
© 2015 Todd Penner and Davina C. Lopez. Published 2015 by John Wiley & Sons, Ltd.

In other words, there would be a separation between our modern concept of "Judaism" and the ancient one. A major implication of such a shift in meaning would be that the New Testament texts that, say, blame Jews for the death of Jesus could not be deployed or simply understood by modern Christians as legitimation for any type of anti-Jewish or anti-Judaism sentiment, such as is often found in contemporary conservative Christian communities, which also spills over into a more general cultural sentiment with a long legacy in the West.

After the horrendous acts of the Third Reich with respect to Jews, culminating in what we now call "the Holocaust," New Testament scholarship took a dramatic turn in its thinking about Judaism in antiquity. To be sure, many of the specific ideas regarding the ancient Judaism of the New Testament period were not new after World War II. Rather, there was a dramatic shift in the general orientation of scholarship as a whole, seeking to rectify, in some respects, the quite antagonistic portrayal of ancient Judaism by Protestant, particularly German, scholarship. Therein the focus was almost solely on the negative characterization of Judaism as a religion of legalistic, slave-driven mentality, which had little sense of a "true relationship" with the divine, let alone any comprehension of conceptions such as "grace," "faith," and "freedom." There are plenty of studies that have focused on German scholarship of the late 19th and early to mid-20th century that demonstrate a trenchant positioning of Judaism as a religious phenomenon out of which Christianity arose and then transcended. Of course, the socio-cultural and politico-nationalistic positionings of German society of this period, and already earlier in the beginnings of Jewish emancipation in Europe (late 18th century), make clear that the relationship between ethnic and religious identity was closely woven into the very fabric of the conceptualization of "Jewishness," which largely accounts for the origins of "anti-Semitism."[4] Post-1950, however, biblical scholars began to reconceptualize Judaism in antiquity in categorically different and oppositional terms to earlier views. This shift gradually resulted in a substantively different conceptualization of Judaism as a religion in antiquity, as one that was not as fixated on "law" and "observance" in the way that the German Protestant scholarly trajectory had insisted. Rather, there proliferated an array of faith positions held by ancient Jews that in a variety of ways demarcated the "people of God" as separate and distinct without necessarily involving the myriad of modern stereotypes that had surrounded Judaism.[5]

The question for the reader, naturally, will be why, in light of the rather denigratory usage of "Jew" and "Judaism" in Western tradition, would Reinhartz insist, over against many others, that *ioudaios* in the New Testament be translated as "Jew" rather than as "Judean"? Those choosing the latter designation insist that it is the "mistranslation" of *ioudaios* that has led to so much misusage in Western intellectual and cultural heritage. Such scholars insist that if *ioudaios* had been translated as "Judean" in the first place then the contemporary "Jew" would not have been branded with the negative characteristics frequently associated with the term *ioudaios* in the New Testament. It is, of course, difficult to know how the history of Western culture would have developed one way or another. That said, Reinhartz is adamant that "Jew" and "Judaism" need to be reinserted, at least in many instances, back into the New Testament. In her estimation, drawing on her extensive research and writing on the Gospel of John, New Testament writers and early Christian readers need to be held responsible for the inceptive moment of anti-Judaism in Western tradition. The writer of the Gospel of John, who declares that the "Jews are children of the devil" should not have his strong sentiments mitigated by the rephrasing of that statement to "the Judeans are children of the devil." It is arguable that ultimately such considerations change little the impact of words like *ioudaios* as they are recontextualized in differing moments of history. Further, we truly cannot know for certain whether or not the growing fascination with and fixation on Judaism as an oppositional force over against Christianity in historical perspective can be traced back to these negative characterizations in the biblical text.

Reinhartz's argument about Jews, Judaism, and Judeans in and around the New Testament draws our attention to a critical problem in conceptualizing not just the past, but even more importantly, the *backgrounds* of our interpretation of the texts from the past. There are significant and serious consequences to how we read these ancient texts beyond the insularity that religion is thought to provide. The forces that may seem benevolent and lead us to a positive reconstruction of the New Testament as not actually (or entirely) "anti-Jewish" or against "Judaism" could also be seen, from another angle – particularly one inhabited by a contemporary self-identified Jew such as Reinhartz (a point she makes clear in the introduction to her essay) – as letting the New Testament and its writers off the hook as "misunderstood." In fairness, those scholars who deploy the translation "Judean" are not of necessity trying to "whitewash" or "save" the New Testament and early Christians from the charge of anti-Judaism. At the same time, it is noteworthy that such conversations about *ioudaios* take place in a context in which scholars have a larger historical milieu in which to place and assess the receptive history of such terms. In other words, the conversation about whether *ioudaios* should be translated as "Judean" or "Jew," as a signifier of ethnic, if not simply geographical, identity versus a religious-ethnic combination, can ultimately only take place in a situation informed by the historical self-reflectiveness occasioned by a massively horrific event such as the Holocaust. Indeed, even the question "Can we, or should we, translate this terminology in a way that might allow early Christian texts and writers and communities to somehow become non-complicit in the effective history of Christianity *in its relationship to Judaism*?" only makes sense within a system in which we can look back on the tragic consequences of such a relationship.

We will likely never know exactly what ancient writers had in mind when they used the term *ioudaios*. The best we can ever do in historical research is to approximate the meanings based on alignments with other texts and concepts to which we have already assigned a particular meaning and purpose. As should be clear from the basic contours of this book already, any historical research is only ever an approximation of a historical "reality" and, even then, we are only ever broadly approximate. In our view, the debate over the translation of *ioudaios* reveals three very important facets that must be kept in mind in looking at ancient texts like those in the New Testament. First, the term *ioudaios* has an ancient context in which it is read and interpreted, but it is unlikely that every person inside and outside of Judea, inside and outside of Judaism/Jewishness, used this term in the same way. Indeed, as we shall see below, the ancient world does not represent or, more importantly, present to us, a unified perspective on anything. Hence, even if we had direct access to ancient "meanings" we would only ever be able to assess these in particular renderings and not in a broadly or universally applicable manner.

Second, the fact that we can engage the term *ioudaios* in the way we do, debating whether it should be translated as "Judean" or "Jew," is a product of relatively modern trajectories of ways of thinking. In other words, the very question of whether one should translate the term this way or that way only makes sense within a history of social and cultural production of meaning that has taken place over the past two centuries. Ours are not questions that necessarily would have made sense to someone, Jewish or Gentile, living in the first century CE. This does not mean that the debate itself is entirely a product of the modern imagination, since it does address real historical issues and evidence from the past can be used to argue for one position over another. However, it is critical to understand that many questions we ask of the ancient biblical texts can only be posed when specific concepts, vocabularies, and historical realities that produce the former arise in historical moments and then become shaped and transformed over time. Had a conceptualization of Jewish ethnic and religious identity never arisen in Western discourse in the way in which it did, and had there not been a highly negative consequence to said discourses in many parts of Europe (and elsewhere), it is unlikely that the debate over the translation of *ioudaios* would or even could in fact exist now. It is only because of particularly unique developments in discourse with resultant actions in the "real" world that such questions come, over time, to articulation and prominence. The ethical question that Reinhartz poses – should we use translation as a means to absolve the New Testament writers and communities of their role in the development of anti-Judaism in the West? – makes sense only in the context in which such discourses about Jews and Judaism in the West developed, and in which it could make sense to link the events of relatively modern history with texts from some two millennia ago. That "linking" of ancient and modern is neither obvious nor inevitable, but, from the vantage point of where we stand now looking back, making such connections amongst the discrete literary remains of Western traditions does seem like a natural thing to do.

Third, and finally, in terms of historical research, considerations, and evaluations, making connections between concerns/questions only available in the present and the approximate realities of the past represents a complex correlative enterprise that ultimately forms the crux, and perhaps also the Achilles heel, of any interpretive effort related to the New Testament and early Christian literature more generally. That is, since our questions of the historical material are largely driven by modern conceptions, vocabularies, and ways of thinking, the only way to address them is to utilize the remains of the past in a way that coheres with these modern sensibilities. It might be too strong to say that we are required to bend the past to meet the needs and desires of the present. At the same time, there is always a bending of the past toward the present, even as there is also a straining of the present toward the past. This "gap" has often been described as the hermeneutical or interpretive horizon that exists between the past and present. In our view, however, the situation is more complex than that. The past itself is configured in part by the present and, to be sure, the present does not escape the haunting presence of the past. There is a correlation between the two, even as we believe it is difficult, if not impossible, to precisely articulate that relationship. All of that said, as we approach New Testament texts from the perspective of the present, as is clear from the debate over the translation of the term *ioudaios*, we require some context in which to make our historical queries make sense.

Thus, we are, of necessity, required to choose some kind of background in and against which we can develop particular historical readings that address modern concerns. Whether our research on the term *ioudaios* is driven by "historical" questions with "ethical" considerations, or "ethical" questions with "historical" ramifications, the basic question of which data set will be deployed and assessed in order to support our particular rendering of the meaning of these past texts remains the same. The importance of this last point cannot be overemphasized. For most students of the New Testament and early Christian literature the deliberative selection process, as well as the critical concerns that drive that process, are frequently hidden from view. Presented for the reader's review and assessment is precisely the end product of a much more complicated and involved process that shapes the manner in which the questions are posed and in which they make sense. "Pick a card, pick any card," the illusionist says. We all understand, of course, that the set of cards is limited. At the same time, at the very moment we pick "that card" we also know, or at least hope, that the result is predetermined. And then the "trick" works and we are surprised, even as the whole process of how and why it works, not to mention the basis of our own marvel and wonder at the process itself, is obscured. We have a certain "faith" in the outcome, even as we know it is a "trick."

In our view, reading and interpreting the New Testament functions in a similar way to the illusionist's card game. While many believers assert that they have "faith" in the content of the New Testament, ultimately the true "faith" is in the historical scholarly products that have been shaped by framing meaning within particular contextual horizons. Do you believe that the "Jews" killed Jesus or that "Judeans" did – and is that a difference that is significant, and on what terms is it so? In principle, the final decision for most readers has been set forth in the interpretive process that is hidden from view. And this is something of the "trick" in which scholars and introducers of the New Testament are involved, even if for the most part, we would suggest, unwittingly. In the end it is the process of analysis and interpretation that needs to be questioned, the very substructure that provides the basis for producing meanings of these ancient texts, and not the actual products of meaning themselves. In many respects, the actual products are much less significant for thinking about and with the New Testament than the processes that are hidden. It is the latter that demonstrate the profoundly human nature of interpretation and the modern configurations of meaning that only make sense for and to us.

Introducing the New Testament: Making Meaning with the Context

When one turns to many modern introductions to the New Testament and the other literatures of the early Christian communities, one immediately finds the discussion framed within the context of some kind of "background." The production of such backgrounds is related to a whole host of questions: What were the historical and cultural circumstances and histories out of which both Judaism and Christianity took shape? To which community was this text written? By what kind of author? Was the author Jewish or

Gentile? Was the community Christian, and if so, what kind – Jewish, Greek, Roman? Was the Gospel of Mark written for or from a context in Rome, Antioch, or Alexandria? How do we account for the earliest development of the stories of Jesus? Where do we position these stories and traditions? How do we account for a literary document like the hypothetical text "Q"? What are the precedents we have for such collections in antiquity? Was Paul truly a practicing Jew in the fullest sense of that word? How do we account for Paul's view on the Jewish law? And in what social and cultural context does it make sense to think about "law" in ancient Judaism? How do we account socially and historically for the shifts between the ministries of Jesus and Paul? Where do we situate the early communities to which Paul wrote? How and in what way do we account for the ways in which Paul used Hebrew Bible scriptures to articulate his "gospel" message? How might we conceptualize the growth and development of the early church? Did early Christians meet in households or in other ancient social venues? Against what background does one account for the symbolism present in the letter to the Hebrews? How do we make sense of the historical context in which the Apocalypse was written, especially given the apparent references to the Roman Empire that appear throughout? Further complicating the picture is a tendency to denote the New Testament texts as belonging to distinct literary genres, demanding that we ask, for example, whether Acts is a "history" or a "novel," whether Matthew is "midrash" or Mark a "drama," whether John is a "mystical" text, and so on. The genre, in its historical setting, should, in theory, dictate for the reader how to understand the text's argumentative strategies in their "proper" literary and historical contexts. This rather rudimentary set of questions just begins to scratch the surface of the various contextual matters that concern scholars of the New Testament.

Although it may not always appear to be the case, every description or interpretation of a New Testament text has been shaped by a pre-existing set of *background* coordinates that help determine the means by which the material is presented to readers. A "good" introductory text will usually begin with some discussion of the history that has shaped the "world of the New Testament," which includes both the history that has shaped first-century Judaism as well as Greek and Roman spheres of influence. One will usually begin with the imperial expansion of Alexander the Great, or perhaps with the earlier Persian period. For certain, the Hasmonean kingdom of the Jews will be mentioned, particularly the conflict between Jews (or Judeans!) and the Greek Seleucid empire that, together in conflict with the Ptolemaic kingdom of northern Egypt, laid claim to the territory of Judea. One will learn of the Roman conquest of the region, the establishment of a "puppet" government under Herod the Great, and then the successive political changes that take place through the latter part of the first century BCE and the beginning of the first century CE. The rise of Augustus Caesar is generally a high point, given the expansion and solidification of the Roman Empire during the time of Jesus. And the Roman presence in Jerusalem will likely be accented, as it provides a larger context for the Roman invasion of Judea in the 60s CE. This all culminates in the fall of Jerusalem to the Roman army, the destruction of the Jerusalem temple under Titus, and other subsequent Roman military victories over the Judean/Jewish resisters such as the one at Masada.

One could go on, but those mentioned above are some of the basic highlights that are usually noted in contextualizing the New Testament writings historically.[6] Such historical moments also had significant influence over the geographical and territorial divisions in "New Testament times." Roman Corinth, Syrian Antioch, Jewish Jerusalem, and so forth are situated in terms of their relationship to the geopolitical shifts that took place in this period. Of course, this has a direct bearing on how and on what terms we understand the formation, production, and dissemination of early Christian literature, as well as the interrelationship of the diverse communities and texts that make up the larger landscape in which early Christians are to be historically situated.

Aside from the historical background of this period, in order to be properly introduced to the New Testament one must also pay specific attention to the social and cultural history of the time period. There is probably no better entry into this vantage point, and no better way to understand how New Testament introductions deal with such material, than the seminal study by Joachim Jeremias, *Jerusalem in the Time of Jesus*.[7] This book, in many respects, represents a model for how one conceptualizes the socio-cultural configuration of the context in which one interprets the New Testament materials, in this case those texts most closely related to the life and ministry of Jesus. Jeremias's division of the various categories of the book is most helpful for understanding the broader range of how "backgrounds" functions as a category in the history of New Testament scholarship. He begins with "Economic Conditions," under which he details "industries," "commerce," and also the "foreign visitors" who came to Jerusalem for social and economic reasons. His second category is "Economic Status," which addresses the range of what we would now consider to be largely modern concepts: the "rich," the "middle class," and the "poor." Jeremias then turns to "Social Status," which includes the sub-sections "clergy," "lay nobility," "Sadducees," and "Pharisees." His final section focuses on "The Maintenance of Racial Purity," and emphasizes the diverse range of "insiders," "outsiders," and those in the "middle" with respect to Jewish "purity," which also includes discussions of slaves, women, and Samaritans.

Jerusalem in the Time of Jesus is just one example – a multitude of other books could be drawn into this discussion. However, Jeremias offers a classic paradigm of the kinds of considerations that are involved in thinking about, in this case, the origins of Christianity in Jerusalem and its environs. One thus needs to bear in mind that this is "Jerusalem" in the "time of Jesus," and that the content is limited to issues related to the historical Jesus and the communities of Jesus-followers, and perhaps also situating some of the earlier alleged debates in the incipient Christian movement as it moved to include Gentiles. The reason why his study is considered a "classic" is precisely because it covers the main issues of economics, social class, and religio-cultural identifiers (e.g., law, purity, ritual), which can quite readily be applied in any number of ways to other sites of perceived importance to early Christianity.[8] It is assumed, then, that delineating the larger context will enflesh the texts relating to Jesus and the early Christians in more meaningful ways. The fact is that, unless one has some idea of what a "Pharisee" is, the conflict between Jesus and the Pharisees in the Gospels means almost nothing. It is by knowing something about the beliefs and commitments of Pharisees or Sadducees, or the social location of scribes, that one can then draw inferences about the meaning of particular Gospel texts. For example, William Arnal, in his study on the hypothetical document "Q," used an even more sophisticated social analysis of the ancient world to detail conflict between Jesus and the scribes in Galilee, seeking to demonstrate that the diverse issues that were at play in the city of Jerusalem extended well beyond into the more Greek-influenced regions of Israel.[9] Herein the delineation of a specific background functions to assist in efforts to better understand the New Testament texts.

Indeed, debates about the composition and nature of the Galilee region in the "time of Jesus" are equally as important in terms of configuring the meaning and placement of both the literature and the historical personages behind the New Testament materials. The German tradition of scholarship had long held the position that the Galilee region, the territory in which Jesus is said to have grown up and undertaken a significant portion of his "ministry," was largely Hellenized and was relatively devoid of "traditional" ritualistic Judaism. Indeed, some studies at the turn of the century went so far as to promote Jesus' "Aryan" origin, suggesting that he himself was not biologically Jewish. More recent, particularly American, scholars have made a concerted effort to demonstrate that the Galilee region was every bit as Jewish as the so-called "Palestinian" region of Judea.[10] To be sure, scholars have also focused on Jesus' alleged familiarity with Greek language and Greek customs from cities such as Sepphoris, some 5 miles to the south of Nazareth. Although not mentioned in the Gospel accounts of Jesus, Sepphoris was one of the crown jewels in the Hellenistic panoply of northern cities. While the particular debates about Jesus' background and familiarity with Judaism are quite beyond the scope of the present book, it is worth noting what is at stake in such discussions: namely, the question of precisely how Jewish Jesus was, and whether we can understand his conflict with more apparently stringent observers of Jewish law such as Pharisees as a conflict based on social class and geographical location.

The point to reinforce in this discussion is that context – here social and economic and political – makes a difference to how we configure the relationship of texts and characters in historical perspective. At a very basic level, one can raise the question of whether the New Testament reflects a prevalently Jewish or Gentile/Greco-Roman perspective in terms of configuring the major themes of the "gospel." For instance, Paul Billerbeck's famed 19th-century collection, *Kommentar zum Neuen Testament aus Talmud und Midrasch*,[11] details the close parallels between the New Testament texts, rabbinic materials, and other Jewish texts, promoting the notion that the New Testament had substantial relationships with Jewish traditions of interpretation.[12] The main four volumes are meticulous and detailed, leaving one with the impression that, whether in agreement or in contradistinction, one could not understand the New Testament apart from a knowledge and appreciation of the rabbinic interpretive tradition.

By contrast, one could turn to the *Hellenistic Commentary to the New Testament*, which decidedly lays out the diverse connections between the New Testament literature and Hellenistic, non-rabbinic texts, from parallel stories to paraenetic materials that potentially illuminate the meaning of the New Testament.[13] Of course, it would be unwise to see this project as an entire juxtaposition to Billerbeck's collection of talmudic and other midrashic texts. Still, one should note immediately that there are radically different ways of situating the early Christian materials in a socio-cultural comparative perspective. While these are not mutually exclusive, the portrait that emerges of the New Testament is so significantly different that one has to pause and raise the question of how scholars can come up with two quite different frameworks for configuring the meaning of these early Christian texts and traditions. Ultimately the debate herein revolves around what historical, contextual, and conceptual frameworks have informed and influenced the development of early Christian ideas and theologies. That is, do we look to the Jewish tradition – and if so, which Jewish tradition? A Jewish tradition that is more inclined toward a traditionally conceived ritualistic structure, or one that is more open and liberated, often configured in terms of the "Palestinian" versus "Hellenistic" divide? Or do we look elsewhere, perhaps to the Greeks or at least regional traditions influenced by Greek religious and cultural concepts? Of course, in all of this is embedded a much larger debate – and perhaps greater anxiety – about the origins of Christianity.

Is Christianity something new and original? Is it something borrowed from elsewhere? To what degree does it present innovative and inspired social, religious, and cultural insights? One cannot overestimate the importance of concerns such as these in terms of configuring the search for the "backgrounds" that shape the meaning of the Christian tradition as we understand that today.

So far we have touched on some broad issues with respect to how we understand and assess backgrounds in relation to the New Testament, its literature, and its social-historical milieu. Perhaps the best way to summarize the above discussion is simply to note that whenever one talks about ideas or particular texts that are found in the New Testament, or reflects on historical realities and personages behind the same, one is constantly contextualizing the readings within a historical, socio-cultural, religious, economic, and political framework that helps contemporary readers make sense of the meaning of the words and the broader concepts that are communicated. There is no meaning without contextualization. To be sure, many introductory materials on the New Testament may already assume a certain knowledge of its socio-cultural and religious background so that when, for example, the terms "Jewish law" or "Torah" are invoked readers already have some sense of what the intended signification of those terms might be. That said, in many cases those seeking to introduce the New Testament set forth the basic context in which they intend their interpretation of a particular text or historical datum to be read.

This discussion may seem very basic, not in small part because so much if not all of human knowledge and communication in general relies on contextualizing practices. It could be said that we constantly process "context," whether or not we know it. Nevertheless, these are practices that we frequently take for granted and to which we often give little attention in biblical scholarship. If the "context" or "background" for any statement regarding the New Testament is quintessential in understanding its basic meaning, then changing the context will make every bit of difference. Indeed, one could well claim that it is not the words of the New Testament that are important, but rather the context in which we place them to give them meaning, for it is the latter that informs our understanding of the texts, traditions, and socio-historical realities underlying the New Testament. Now, we should remind ourselves that many New Testament introductory textbooks in fact presume, and also create, the background against which the interpretation that follows will proceed. There is no escaping this practice. There is no outside of context – there is only the stepping back and examining the meta-contextual issues regarding what difference a different context might make for understanding the same piece of datum.

Basically, what we have noted here is the "problem" of language: all statements have to be embedded in particular systems of signification for them to have any meaning or purpose. As a result, as part of a process of de-introducing the New Testament we are not suggesting that we can move outside of "backgrounds" with respect to grounding meaning in early Christian texts. Rather, we are invested in highlighting the essential role that conceptual "backgrounds" play in signifying meaning-making practices in the present. In other words, the only way to change meaning in any New Testament text is to reconfigure the system of significations that gives meaning to the signs in the text. And the focus on backgrounds is the key facet involved in such configurations and reconfigurations.

The entire corpus of scholarly writing on New Testament literature can, in fact, be understood as a grand and lively debate about what contexts should inform our reading of this ancient material. That is, in fact, what scholarship does – it functions to create the structural relationship between the context and the production of meaning that results. And any debate about meaning in the early Christian literature is, fundamentally, an issue of realigning the contextual configuration that helps us produce meaning with texts. Even the smallest twist to a context, the most minute shift, can have a dramatic effect on the meaning of a given text. Backgrounds or contexts are not simply one element to consider among others – they are the only things that matter in terms of structuring the "trick." The problem is that scholars themselves often are unaware of the frequently arbitrary nature of the construction of contexts themselves, and certainly pay little heed to the complexity of backgrounds. Aside from there being a context for meaning in the first palce, one also has to assume a stable context in order for there to be stable meaning in texts. While we might experience a world of constantly changing motivations and random orientations that often shift midstream, in order to have firm and certain readings of New Testament texts we have to configure the backgrounds that produce the meanings of the texts to be secure, firm, and unchanging – or, if they do change, they do so in relatively stable and predictable ways. It is only in this manner that we can have any faith in the outcome of the interpretive process. In some respect, it is the same with the illusionist's card trick noted earlier: we all know where it is going, and, while surprising, the end result is still predictable (and if not – the illusionist is, well, not all that good at her or his profession). But should a card trick all of a sudden result in pulling a rabbit out of a hat we would see a fundamental disjunction in the logic of the "game." Thus, even the surprises we experience in the interpretive effort still depend on a stable regime of analysis that frames the entire experience of interpretation.

Therefore, we encounter two main problems as we proceed to investigate the matter of backgrounds more fully. The first is that differing backgrounds produce variant interpretations, and there are strong cases to be made for one background over against another. These debates can be carried on – persuasively one might add – endlessly. The second is that there is a particular commitment to stability and coherence that is required for focusing on backgrounds in the way that we tend to do in the field of New Testament studies. Complexity can and sometimes does enter into the conversation, but more frequently the contextual structural basis of the configuration of meaning is necessarily related as static, immovable, and impervious. Such understandings become crucial in terms of making certain that the meanings we derive from texts can in fact bear the weight of the certitude we have come to demand.

Backgrounding the Backgrounds Approach

In the above section we have highlighted the fact that all interpretation of the New Testament – its literature, its concepts, its practices, its social histories – only makes sense through being situated in a background context that illuminates and nurtures interpretation. We also noted that there are myriads of differing backgrounds that can be deployed to shape the meaning and interpretation of texts, concepts, practices, and social histories in one direction or another. Use of these backgrounds bends meaning toward a particular purpose, one that has more to do with our present interests, concerns, investments, and ideologies and less to do with being a product of objective historical investigation and recovery. Fundamental, in fact, are the assumptions and values that go into the scholarly work on selecting particular backgrounds and then moving to construct those backgrounds in specific ways. Any background, once selected, can be construed in innumerable ways depending on the larger matrices that the interpreter deploys to configure the "stable canvas" against which our contemporary interpretive artistry comes to life.

Frequently, especially in scholarly discussions of the New Testament, part of the treatment of a particular subject is to delineate what backgrounds have been used in the past to understand it, some of the problems for interpretation those backgrounds have posed, and how a proposed reconfigured or altogether different background will help us see the phenomenon in question in not only new but also better ways. Seldom do scholars reveal their own personal predilections for one background over another, and rarely is the choice value-neutral. In introductory materials, the backgrounds used for interpretation are frequently referenced but without extensive discussions regarding alternative options. Moreover, at times the background that informs the interpretive work on display is hidden from view and, not surprisingly, even the scholar producing the work may be unaware of the operative background that informs her or his analysis. In other words, it is important to bear in mind that there are received traditions of interpretation that rely on particular backgrounds that often do not demand reflection or even evoke skepticism in their reception by scholars at a later point in time.

For instance, the idea that Jesus as a historical figure must be placed in some kind of messianic or prophetic conceptual and historical context comes as a fairly obvious assumption to many scholars, and certainly bears a distinctively conservative mark in terms of linking the historical and literary figure of Jesus to the Hebrew Bible traditions and scriptures. Thus, scholars will move forward with a position on Jesus, either as historical character or as represented in the Gospels, within a well-entrenched history of interpretation that links Jesus to a traditional form of Judaism, which provides the basis for understanding the controversies and actions associated with his mission and message. That said, there is a strong counter-tradition among scholars who see Jesus as a Cynic-like character or someone heavily steeped, or at least contextualized at a literary level, in a wisdom tradition that predates the apocalyptic and even prophetic accouterments that were added to the Jesus traditions. In this trajectory, the "original" Jesus had more in common with the kinds of teachings we might find in the *Gospel of Thomas* than what we find in the final edition of the Gospel of Matthew. Thus, the background one selects not only offers a particular portrait of Jesus as a historical figure, but it also has implications for the oral and literary growth of the Gospel traditions, including how one conceptualizes the movement from the teachings of a historical personage to the accumulation of such sayings within larger narrative contexts that bring in other types of backgrounds that shift and mutate the potentially "original" portrait. We have examined in Chapter 1 this question of the "original" as somehow foundational for much of how we think about and conceptualize the New Testament and its afterlives. For the moment we are focusing on the ways in which these background conceptions play out in interpretation, often at the level of simply being assumed and presented as givens.

Further, it is critical to note, as the above example regarding Jesus suggests, that every decision about backgrounds with respect to one text of the New Testament necessarily reconfigures larger aspects of interpretation regarding early Christian concepts and traditions. How one configures the "historical Jesus" will shape the way that one delineates the origins and growth of the Jesus traditions and, finally, the composition of the Gospels, including implications for their interrelationships, both textually and conceptually. Moreover, if one considers Jesus to have been a resister of Roman imperial rule, then one also has to think more broadly about how that kind of resistance is transmitted to other early Christian groups. If the Gospel message is essentially shaped by resistance to the rule of imperial powers, those above Earth and those on Earth, then that message will play out in other texts of the New Testament, perhaps even all of them! Thus, one always has to consider the broader ramifications that particular backgrounds choices bear, especially in relationship to assumptions regarding the formation and development of early Christianity as an emergent movement in the ancient world, itself based on particular models that one draws from other background parallels. The complexity of the structure for signification of meaning is apparent.

In this section we aim to briefly delineate a broader paradigm for conceptualizing the use of backgrounds in New Testament scholarship. We should emphasize that this is a *heuristic* framework – we are not suggesting a universal, univocal, and naturalized system of structuring approaches to the backgrounds of the New Testament and early Christian literature. However, in order to provide an analytic lens through which some of the larger issues related to New Testament interpretation can be assessed, and, in line with the aim of this book, problematized, we offer two main categories of contexts for interpretation, both with qualifications: Judaism and Greco-Roman influences. In the category of "Judaism," we include two basic types: "traditional" Judaism, often in the past designated as "Palestinian Judaism," by which was meant a more conventional and con-servative Judaism especially in relationship to the maintenance of Jewish law and identity, and "liberal" Judaism, one referred to in past scholarship as "Hellenistic Judaism" and understood to denote the Greek influence on Jews, largely believed to have occupied the diaspora, outside of the Palestinian region proper. The term "Greco-Roman" denotes the "other" side of the equation, which represents a host of traditions and influences on the New Testament and early Christianity that is not related to Judaism per se, although admittedly there may be an intermingling or syncretism pro-ducing a hybrid that might not be considered strictly "Hellenistic Jewish" in our heuristic framework. Naturally, this category is extremely broad, and in some sense is relatively unhelpful for precise analysis of "non-Jewish" elements in the New Testament. One can, for instance, scarcely consider Egyptian and Parthian traditions as strictly evoked by the term "Greco-Roman." Still, as a heuristic tool it is a phenomenon with which to think and plot out some larger structures of meaning that inform much of modern interpretation.

It should be noted that any strict categorization of concepts and social-historical realities into precise "camps" is simplistic, as it assumes a fairly stable relationship between spheres of influence and, to be sure, that indi-viduals and communities in disparate parts of the Mediterranean world are similarly stable and naturalized – that every person in a community will embody the confluences of differing social and cultural realities in similar if not exactly matching ways. In fact, one of the major points we hope to convey in this book is precisely that all of the assumptions we make about the New Testament in terms of how we talk about and represent the data in many respects assume a fairly "cardboard" and "stick figure" historical world. In other words, the body, as a site of basic biological, social, and psychological interactions, cannot be universalized even at the level of the body itself, as the individual is constantly in flux not just throughout a lifetime, but also within any given moment. Thus, to make statements that encompass a static view not only of individuals but, even more so, whole communities, regions, territories, and empires, is ultimately unhelpful. Useful, however, is to think about the frameworks scholars have deployed and continue to deploy in terms of framing the data that is presented, even if in "cardboard-cutout" or one-dimensional fashion.

Each different era of New Testament studies configures, deploys, and relates to these differing backgrounds in distinctive ways. It is noteworthy, for instance, that while the deployment of Greco-Roman religious traditions as a context in which to explore the rise of early Christian concepts, practices, and texts was considered problematic in many quarters a century ago, we see, today, a marked shift in attitude. And even in a given time period particular regions and groups of scholars positioned themselves differently vis-à-vis a particular background. It was often the case that, especially in earlier German scholarship, deploying Greco-Roman parallels for understanding facets of the New Testament implied that these particular facets were more removed from the originary impulses that lay behind the messages of Jesus and Paul, and in some sense were "less authentic" elements as a result. While the precise meaning of "less authentic" would differ from scholar to scholar, one can generally say that the more Greco-Roman a phenomenon was the more likely it was to be considered less authentically Christian – which often, of course, meant "less Protestant." Indeed, the Protestant/Catholic divide across Europe has to be understood as a driving force in these discussions. The animosity that led to political conflicts and wars undoubtedly factored into how backgrounds were deployed in the scholarship of the era. At the same time that the (largely Protestant) German tradition was seeing the increasing distance from "original" Christian ideas, concepts, and practices as one moved further out into the Greco-Roman world, so also were the French Catholic scholars relying quite comfortably on seeing parallels between ideas and practices in Paul's letters and Greco-Roman religious traditions without perceiving therein any challenge to the authenticity or revelatory nature of these early Christian concepts.

Religious affiliation thus played a role in how one was oriented toward the background materials. For example, any potential influence by the Greco-Roman mystery religions on early Christian perceptions of ritual was considered by German scholarship to be the result of a degeneration of earliest Christian worship practices. To be sure, these earlier scholars did see the development and deployment of elements like the mystery religions in "their" materials, but these were thought to be facets of later development in early Christianity, which were, again, a degeneration of the "true" and "authentic" religious impulses among the earliest Christians.[14] French Catholics, by contrast, had much less to lose by acknowledging parallels between early Christian rituals and Greco-Roman religious traditions, since Catholicism was steeped in a highly ritualized practice. In short, one's orientation to one's own religion and culture – and particularly one's own understanding of the key concepts and principles that are held as core, authentic, and perhaps even "revealed" – shapes the manner in which one relates to and experiences the contextualization of the New Testament in one environment or another.

Given this general framing, then, it is not difficult to understand how Judaism in the 18th through mid-20th centuries was a problem, especially for Protestant interpreters in Europe. Of course, the bastion of the development of the modern critical study of the Bible, and particularly the impulse to separate out the historical interpretive task from church dogma, was thoroughly situated in the Germanic region. Within this environment, Judaism would prove to be a particularly contentious theoretical and religious category for New Testament interpreters. In short, Protestantism arises as a movement in opposition to a perceived rigidly legalistic and overly ritualistic Catholic Church. At the same time, Judaism in the history of Western thought and culture has always posed a problem, given the identification of Judaism as somehow in opposition to early Christianity – and especially to the figure of Jesus. Christianity, then, has in some sense evolved in opposition to Judaism – and defined itself on that basis. And once Protestantism emerges as a viable and volatile force in Europe, it is not a stretch of the imagination for some interpreters and theologians to begin to equate Judaism and Catholicism as fundamental oppositions to the freedom, faith, and individuality of the Protestant expression of the Christian tradition, even as Protestantism itself had a myriad of variations on its core themes.

It is in this context that German scholars, particularly under the influence of a group of biblical critics working out of the University of Göttingen, formulated something of a specific "backgrounds" approach to the study of the Bible. Designated as the "History of Religions school" of biblical interpretation, often referred to by its German title *Religionsgeschichtliche Schule*, this approach or movement, or what we might call for all intents and purposes a larger interpretative horizon that overlapped with what scholars were already doing in their research elsewhere, focused on reading biblical texts within their ancient contexts, paying particularly close attention to parallel phenomena in other ancient religious traditions. So, someone studying Hebrew Bible/Old Testament literature would pay close attention to Babylonian and Assyrian parallels, or perhaps Zoroastrian/Persian traditions, depending on which portions of the biblical text were in view. Someone studying the New Testament would examine the larger Greek and Roman parallels that helped illuminate the kinds of expressions, concepts, and practices that arise in the early Christian materials. The underlying commitment or assumption was that all ideas in any historical context are influenced by and interact with the larger ambient cultural, social, and religious spheres in which they arise. And identifying parallels provides an accessible means by which to understand the rise, development, and meaning behind these specific ideas and practices. This is not a difficult notion. It does, however, take seriously the view that there are no truly "original" ideas per se, but that new ideas arise through interaction, mutation, and transformation in interaction with a larger environment.

To be sure, there is also a debate here, especially in terms of the extent to which revelatory or "divinely inspired" concepts are present in the formative period of Christianity. And there is a controversy that grows out of precisely this issue that has in some sense continued into the modern period – namely, to what degree does religious experience account for new ideas, so that there is something outside of culture, society, and religion that stands alone, even as it is also fully expressed within a cultural matrix? One might consider this an "incarnational" issue at its core, and it is a matter we will return to again in this chapter. For the moment, however, it is important to note that the *Religionsgeschichtliche Schule* was foundational for the development of modern scholarly approaches to the New Testament. Strictly speaking, many scholars only use this term to refer to the specific individuals and movements that identified with this approach and its concomitant methodology. However, we use it more broadly to highlight an expansive approach to the study of the New Testament that is committed to fully contextualizing the material within the religious and cultural worlds of antiquity.

In considering the early Christian materials, Judaism obviously comes to the forefront. The New Testament texts are flooded with historical referents and religious images drawn from Jewish traditions more broadly and Jewish scriptures more specifically. One can imagine the problem this posed for German scholars of the late 19th and early 20th centuries. On the one hand, one has to acknowledge the deep-rooted indebtedness of early Christianity to Judaism in terms of its basic concepts and practices. At the same time, particularly from a Protestant reading of the New Testament, it could appear that Jesus and Paul stand fundamentally opposed to the legacy of law in Jewish tradition. In such a framework, the New Testament both needs to look like, but also be different from, the Jewish background out of which it arose.

Similarly, one also has to recognize that there are large portions of the New Testament, particularly the Gospel of John and many of the concepts contained in Paul's letters, which do not seem to be closely connected to traditional Judaism in terms of its expression and focus. At the same time, while Judaism could be a problem in this earlier scholarship, it is also a categorical necessity, since the possibility of Christianity arising out of purely Greco-Roman matrices is also unacceptable. What would be worse as a source, the thinking might go: "paganism" or "Judaism"? At least in the latter case, there is a proximation of concepts and identity to what we find in early Christianity, since the latter draws so heavily on the Jewish scriptural tradition and monotheism. The proximate other, in many respects, is a safer bet than the completely other, or at least this was the assumption embedded in the larger structural framework in which many scholars of the period were operating.

The distinction between "Hellenistic" and "Palestinian" Judaism is largely born out of the above-mentioned dilemma for scholars. On the one hand, there is a type of Judaism of the law and ritual that scholars believed early Christians opposed and beyond which they moved. On the other, there are numerous Jewish concepts that are critical to New Testament ideas and practices that seem to be influenced by Greco-Roman religious matrices. That is to say, there appear to have been Jews living in Palestine who were traditional and legalistic, and with whom early Christians were generally not to be identified. And there were Jews living abroad, in the diaspora, who had already for a long while imbibed the religious and cultural ethos of the Greeks and the Romans, but particularly the former. They were less legalistic in focus, more interested in assimilation, and less tied to the mundane rituals of so-called traditional Judaism. Indeed, they may well have reconfigured their own rituals under Greek influence, perhaps at times drawing on mystery religions for inspiration, and they may even have moved away from Judaism altogether. Thus, we have two distinct types of Judaism, each possessing distinctive geographical elements. As Christianity spreads out of Palestine, but is still within the ambient sphere of Judaism, it draws some of its ideas from Hellenistic Jews, which accounts for some of the unique developments in early Christian thought and practice without sacrificing, in some respects, the "biblical" connection of that tradition. Hellenistic Judaism becomes something of a buffer, then, for emergent Christianity. And to be sure, scholars understood that it does gradually become more corrupted as it moves outward, but it is corrupted in a way that still makes it consonant with its beginning. At the moment that Christianity draws fully on Greek and Roman religious traditions, according to this older framework, it has become diluted and degenerate. For many Protestant interpreters, of course, this dynamic signified the development of Catholicism.

The sketch above is generalized in a way to make obvious its heuristic potential. The key points of Judaism (broken into "Palestinian" and "Hellenistic") and Greco-Roman influences (paganism) represent components on a spectrum that allows one to plot the development of and shifts in the field of New Testament studies as it deploys backgrounds to help illuminate early Christian materials. One way to map how this looks in practice is to locate four different points over the last century in the development of the discipline of New Testament studies as it relates to examining the evolution of Christology. Christology is a particularly good example for us to survey herein, since it represents one of the core identifying beliefs of early Christians: that Jesus, the Galilean man, came to be worshiped as Christ and Lord. Indeed, Christianity is distinct in precisely the fact that Jesus came to be worshiped alongside and equivalent with God. For Wilhelm Bousset (1865–1920), one of the key proponents of the *Religionsgeschichtliche Schule* and one of its chief architects in terms of its becoming an identifiable movement of interpretation, the worship of Jesus as Christ and Lord is something that developed gradually, as the early Christian movement extended well beyond the borders of Palestine.[15] For Bousset, it was not possible for a deification process such as this to take place in a cultural and religious matrix so closely aligned with traditional Jewish Palestinian beliefs and practices, particularly the strong commitment to monotheism. It was only as Christianity moved out and encountered Hellenistic Jewish influences that it slowly began to develop more complex concepts related to resurrected and risen divine figures. Indeed, Hellenistic Judaism, already influenced by Greek notions of divinity, would have provided a resource for early Christians as they began to develop expansive ways of conceiving of Christ beyond the man Jesus.

Half a century later, the German scholar Martin Hengel (1926–2009), who was probably the most influential New Testament critic to have adopted the *Religionsgeschichtliche Schule*'s general framework, established himself as an adamant opponent of the interpretations of scholars such as Bousset and Rudolf Bultmann (1884–1976). Hengel sought to undo the dichotomy between Hellenistic and Palestinian Judaisms, and is considered largely to have achieved that goal. Through a massive study on the relationship of Judaism and Hellenism,[16] and then a host of other studies that expanded on and developed the ideas set forth in his initial analysis, Hengel demonstrated that, by the time early Christianity arose in Jerusalem, Hellenism – that is, Greek concepts, practices, and religious notions – was well represented in Palestine. Indeed, there was always good evidence for this position in the Maccabean literature, where substantive conflicts between Jews loyal to Torah and Jews seeking to assimilate to the practices of the reigning Greek empire are well depicted. Hengel drew this basic facet out much further, though, showing that, even in cases where Jews still remained "traditional" and adhered to the law, they none the less adopted Greek customs, practices, and also, in many cases, the language. Thus, Jerusalem was, for all intents and purposes, thoroughly Hellenized. As a result, for Hengel, the basic notion of worshiping Jesus as Lord could easily have developed right at the beginning of the Christian movement, albeit still being associated with the Hellenistic Jews of Jerusalem.

Hengel agreed with Bousset that Hellenism was a critical background for understanding the rise of Christ-devotion in early Christianity. Unlike Bousset, however, Hengel wanted to make the case that such devotion happened early on among Jerusalem Christians. Further, Hengel is adamant that Christianity does bring with it a new experience of the spirit, which dramatically transformed conceptions from the very beginning. For Hengel, there is a clear evangelical and pietistic commitment to the uniqueness of Christianity, which stands over against the more liberal positions of Bousset and Bultmann. At the same time, it is important to bear in mind that Hengel still does want to see Judaism as something other than Christianity, and in the moment that he Hellenizes the Judaism of Palestine he also in many respects makes the Judaism of the diaspora much more nationalistic and Torah-observant than previous scholars like Bousset were willing to do. In this way, Hengel still uses Judaism as a buffer-zone and constructs a fairly concrete conception of the proximate other over against which Christianity, whether in Palestine or beyond in the Greco-Roman regions, can be defined as something new and distinct. Here one can observe the palpable influence of the German Protestant tradition's engagement of Judaism, which well after the Holocaust still had traction, even if much less open and obvious. For Bousset, Judaism was both a (Palestinian) oppositional facet in, and also a (Hellenistic) buffer-zone for, the development of Christian concepts and practices. For Hengel, Christianity does need Hellenistic Jews, but these Hellenistic Jews are already in Jerusalem and they are already oriented toward a more "law-free" approach to the deity, which makes them ideal conduits for the revelation of Christ and the law-free mission to the Gentiles. Herein, then, Judaism proves to be an oppositional element, whether in Palestine or abroad in the diaspora, and only in so far as Hellenistic Jews become thoroughly immersed in the early Jesus movement in Palestine do they represent something beyond Judaism. And, to be sure, that "something" is that they are a channel, a mediator, for the fullness of Greek ideas to be brought to their most complete expression in earliest Christian theology and practice.

More recent scholarly engagement of the issue of worshiping Jesus as Lord, however, has gone in quite divergent directions from the likes of Bousset and Hengel. For example, Larry Hurtado's seminal work, *One God, One Lord*,[17] which was intended in many ways to lay the groundwork for his larger study that would seek to offer a replacement to and challenge of Bousset's *Kyrios Christos*, situates the worship of Jesus within the Jewish tradition. While not avoiding Hellenistic Jewish literature as such, Hurtado is fully comfortable seeing precedents in non-Hellenistic Jewish literature that clearly could "mutate" into the divinization of Jesus within a "binatarian" system of belief. Hurtado thus both follows Hengel's lead by dating the full worship of Jesus as Lord very early in the emergent Christian movement, but also does not hesitate to connect such conceptions even to trajectories in rabbinic literature. In some sense, as we will note again below, there was much less antipathy toward a more "traditional" Judaism in the post-Holocaust period, especially among anglophone scholars. The Holocaust was a definite wake-up call, for sure. However, it was not the only element. In the historically more conservative trajectories of anglophone scholarship, there was also a desire to connect the New Testament more closely with the Hebrew Bible/Old Testament, as a means of showing God's continuity of working in history, and more traditional post-biblical Judaisms were often seen as being in continuity with the latter.

While no one denies that Judaism developed in the diaspora in vibrant and sometimes radically differing ways than one might think of as "Hebrew Bible Judaism," or that there were without a doubt multiple Judaisms in the ancient world (even in Palestine proper), there is also an inherent desire, particularly in the more conservative strands of anglophone scholarship, to link a conception of "Hebrew Bible Judaism" with the development of incipient Christianity. In this configuration not only was Jesus Jewish and the early Christians similarly so, but the language and imagery used to express much New Testament "theology" or "religion" are drawn from the Jewish tradition that is thought to be represented in the Hebrew Bible, without regard to the difference between Judaism and, say, Israelite religion and culture. We leave aside here the question of just how much one can speak of "Hebrew Bible Judaism" beyond a kind of fictional construction of modern scholarship itself. There is a biblical theological commitment that underlies this connection, of course, but in many respects the two canons of literature lend themselves to thinking in this direction. The "New Testament" stands as a "follow-up" in some respects to the "Old Testament" in the Protestant Christian tradition, and for the longest period early Christians would see the prefiguration of Christ throughout the Hebrew Bible and certainly continue to do so in key passages such as Isaiah 53. Such associations between the two testaments are not new, and such typological readings go way back to the earliest patristic interpreters and even to the New Testament writers themselves. It is telling that German New Testament scholarship has been much less invested in aligning the two testaments than has anglophone scholarship, but that says much about the orientations of the intersection of religion and culture in these regions.

More recently, a new focus in anglophone scholarship on the Greco-Roman or "Gentile" background of the worship of Jesus as Lord has precipitated another variation in the use of backgrounds in the study of the New Testament. Luke Timothy Johnson's *Among the Gentiles*, which examines the deeply rooted nature of the development of Christianity in Greco-Roman religious traditions, is a prominent example of this major shift in scholarly focus. Here not even "Hellenistic Judaism" is that much of a concern; as Johnson himself acknowledges, no matter how much one may think Jews were rooted in Greco-Roman culture, Christianity was much more so and for much longer.[18] The point to be made here is that the shift in emphasis from Jewish traditions to Greco-Roman contexts is quite marked, and, while not completely new per se, this shift does highlight broader changes in the field. For example, two recent scholars who focus on the rise of "Christ-worship" in early Christianity, Michael Peppard and M. David Litwa, both, in varying ways, focus on the Greco-Roman world for providing the context in which the early Christian belief that Jesus was Lord took shape. Peppard accents the emperor cult and its various political and social affiliations, while Litwa looks more broadly at Mediterranean deity worship and the widespread practice of deifying individuals.[19] For our purposes here, the specifics of each case do not matter. Rather, they highlight for us the shift away from more "traditional" moorings of scholarship, whether in Hellenistic or Palestinian Judaisms.

As it turns out, more recent New Testament scholarship does not appear to feel indebted to the Jewish tradition in particular in terms of explaining how Jesus became (a) God. Rather, contemporary considerations of that question, among many others, freely move beyond the former "boundaries" that once defined the construction of early Christian belief as far as its backgrounds and influences are concerned. Anything is fair game, in this respect. It is definitely not the case that scholars who follow this interpretive trajectory are in any way leaving Judaism behind, although no doubt some critics might accuse them of that. Rather, Judaism as a background for early Christianity simply does not play the same role it once did in studies of the New Testament, either positively or negatively. Now, to be sure, not all scholars of early Christianity would agree with these conclusions, nor would they concur that Judaism is somehow less important than it once was for understanding early Christianity. As we will argue below, within Pauline studies Judaism is still critical as a background and context. Yet the shift in focus should be noted, not least because it suggests that a newer generation of scholars does not see an obvious connection, whether genealogical or not, between the formation and development of Christianity and its broader Jewish context, which seems to loom large in the New Testament. It is rather likely that this shift will continue to have prominence in future scholarly agendas.

By way of summary, then, we note that in the above analysis we have sought to highlight several key points with respect to backgrounds. These are as follows:

First, utilizing historical and socio-cultural backgrounds as a method and approach to early Christian texts has a long history in studies of the New Testament and early Christianity. It is in part a product of the modern development of historiography itself as a discipline wherein past phenomena are understood to have a concrete historical context that necessarily affects how we understand and interpret those materials. One cannot simply say that such approaches rose to prominence solely in the 18th and 19th centuries, as during the Renaissance period the development of philology as a key to understanding translation already demanded a sense of "backgrounds." Nevertheless, it is the case that the broader contextualization of the reading of the New Testament in the context of its backgrounds is a relatively recent development in scholarship. It is, in principle, a modern approach and solicitous of modern questions and concerns. In this respect, one of the major modern shifts in understanding the New Testament materials was a turn to contextualization, whether it be simply understanding the historical events in which a text was written and to which it responded, or assessing the influences that shaped concepts, beliefs, and practices. Readers of the Bible can readily appreciate that, without some contextual background to help us formulate and tease out the meaning of the texts, we are left adrift in our efforts to access that meaning. The upshot of this emphasis, of course, is that there is nothing ever truly "new" in terms of expression of ideas, but rather everything is in some sense a product of its environment, even as emergent ideas may offer something different in orientation and scope, and even at times radically so.

Second, we note that attempts to contextualize the New Testament materials are vastly more complex than is often presented. We have attempted to delineate some of the overarching aspects of the "backgrounds" approach and to provide a historical and intellectual context in the 18th and 19th centuries that helps explain something of the way in which Judaism was deployed in early backgrounds scholarship. Moreover, our aim has been to distinguish some of the broad choices that are utilized in the contextualization of the New Testament, and particularly Palestinian and Hellenistic Judaisms alongside Greco-Roman backgrounds. Of course, these categories are general and are meant to be heuristic and illustrative rather than structurally determinative. That is, every concept, belief, and practice is contextualized historically in ways that are almost impossible to fully recreate. We can access threads of meaning and connections, but the broader backgrounds will always remain elusive. All regions and the peoples within them, both in the same time period and also over time, exist within a confluence of contexts that are continually being reconfigured, and not in the same way for every person.

Every context, then, is itself a continuing product of and participant in the creation of ever new and often more complex contexts. Moreover, we know that Judaism is different in Egypt than in Persia, and that "Greco-Roman" covers a time period that includes cultures as diverse as the Gauls, Dacians, North Africans, Spaniards, and so on. The most that the categories we have deployed here suggest are the kinds of larger choices that scholars make in terms of interpreting the New Testament. Thus, we will always of necessity be generalizing when we interpret the meaning of a concept in the context of a background.

Third, while we acknowledge that the deployment of these contexts is complicated and convoluted, we also highlight an emergent pattern. On the one hand, even as post-Holocaust scholarship has moved the backgrounds discussion in differing directions, particularly regarding the portrayal of ancient Judaism, there still remains a fairly coherent conception of what ancient Judaism is. What has changed is the assessment of its usefulness, importance, and the character of its contribution (e.g., Judaism's influence on the New Testament might not be so "bad" after all). It is true that more complexity and nuance have been added to our understandings of ancient Judaism, but Judaism as something essential – as a religious and ethnic phenomenon in the ancient world – is still a core principle of scholarship. In this respect, as it is understood as a background for early Christianity, Judaism represents something essentialist, particular, and, in early German scholarship (and to some extent even today), it signifies "blood" and "race."[20] It is a biological concept in many respects, even as the term "ethnicity" is also deployed to create some distance from the scientific category. Granted, the earlier idea that Judaism represents "enslavement to law" over against early Christianity's relatively "law-free" orientation, offering a major contrast between slavery and liberty, has been challenged by contemporary scholars. However, there is still a sense of essentialism and particularism that runs through the representations of ancient Judaism in which earlier conceptions continue to have influence, often unbeknownst to contemporary scholars. To be sure, we may still make distinctions like "less law-bound" Judaism and "more law-bound Judaism," or "legalistic Judaism" and "prophetic Judaism" (the former being focused on law, the latter on justice), but in these cases there is still an attempt to configure Judaism in a particular way so that it helps us better understand early Christian concepts, beliefs, and practices. In other words, Judaism is essential as something isolable, particular, and knowable so that Christianity can, in multiple and creative ways, be defined against it.

Fourth, and similarly, with respect to the Greco-Roman contexts, what we might term the "Gentile background" of early Christianity also has a particular role and purpose. In the broader and more general contours of this shift, the Greco-Roman tradition stands opposite Judaism as something that is not based on commitment to theocratic law, but rather on a moral code offered by humans. It is not law-bound, but rather has an accent on liberty and justice. It is civilized, as opposed to the frequently implied characterization of Judaism as something that is less so. To be sure, the ancient non-Jewish world was filled with all kinds of "strange" practices and beliefs, and, while these may have had some influence on Christianity, for many historical interpreters Christianity did not in essence arise directly from these traditions – and that distance makes a categorical difference for interpretation. The point to be emphasized, then, is that New Testament scholars have always needed and still do need a particular construction of Judaism and Greco-Roman influences in order to produce a specific form of ancient Christianity. Driving our choices as far as context is concerned is a commitment to the discursive production of an early Christianity that happens to fit with our perspectives and commitments, be they historical, cultural, political, and/or religious. Early Christianity thus emerges and stands out when placed against the background we select, being brought into existence through comparison and contrast. That is not to say that the New Testament materials somehow do not exist outside of an ancient context. However, in order to make sense of the texts, concepts, beliefs, practices, and social histories of early Christianity, we need models and frameworks to help contextualize its distinctiveness as an ancient religious movement. True, it is not out of necessity that we focus on "distinctiveness," and yet, given the role that Christianity plays in the modern world, it is usually the main lens through which we examine Christianity in its ancient historical context. In so far as early Christianity is understood to be "the same" as other traditions, it vanishes from our viewpoint, and certainly does not thereby stand out as a unique or necessarily transformative world religion.

Thus, there is no neutrality in the decisions that scholars make about the backgrounds for understanding the New Testament, and there is no random or innocuous mediation of the past for the person first learning about the New Testament and early Christian movement. In this way, it is important to bear in mind that so many other choices could be made to aid in illuminating the ancient materials, but multiplicity and complexity are usually sacrificed for singularity and simplicity, especially in introductory works, which serve to reify the general notions of early Christianity that even the most adept scholars tend to replicate in advanced analytic work. This situation reveals a major component of modern study: context helps create the subject, even as the context is in turn shaped by our prior understanding of that same subject. In the process, ironically, the very background that elucidates early Christian materials also becomes that entity from which Christianity in turn must be differentiated. The context arises only to then vanish or to be superseded.

Fifth, and finally, one of the key themes to take away from our discussion herein is that, no matter how much difference of opinion may exist among scholars in terms of the context shaping the New Testament, they all agree that some background is vital in order for New Testament scholarship to proceed. In other words, no one suggests that somehow early Christian concepts, beliefs, and practices arose in a vacuum or can be understood as such. There is consensus, rather, that culture and history shape how ideas are manifested and expressed. To be sure, as we just noted in the previous point, this is part of the problem as well: Christianity is generally only recognized in its distinctiveness rather than in its similarity. That said, it is evident that scholars automatically move to present information about early Christianity or argue a particular point of interpretation by appealing to a context or set of contexts. Meaning only takes place in a historically conditioned and contingent manner, which itself is one of the hallmarks of modern approaches to the study of the Bible. To have a Bible to talk about at all is to have a Bible that is contextualized. And should someone no longer be invested in talking about the Bible in its ancient context, they still will talk about the Bible in *some* context. Even the most "radical" interpreters working within a postmodern theoretical framework, for example, cannot think about the Bible apart from a context – it might just be that they are not interested in the ancient context as that which drives interpretive efforts. In what follows in the final section of this chapter, we tease out some of these themes a bit further with reference to a particular example of how scholars have continued the push and pull between varying backgrounds for studying particular early Christian beliefs and practices. We will focus on two main issues that one frequently encounters in reading contemporary New Testament scholarship, both at the introductory and more advanced levels: Jewish law and Roman rule.

Backgrounding the Character of Early Christianity: Liberty against Tyranny

If one follows the argument we have outlined thus far in this chapter, backgrounding the New Testament and early Christianity as a whole is not simply about an objective enterprise that involves the modern scholar picking the "right" historical and socio-cultural context in which to place an early Christian concept, text, or practice in order to interpret that element "correctly." As we have noted, there are a variety of factors that go into engaging early Christianity in context, and in many respects there is not one "right way" of doing so. The scholar's own historical context and social positioning, assumptions, values, and audience play a formative and often decisive role in choosing the background that will be used in the interpretive enterprise. That said, the process is not simply random either, as if anything goes. In fact, there is a limit on contexts that can be useful, and most often scholars will review and assess a variety of these before selecting what they believe is the most productive for meaning-making.

As we have noted, there is not really a true "context" that itself is not already interconnected and imbricated with a variety of other contexts,[21] making the selection of "just one" background an unrealistic overarching framework for studying the New Testament. Obviously the more complex and convoluted the background, the more attuned that interpretation is to the nuances of the historical and socio-cultural context. It is another matter to assess more broadly how differing backgrounds may be deployed by scholars to support interpretations of early Christianity that are quite similar. That is, it is one thing to engage the notion of backgrounds, examining the ways in which one can contextualize early Christian materials. We might ask, for example: which background is best for understanding the rise of Christ-worship in earliest or earlier Christianity? This question involves a matter of examining differing backgrounds to see which one "best fits." However, there remains a larger methodological question regarding how diverse backgrounds may in fact serve to affirm and solidify similar interpretations of early Christianity. Here we are inquiring as to how "backgrounds" as a methodological approach may, in variant ways, serve our own interests in constructing particular understandings of the New Testament. If we take seriously that at least one accent in the study of New Testament backgrounds involves our own commitments and orientations vis-à-vis this ancient material, then it should also be possible to trace the manner in which these larger themes work in tandem, although not necessarily in obvious ways, to reify specific structural commitments about the character and intrinsic meaning (for us) of early Christianity and the New Testament. The point of the following discussion, then, is to demonstrate how the backgrounds approach also functions, precisely in the midst of its diversity in application, to produce nevertheless a coherent and consistent version of early Christianity.

In order to explore these issues more fully, we utilize two quite distinct contextual issues that are prominent in the study of early Christianity. The first involves the relationship of New Testament beliefs and practices to Jewish law and the second concerns the relationship of early Christians to the Roman Empire. The question of how Jesus, Paul, and the earliest Christians viewed and related to Jewish law has been on the New Testament scholarly docket for a long while. With roots in German Protestant scholarship, it has been, and in many ways still is, one of the dominant issues that New Testament interpreters address. The question of the Roman Empire is something of more recent scholarly interest. While the Roman imperial context of the New Testament has long been a factor in interpretation, it is only more recently that scholarship has taken a decidedly "empire-critical" turn. Both of these accents – law and empire – are important, as both focus on early Christian resistance to tyranny in concept and practice. In other words, whether it be tyranny of religious law or tyranny of political rule, early Christianity is seen to be an entity that challenges autocratic systems of authority, religious and/or political. Contextualization here, despite being quite distinctive in terms of the fields of reference, serves to reinforce particular notions of early Christianity that have been embedded in New Testament scholarship since the inception of modern critical study.[22]

Early Christianity and Jewish law

It should not come as a surprise to even the novice who is being introduced to issues in the study of the New Testament that one of the enduring characterizations of early Christian interaction with Judaism is the striking challenge that early Christianity raises to Jewish law. Throughout the Gospels one comes across story after story where Jesus confronts and challenges the laws of the Jewish authorities. Even as in each Gospel these challenges and confrontations take on specific meanings and functions, and scholars have long recognized the influence of the differing perspectives of the writers of these Gospels in terms of shaping the stories about Jesus' responses to Jewish law, the importance of conflict and contention over Jewish law in some form has proved to be a prevailing theme in New Testament interpretation. Scholarly nuances have proliferated over time, as more recent interpreters, in response to earlier German Protestant scholarship, began to insist that Jesus must be considered Jewish and, for all intents and purposes, also law-abiding. During the past several decades, the conflicts with the Jewish authorities over legal matters have taken on greater nuance in New Testament scholarship. There is some measure of recognition that different Judaisms existed in the ancient world, and that this diversity yields variant interpretations of law and its application.

Some ancient Jewish authors such as Philo attest to an allegorical reading of Jewish law, demonstrating that Jewish conceptions were not literally about the body but about the mind and soul. Philo's particular perspective on the actual practice of Jewish law, and his own practice itself, are more difficult to ascertain. Other Jews, such as those represented in the Dead Sea Scrolls/Qumran Texts, seem to have held stricter views on legal regulations than many other practicing Jews of the same time period. And there were certainly intra-Jewish debates about the application of particular laws as well. For example, texts like the book of Jubilees, dated to somewhere in the middle of the second century BCE, offer a fairly extensive and insistent demand that the Jewish calendar needs to be based on solar calculations rather than the traditional lunar readings. Moreover, different feasts and holy days are added in the process. Obviously, there was debate – quite likely widespread – over the role and interpretation of Jewish law. Jesus can be situated within this larger context as someone who also had variant interpretations of Jewish law, and who came into conflict with differently oriented Jewish authorities as a result of such variance.

However, it has been difficult for scholars to shake the notion that there is more than mere variation between Jesus and the Jewish authorities: that conflict must be the arc that defines how we understand Jesus in history and narrative. "God demands mercy and not sacrifice" (Matt. 12:7) is often held up as a place wherein the traditional, more stringent application of "working on the Sabbath" is challenged by Jesus, who utilizes the story about David and his men, being ravenous on the Sabbath, having to violate the law by eating consecrated bread. Now, one may well read such responses by Jesus as the alternative views of a rabbi, responding to other religious authorities, wherein there is debate or alternate interpretation but not outright conflict. That said, the predominant image of the New Testament as a whole in relationship to Jewish law is more clearly shaped by the positioning of the apostle Paul than Jesus himself. Indeed, in so far as Jesus is read as "anti-law," such readings frequently depend on viewing Paul as being so himself. And here the role of German Protestant scholarship, from the period of Martin Luther (early 1500s) onwards, has proven to be critical in determining the contours of the New Testament "response" to Jewish law.

One of the predominant images of Paul is that of a "convert," which should not be underestimated as a useful category for scholarly understandings of the New Testament in relation to Jewish law. Indeed, Paul is frequently considered the "first" convert, leaving behind his Jewish heritage and becoming a follower of "the risen Christ" who confronted him on the road to Damascus while Paul was, according to Acts, headed to persecute the early Christians (Acts 9). As a "convert," Paul is often configured as the "true founder" of the emergent Christian movement, and certainly the originator of the universalizing message of early Christianity that moves outward toward non-Jews/Gentiles. The New Testament "story" of Paul and the Gentile mission is actually more complicated, at least in terms of how it is portrayed in Acts and from what we can glean from Paul's letters. However, the vast majority of readers and a significant quadrant of scholars nonetheless consider Paul to be the innovator, even though there may have been forerunners, of a "law-free" mission to the Gentiles.[23]

Read in light of a move toward Gentile Christianity, Paul's letters – particularly Romans and Galatians, often considered to be his most "important" missives – are traditionally understood to represent his departure from Judaism, highlighting his fundamental antagonism to the Jewish law he once held so dear. Certainly an "anti-Jewish-law Paul" has been of fundamental importance in shaping the discourse on Paul and Pauline studies for more than 200 years. And to be sure, this antagonism has often been spread to the social origins of early Christianity as well, where Paul is seen to oppose the "Jerusalem apostles," such as James the brother of Jesus and the Apostle Peter, who are both viewed as law-observant in their orientation. The story of Peter and Paul in Antioch (Gal. 2), and the "incident" that arises when "men from James" arrive and Peter separates himself out from the Gentiles for purity reasons, highlights for many scholars the persistent issues that were present in a movement that was both deeply rooted in Jewish tradition and practice and yet at the same time was expanding out to Gentile converts and adherents. Certainly Jewish law forms a critical component in the modern interpretation of the emergence of early Christianity in its social interactions, including its rapid expansion out of, and away from, more traditional Jewish frameworks and locales, which in some sense becomes a footnote to the history of early Christianity.

The above description offers the broad contours of the structure that has shaped much of New Testament interpretation over the past two centuries, regardless of the specific method or approach adopted. In such a framework, the forerunners of the early Christian movement, particularly the apostle Paul, are viewed as individuals who solidly placed individual freedom and liberty at the heart of the "gospel message." While social justice finds expression in Paul's writings, the implicit conception is that ethics proceeds from the liberation of the individual. Martin Luther's reading of Augustine on "justification by faith" as something that is based on "faith" and not "action" is deeply rooted in a Protestant religious commitment. The juridical nature of this declaration, wherein a sinner is deemed "righteous" through God's proclamation based on Christ's atoning sacrifice for human sin, is not a surprising theological focus in the evolving nation-state of the Prussian Empire. In the coalescence of the rise of the nation-state and its concomitant commitment to individual freedom, liberty, and due process, it is not surprising to see theological formulations that accent human liberation brought to the forefront. Indeed, it is not difficult to understand how, in this context, Pauline literature could come to be viewed as something of a human civilizing project, initiated by God's own direct act. In this light, although Jews themselves were understood to be emancipated in Europe toward full citizen rights in their various political and legal contexts, Jewish law – which was often simply a signifier for "Judaism" or "being Jewish" – became a marker of slavery and irrationalism which, in Pauline literature, could be counterbalanced with the irrational lawlessness of the Greeks as represented in, for example, Romans 1. Christianity is then configured as that which is about liberation from slavery to sin and the embracing of a rational existence. Jewish law, in this framework, is in many respects a stand-in for "slavery to sin."

The representation of Jewish law as that which enslaves its adherents is most implicit in early New Testament interpretation. It is an important element in terms of just how vitriolic some interpreters became toward Judaism as a whole, especially in the late 19th and early 20th centuries. In this way, Jewish law as a religious, cultural, and legal context for reading Paul in particular, and the New Testament more generally, becomes a means by which the character of early Christianity is clearly defined as liberative in orientation. Freedom – especially freedom of the individual – becomes a concept that lies at the heart of the Gospel message. As a result, Christianity is also understood to resist tyranny and oppression, becoming, in many respects, the ultimate expression of redemption from domination by sin, despotic laws, or other principalities and powers, national or political or other. Further, out of this liberation toward "true" freedom comes a rational law, one which is followed freely by free individuals, and which represents the civilizing project that arose within Christianity. Along with this freedom one also finds the expression of a "truly" spiritual (even pietistic) religion, one not demanded by outside authorities and one not exemplified in rote actions, but something that flows outward, from the human heart.

The turn in more recent studies toward an appreciative and contextually nuanced assessment of Judaism in antiquity has prompted differing takes on the relationship of early Christians such as Paul to his Jewish background. Rather than seeing Paul as someone who walked away from Judaism and denounced its law and practices, scholars, particularly those in the anglophone tradition, have come to view Paul not only as someone deeply indebted to his Jewish past, but also as someone who continued, even after his so-called "conversion," to remain in the Jewish religious tradition. Obviously "conversion" as a conceptual category becomes a problem in this framework, but then the Pauline texts also do not accent this well-entrenched modern model either.

Contemporary Jewish scholars who have taken up the New Testament as a point of study have been influential in terms of pushing scholars to consider more broadly the Jewish context not just of Jesus and Gospels like Matthew, but also, and perhaps most importantly, Paul and his letters. At the same time, over the past several decades the so-called "New Perspective" on Paul has gained significant traction among scholars, with many if not most interpreters acknowledging that Paul was much more deeply rooted in his Judaism even after his "risen Lord" experience than earlier scholars had acknowledged.[24] For proponents of the New Perspective, Paul continues as a practicing Jew after his encounter with the risen Christ. Whatever considerations may have been granted to Gentiles with respect to Jewish law, Paul remained fully committed to the validity of that law as revealed by God in the Hebrew Bible. In other words, in the New Perspective the contours of Judaism are redefined in terms of what it means to be a "covenant people," but the basic structures of Judaism do not change. In this view, Jewish law was never really the issue. Rather, at issue was the manner in which the Jewish community was to be demarcated as a result of the new experience that Jesus-messianists had with the risen Lord. Some scholars have gone even further and challenged, for instance, the legitimacy of the long-held fundamental Pauline principle of "justification by faith." Although this shift is hotly debated and, to be sure, not all New Perspectivists go this far, there are scholars who argue that "justification by faith" has no place in Paul's understanding of faith commitment. Rather, it is "obedience" and "imitation" of Jesus' own faith/faithfulness that is the cardinal "doctrine" for Paul. Removing the juridical nature of "justification" in Paul strikes at the heart of nearly 500 years of Reformed/Protestant readings of Paul, but it does have some basis in the text, wherein ethics surfaces as the primary principle of early Christian identity and belief.[25]

Even with the shifts in interpretive practices such as that which the New Perspective proposes, we still see a certain stability of the Jewish background against which Christianity is measured and understood. Jewish law has to be an issue in scholarship – even as how exactly it is an issue changes, and necessarily so. Yet without the concept of law modern scholars cannot seem to fully account for Paul's message in his letters – or his significance for early Christianity and subsequent epochs, including the present. And to be sure, even with the changes represented by the New Perspective, scholars continue to accent Jewish distinctiveness even as Paul may now be configured as someone who is more enmeshed in that distinctiveness. That is, we still need a Judaism against which we can discuss, define, and understand early Christianity, even if its foremost apostle and perhaps even its founder is deeply embedded in Judaism. Of course, regardless of how that looks in the end, Gentile Christianity still arises as something different – and it is that distinction that remains critical. It becomes more of a question as to what kind of bridge Paul himself becomes. Does he function like "Hellenistic Judaism" did for understanding the rise of Christ-worship in early Christianity? Is he the middle term that links Judaism and Christianity or brings Christianity close to its roots – but still allows it to remain distinct? These are fair and important questions. However, for the moment, it is critical to recognize that even if Jewish law fades into the background in some trajectories of modern, mostly anglophone, scholarship, there is still a prominent accent on how early Christians negotiated Judaism and how the two interrelated, irrespective of whether Jewish law is foregrounded. In other words, there is still *difference*; it is now just difference of a different kind.

Most importantly for the argument we are developing here, no matter from which angle one approaches the matter, Judaism still serves as the background against which early Christianity emerges as something distinctive and identifiable. The fact that Paul (or Jesus) may somehow be an "in-between" figure does little to change the larger function and structure of differentiation, although it does serve to mute in considerable ways some of the egregious characterizations of Judaism in earlier New Testament scholarship by showing that the earliest Christians were not themselves opposed to Judaism or Jewish law. That is, the conflicts have been recast as "intra-Jewish" and part of a broader multiplicity of Jewish identities attested in the ancient world rather than as something essentialistic with respect to the differences between Christianity and Judaism. Still, as we have noted, there are nevertheless differences, and early Christianity can only be understood in its distinctiveness through comparison and contrast with Jewish concepts, practices, and beliefs. In the next section, we turn to see how the Roman Empire, as an entirely different context for analyzing early Christian engagement, yields surprisingly similar results.

Early Christianity and Roman rule

To reinforce the argument we have been developing in this section, we now turn to "empire-critical" New Testament scholarship, which is an approach to the texts, contexts, and histories of interpretation that focuses on early Christian resistance – politically, theologically, and socially – to the Roman Empire. In our estimation, the Roman imperial thread as developed in more recent scholarly analysis of the New Testament serves to make sense of Christian community identity and theological claims in much the same way that Judaism has. Scholarly disagreement with respect to the specifics of how the New Testament engages the Roman Empire, or whether the New Testament engages the Roman Empire at all, does not change the stable entity that provides the backdrop against which early Christian responses can be measured and engaged.

Before exploring further how scholars of early Christianity have taken up the cause of empire-critical scholarship, it is worth inquiring as to the nature of the definition of "Roman Empire" in the first place. That is, whose concept of "Roman Empire" are we working with? While we did not raise this issue with the Jewish law example above – although it equally applies there – it is important to put this question on the table at least once in this chapter's discussion of categories and frameworks. For instance, classicists and ancient historians hold a variety of positions on what, exactly, constitutes the "Roman Empire," which in turn affects how one might read the terms on which the interactions between early Christians, the Jesus movement, their representations in the New Testament, and the Roman Empire take place.

Unlike many classicists who make a relative break between Hellenistic and Roman epochs that is largely indebted to the work of Sir Ronald Syme,[26] those who advocate for a "cultural approach" understand the Roman Empire as slowly evolving out of the world that came before it, and tend to place a higher value on the benevolence of Roman culture as that which fosters a "new humanity" that is responsible for a "golden age" of cosmopolitanism and innovation in all areas of life – political, social, religious, and domestic.[27] Herein the desire for, and performance of, authority and hierarchy is not simply the province of an emperor who rules through dominating his powerless subjects. Hierarchies are formed through local networks and relationships, and such expressions of *auctoritas* are central to the discourse of "being Roman." Within this framework, then, what some might call "systemic violence" can also be interpreted as another means by which authority is affirmed on local levels – that is, through the policing and surveillance activities of the state that are necessary to stabilize and protect the "Pax Romana" outside of the capital city. The expansion of the Roman Empire, which might otherwise be couched in terms of forced submission to Roman power, can be assessed as an unparalleled achievement in the evolution of world civilizations, with all the expected casualties and spoils of war that accompany such triumph. In other words, the newly acquired and built Roman cities in provinces across imperial territory require the military machinery of empire to keep their luster. What some might call "imperialism," others might call "trade"; as far as empire's effects on a vast and diverse population of Romans and "barbarians" are concerned, what some might call "slavery," others might call "labor." Being Roman and living in Roman culture, then, can be seen as that which necessarily involves living in a state where power is unevenly distributed.

Such a view of the Roman Empire stands in stark contrast to how the Roman Empire functions for some New Testament scholars, especially in the past several decades, and most particularly among North American scholars since the events of September 11, 2001.[28] As Judaism in some sense faded into the background as a major contentious issue for understanding emergent Christianity, the Roman Empire, at the very same time, arose as a critical piece of the new conversation that would replace the former. Some scholars have tried to make sense of the complex portrayal of Rome throughout the New Testament by postulating a developing trajectory that moves from the resistance practiced Jesus and Paul themselves to the accommodation portrayed in Luke–Acts. Some have posited that, while the New Testament may not seem like it is explicitly deploying rhetoric against empire, the texts function more like a "hidden transcript" which, if decoded properly, reveal themselves to be profoundly (if cleverly) anti-imperial.[29] Others have noted a more complex picture wherein even in the same author/text there exists a diversity of positions.[30] Whatever the precise formulations look like, most New Testament scholars would agree that early Christians, as a "minority" group, contended with empire in one form or another and that such struggling left an impact on the configuration of their theological formulations, their political positionings, and their practical interactions with and responses to communities with which they were in contact and in which they participated.

In New Testament scholarship, then, empire is ever present. Indeed, he Roman Empire is an objective reality or "macro-narrative" that stands in contrast to early Christianity, which itself is called into being as a subject through the invocation of the objectified structure of empire.[31] As such, early Christianity is a more malleable phenomenon because it is also seemingly more unknowable. In other words, it is much more difficult to find a religion or ethnic group in antiquity than it is to find the Roman Empire itself. As with Judaism, the Roman Empire provides a particularly stable and natural background against which early Christianity can emerge, be analyzed and interpreted, and in some sense then projected as an independent, self-contained entity. In effect, of course, the New Testament is the product of ancient Jews who, in varying degrees, also happened to be Roman subjects, citizens, or in some other relationship with Romanness. With respect to the "big three" in which early Christianity is usually one of the "players," it is noteworthy that amidst Greeks, Romans, and Jews, early Christians are the only group that is image-less and material-less.[32] There is nothing by which early Christian communities or individuals can be identified except through being aligned with the other three (i.e. Greek Christians, Jewish Christians, Roman Christians). And even in these instances, we do not have images that portray anything that is identifiably "Christian" and thus we lack a secure foundation for tracing out the origins or at least earlier threads of a significantly important modern religious tradition that became fundamental to Western thought and development.

Yet it is not just a matter of what empire-critical New Testament studies offers for interpretation and reconstruction of early Christianity that is important for our discussion. It is also critical to note what this interpretive trajectory obfuscates and in some sense erases from the historical conversation. First and foremost, the relationship of early Christianity to Judaism is reconfigured in substantial ways in this arena of scholarly investigation. In initial studies on New Testament resistance to Rome, scholars such as S. G. F. Brandon and others had already made this shift.[33] According to Brandon, in Christianity's earliest phases, followers of Jesus were much more closely aligned with Jewish opposition to Rome, whether or not they participated in meaningful ways in violent resistance itself. There was, in effect, sympathy without identity. In this schema the Romans, and not the Jews,

were blamed for the death of Jesus. The Gospels, however, began to reconfigure that relationship so that Jews emerged as playing an increasingly
important role in Jesus' death. One can see traces of such positions still in
the work of those scholars who want to drive a wedge between a more egal-
itarian Jewish Jesus movement and a later hierarchically structured
emergent Christian movement that deploys Jews and Judaism in more
aggressive and unseemly ways. As noted above, however, in the broader
configuration of recent empire-critical scholarship, it should be noted that
Jews and Judaism largely fade from the scene. Jewish social movements, biblical themes and traditions, and Jewish theological and political tropes play
an important role in providing resources for the early Christian response to
empire. In so far as the broader negotiation takes place, however, Judaism
becomes a fading backdrop to early Christian engagement.[34] In the process,
much of the negative historical and theological sentiment placed on Judaism
in earlier scholarship is now transferred to the Romans. As a result, this shift
away from the centrality of Jewish issues in Pauline interpretation toward
Paul's situation vis-à-vis the Roman Empire offers another way of dealing
with the anti-Jewish (and anti-Semitic) tendencies of earlier treatments of
Judaism.

The scholarly conversation about backgrounds seems to have changed,
or to have been changed by engagements with the Roman Empire. But
the methodological question is whether it really has changed as much as
we might initially think. One could inquire, for instance, whether Jews and
Judaism have actually disappeared and if the well-established legacy of
Christian interpretation has truly eradicated its anti-Jewish history through
positioning the Roman Empire more clearly as a background for early
Christian engagement. In point of fact, Roman imperial power also stands
in as a cipher for what was earlier configured in New Testament scholarship as Jewish oppression of Christians. The shift to Christian negotiations of
the Roman Empire is potentially seductive in this way. That is, that which
vanishes may well reappear in another form – or, one might say, we see here
the return of the repressor, if not the repressed. In so far as Judaism has
frequently been linked to that which stands in opposition to Christianity,
the reification of that principle of oppositionality, now transferred onto the
Romans, continues the legacy of oppressive hermeneutics in Christian
theological history. In other words, Jews and Judaism both disappear and
then reappear in another form as the Romans.

The very principle of oppositionality – "bad" Empire, "good" Christians –
may be what signifies Christianity as that which stands in opposition to
tyranny and oppressive rule. Just as with Judaism earlier, the Romans now
represent the world of the "flesh" and of resistance to the will of God; it is
from this that early Christianity provides a means of achieving liberty and

justice. In that respect, however, the principles of oppositionality once construed with respect to Jewish law still exist as they once did. Romans/Jews and Roman rule/Jewish law are herein elided, and the early Christians remain "victims" who "resist" and "overcome" their oppressors with their "weapons of the weak." We thus may not have escaped the legacy of anti-Jewish scholarship, but rather simply transfigured that former subject into another form. Whatever the specifics might look like upon closer analysis, it does seem to be the case that once again, now in relationship to the Roman Empire instead of Judaism, early Christianity represents the triumph of freedom and the defeat of tyranny. Within the framework of empire-critical scholarship, the Roman Empire, like Jewish law, comprises an irrational system of governance, one enacted by brute force. Early Christianity resists despotism, whether in political (Roman) or religious (Jewish) forms, and is characterized as that which brings freedom to the individual and defeats the forces and powers of enslavement.

In the final analysis, then, the "true" character of early Christianity as conceived by modern scholarship emerges against a background that is configured to help highlight said character. Paul and Jesus may have been Jewish. And perhaps segments of early Christianity were also compromised by and complicit with Roman rule, even if they simply reinscribed Roman imperial power in their own communities and perpetuated oppressive structures in their discourses related to otherness, particularly with respect to Jews, women, and other outsiders. These middle-ground positions do not change the fact that Christianity is defined, either positively or negatively, in relationship to "law" and "rule," both of which can be used interchangeably. And not surprisingly, the picture of early Christianity as it is sketched in scholarship that differentiates it from Judaism is strikingly similar to, if not identical with, the image of early Christianity that emerges when it is differentiated from the Roman Empire. The background and context are substantively different, but the essential structure of early Christian religious identity and stance toward oppressive power remains constant. In the process, the objectivity and stability of the interpretive horizon of, in this case, Jewish law or the Roman Empire, encourage the interpreter to similarly stabilize early Christian resistance, which then paradoxically proceeds to destabilize – religiously, politically, and socially – the very stable horizon that created it. Thus, whatever else we learn from drawing these parallels, it is important to accentuate the role that our preconceptions of the core nature of early Christianity play in how we utilize various backgrounds toward achieving particular ends of interpretation. Ultimately, it might well be the case that the specific background that a scholar chooses for elucidating the meaning of early Christian conceptions, practices, and beliefs matters less than how one configures the context itself to help produce a recognizable version of Christianity for the consumption of modern readers, scholars and initiates alike.

It is perhaps a final irony, then, and not by accident either, that the newest "hot commodity" to hit the "New Testament scholarly marketplace" is the "Paul and the Philosophers" discussion, otherwise known as the "philosophical turn" in New Testament studies. In essence, theologians and philosophers deeply indebted to the Continental philosophical tradition have taken to analyzing Pauline texts within a theo-philosophical framework, evidencing the ways in which the structures of individuality, freedom, personal sovereignty over collective tyranny, universalism, and ontologies of resistance to despotism, among other critical themes of modern liberal thought, are grounded in the discourse of Paul.[35] The scholars involved in these conversations frequently ignore the historical context of Paul's thought and work altogether, moving straight toward a structural analysis of Paul's logic with help from other contemporary philosophers and theologians. New Testament scholarship is frequently sidestepped, if not outright ignored, in these discussions. Occasionally, though, reflections on the Roman Empire and/or Judaism emerge as important calibrators for configuring the internal logics of Paul's discourses. For our purposes here, the "Paul and the Philosophers" discussion is most revealing for how the trajectories of modern New Testament scholarship on early Christianity in relationship to Jewish law and Roman Empire have prepared the way for such apparently "new" conversations and approaches. In essence, then, what appears as a fundamentally innovative means to analyze Pauline discourse is in effect simply another manifestation of the same phenomenon we have seen with respect to Jewish law and the Roman Empire. Herein the character of early Christian innovation rests in its embrace of universality over particularity, that is, in its ability to provide a transcendent universal vision that neither Judaism nor Greco-Roman thought was able to produce.

Even with its updated linguistic garb based in Continental philosophy and its attendant concepts, traditions, approaches, and logics, the "philosophical turn" in reading the New Testament in some ways reveals most clearly what is taking place in the conversations about Jewish law and Roman Empire, and is not unrelated to our discussion of backgrounds in this chapter. Here we find a certain (un)intentional commitment regarding the characterization of early Christianity as that which rises above history, as that which provides the basis of universalism over particularly, of transcendence over contingency, of freedom over enslavement. Of course, such characterizations only make sense in a modern context in which these values are prized and lauded. And therein lies the rub: when we observe these patterns emerging in scholarship, it should stand as a reminder that, no matter how much we think we understand about the ancient world and early Christianity's place in it, we are always in the strange territory of interpreting actual "real" historical contexts and, at the very same time, also producing, presumably unwittingly, structurally consistent readings of early Christianity based on assumptions and values of our own time period, all the while having our own subjectivities "produced" as our values and consciousness are reflected back to us by this very same ancient material. It is a major triangle of interpretive befuddlement in which it becomes difficult to know where to draw the line between the past and the present.

Contexts Matter, Ancient and Modern

The way in which we understand early Christianity as emerging in and through and over against its historical context(s) is clearly shaped by the place where we stand now – the values we hold, the religious and/or theological perspectives we embrace (or eschew), the historical orientations that we espouse. In the end, what we are looking at here is fundamentally a matter of the perspectives, interests, and investments of the New Testament interpreter drawing on a vast array of ancient materials and working to make sense of those. There is no neutral ground when it comes to backgrounds, despite the fact that whenever the New Testament is discussed in scholarship it is usually done under the guise of neutrality. And as different configurations of the modern world rise and fall, as differences in our own particular culture and history shift, so do our interpretations and applications of New Testament contexts. At the same time, as we have noted above, there exist some core observations and principles when it comes to articulating the conceptual emergence of Christianity, and particularly its *character* as a religious movement. These are no less influenced by modern perceptions, but they do transcend the implications and ramifications of particular backgrounds of interpretive choice.

However, as we discussed in Chapter 1 and as we continue to do elsewhere in this book, we do not hold to a historical solipsism wherein nothing about the ancient world or the past in general can be known or quantified. In our view there are very real historical parallels and contingencies that emerge in the study of the early Christian materials. While there may be differences of opinion over which precise background is most helpful for interpreting this or that concept, belief, or practice, the fact remains that historical and socio-cultural backgrounds as a whole do help to illuminate the interpretive and explanatory task. Indeed, given how many different backgrounds can be selected and utilized to interpret even just one concept or theme found in the New Testament, it is clear that the ancient world offers a plethora of contextual possibilities. The fact that we might not ever know which is the "correct" one does not mean we cannot creatively work with the variety of options that are afforded. That said, we also observe how curious it is that, even when a realignment of primary sources and backgrounds is undertaken in scholarship, the characterization of the New Testament, Christian origins, and early Christianity remains largely stable and unchanged.

Moreover, by moving beyond a singular notion of context and background we also come to appreciate how it might be the case that ancient readers, not unlike us, understood the same New Testament concept or theme in differing ways, depending on what particular framework shaped their reading/hearing of the text in question. That is to say, the backgrounds approach may be less helpful in the end for assisting us in finding the *one* context we have been looking for and are sure is "out there" – like the search for the Holy Grail. Rather, the backgrounds approach might better be understood as a historical methodology that aids us in understanding particular epochs of interpretation better, both ancient and modern. We are still understanding texts and traditions historically, but, rather than looking for the original, solitary, and unified structure of interpretation, we find, instead, historical possibilities and complexities. And with every possibility we learn something about how ancient readers/hearers *might have* received a particular New Testament concept or theme or practice, just as we learn, from our own emphases in the process, how contemporary readers *might* receive the same. Ironically, then, while some scholars have called for the end of historical criticism and historical focus on the New Testament, pointing to the highly subjective nature of interpreting the past in light of the social location of the modern interpreter, the historical approach has always contained within it the possibilities of elucidating those same insights. It does not take the "postmodern" call or the latest theoretical fad to get us to rethink how history is done. In our view, what it takes is careful and considered historical work to achieve such reimagination. In fact, without attention *to* historical contexts, there is no escape *from* the perceived limitations and strictures of historical contexts. As we noted in the introduction to this book, it is precisely at this juncture that critics of historical-critical approaches to the New Testament would do well to revisit the potential liberating power of historical work.

In the end, then, despite acknowledging the potential for uncertainty regarding the backgrounds to the New Testament and, in some respect then, also its meaning and purpose, we would still advocate vociferously for historical study and debate. Indeed, as is clear from the opening vignette to this chapter that details Reinhartz's concerns about the translation of "Judean" over "Jew," we learn both about the ancient world and our own in a kind of symbiotic, interdependent relationship when we examine the ancient materials with these questions in view – and, to be sure, both of those moments of learning involve understanding historical contexts, ancient and modern. Both word choices, "Jew" and "Judean," are an option for translation, and, in point of fact, there are probably cases where one is more appropriate than the other but not in a mutually exclusive way. These terms represent two "historical" possibilities among many others. That said, it is clear that the discussion related to ancient background and context arises out of modern concerns and commitments. As we just noted, there is not one "right" option over another, and we have for too long limited our options by virtue of our own limitations.

Early Christianity is a vastly more complicated and malleable entity than our models may allow us to conceptualize at present, in large part because we have focused so squarely on "choosing" one context over another. In our view the problem lies less with the opacity of the ancients than with the modern scholarly compulsion to analyze and to interpret in light of the assumption of a phenomenon's exclusivity, singularity, and linearity, not to mention the focus on a one-to-one correspondence between texts and contexts. And even when multiple backgrounds are chosen as a context for the development of a particular concept or practice, those backgrounds and contexts are always understood as stable and clearly identifiable. The ancient realities, however, were likely much different. The moment that we allow early Christianity to disappear over the horizon of the past, vanishing as something distinctive and unique, might well be the very moment we begin to learn much more about how Christianity, like all ancient religions/ ethnicities/ideologies (Jewish, Greek, Roman, and other), is in fact a richly varied, and not so easily identifiable, phenomenon.

Such recognition, however, would mean that we would likely have to think differently about Christianity in our own world today. The realization that within the "Judean" versus "Jew" translation debate there emerges one constant should give us pause. In either case, regardless of how we translate the term *ioudaios*, early Christianity emerges as that which *resists* and *is resisted by* someone or something – either "Judean" or "Jew." So the character of early Christianity remains the same irrespective of how modern scholars choose to translate the term *ioudaios*. True, the character of the opponent changes – and to be fair, only the surface level of meaning changes, since most people probably hear "Jew" when they read "Judean." It goes to show, of course, that in all of the well-intentioned attempts to redeem Christianity from both its real and alleged anti-Jewish orientations in the past, ancient and more recent, scholars are not really doing any service to the overall structural issues involved in interpretation itself. What should be on the docket is not by which designation one signifies the *opponents* of the early Christians, but rather why the *heroic character* of early Christianity continually surfaces as the central thematic arc of scholarly conversation. And here we note that, while some scholars seek to diminish the anti-Jewish nature of early Christian discourse, and others like Reinhartz insist on its reinsertion into historical discussion so as to ensure that the culpability of early Christians is not erased from historical memory (a worthwhile cause to be sure), no one is querying why it is that we, in the modern world, conceive of early Christianity as that which resists "oppression," real or imagined, in the first place. Thus, we would argue, scholars tend to invest their energies in historical contextual debates that relate to the peripheral issues. Whether Jewish or Christian or secular in orientation, and even if they do not assess the ethical value similarly, these same scholars implicitly affirm the same overall character of early Christianity, which is itself a decidedly modern invention. None of these observations should be taken to mean that we have left the field of *history* or *context* in analyzing these debates and questions. There is, in the end, no escaping context, ancient or modern.

Notes

1. Adele Reinhartz, "The Vanishing Jew of Antiquity," *Marginalia: A Los Angeles Review of Books Channel*, June 24, 2014. http://marginalia.lareviewofbooks.org/vanishing-jews-antiquity-adele-reinhartz/ (accessed July 18, 2014).
2. Reinhartz cites in particular Steve Mason, "Jews, Judaeans, Judaizing, Judaism: Problems of Categorization in Ancient History," *Journal for the Study of Judaism* 38 (2007): 457–512.
3. For a summary of the main issues behind the notion that "religion" as a category is largely a development of modern sensibilities and constructions of knowledge, see Brent Nongbri, *Before Religion: A History of a Modern Concept* (New Haven: Yale University Press, 2013).
4. For further detail and explanation, see Todd Penner, "*Die Judenfrage* and the Construction of Ancient Judaism: Toward a Foregrounding of the Backgrounds Approach to Early Christianity," in *Scripture and Traditions: Essays on Early Judaism and Christianity [in Honour of Carl Holladay]* (ed. P. Gray and G. O'Day; Novum Testamentum Supplement Series 129; Leiden: E. J. Brill, 2008), 429–455.
5. There are many studies one could point to here, including some written around the earlier time period of German scholarship noted above. The standard treatment with respect to Paul, and one which signaled a "sea-change" at least on the North American scene, is E. P. Sanders, *Paul and Palestinian Judaism: A Comparison of Patterns of Religion* (Philadelphia: Fortress Press, 1977).
6. It was more frequent in the past to have separate introductory books, one dealing with the history and socio-cultural context of the New Testament and another being the introduction to the New Testament texts themselves. Frequently we now find these combined into one volume. The former is probably from the German tradition and reflects their theological curriculum, wherein they would do languages, backgrounds, New Testament literature, and exegesis. The North American situation developed differently, with more one-volume introductions

but still set up the same way, even within chapters: culture, background, litera-
ture, and then exegesis/meaning. For an overview of the theological context of
German higher education during the development of biblical scholarship, see
Thomas A. Howard, *Protestant Theology and the Making of the Modern German
University* (New York: Oxford University Press, 2006), and Suzanne Marchand,
German Orientalism in the Age of Empire: Religion, Race, and Scholarship
(Washington, D.C.: German Historical Institute; New York: Cambridge
University Press, 2009).

7. Originally published in German in 1962, the English translation appeared in
1969; see Joachim Jeremias, *Jerusalem in the Time of Jesus: An Investigation into
Economic and Social Conditions during the New Testament Period* (trans. F. H. and
C. H. Cave; London: SCM Press, 1969). The exemplar of this study is Emil Schür-
er, *A History of the Jewish People in the Age of Jesus Christ* (trans. S. Taylor and
P. Christie; New York: Scribners, 1891).

8. One might note here the work of the Koester trajectory, related to situating the
religious, historical, and socio-cultural life of the major Gentile cities associated
with the movement of early Christianity. Koester's introductory New Testament textbook is in fact ordered in this fashion; see Helmut Koester, *Introduction
to the New Testament* (2 vols.; New York: Walter De Gruyter, 1995).

9. See William Arnal, *Jesus and the Village Scribes: Galilean Conflicts and the Setting of
Q* (Minneapolis: Fortress Press, 2001).

10. See Eric M. Meyers and Mark A. Chancey, *Alexander to Constantine: Archaeology
of the Land of the Bible*, vol. 3 (Anchor Yale Bible Reference Library; New Haven:
Yale University Press, 2012).

11. Hermann L. Strack and Paul Billerbeck, *Kommentar zum Neuen Testament aus
Talmud und Midrasch* (Munich: Beck, 1961).

12. The main four volumes were completed between 1922 and 1928, and the project was commissioned by H. L. Strack as an intended replacement to the then-
major study on rabbinic Judaism by Ferdinand Weber, *System der altsynagogalen
palästinischen Theologie: Aus Targum, Midrasch und Talmud* (Leipzig: Dörffling &
Franke, 1880).

13. M. Eugene Boring, Klaus Berger, and Carsten Colpe, eds., *Hellenistic Commentary to the New Testament* (Nashville, Tenn.: Abingdon Press, 1995).

14. One should bear in mind, as well, that there is also a whole tradition of atheist
scholars seeking to discredit the idea that there is any truth to Christianity through
identifying it with parallels to Greco-Roman religious traditions and practices. In
other words, while Protestant German scholars might use Greco-Roman influence
to understand the development of a concept or practice in early Christianity, albeit
one that is not original to the first impulses of the movement, other scholars of
that same time period would use the same methods to suggest that even the originary impulses were themselves fabrications based on Greco-Roman traditions.
Hence, the "game" could be played to a variety of ends, all depending on where
the scholar was to be situated. Arthur Drews (1865–1935) is but one representative
of a "radical" tradition that is often downplayed in modern scholarship but once
enjoyed moderate traction, especially among freethinker circles. See, for example,

Drews, *Die Christusmythe* (Jena: E. Diederichs, 1909), wherein the author drew on the work of Bruno Bauer (1809–1882) to propose that Jesus never existed and was an invention of Greco-Roman culture and mythology that became outdated in its time.

15. Bousset's signal work was originally published as *Kyrios Christos: Geschichte des Christusglaubens von den Anfängen des Christentums bis Irenaeus* (Göttingen: Vandenhoeck & Ruprecht, 1913); see now the translation with a new introduction by Larry Hurtado, Wilhelm Bousset, *Kyrios Christos: A History of the Belief in Christ from the Beginnings of Christianity to Irenaeus* (trans. J. Steely; Waco, Tex.: Baylor University Press, 2013).

16. Martin Hengel, *Judaism and Hellenism: Studies in Their Encounter in Palestine during the Early Hellenistic Period* (trans. J. Bowden; Philadelphia: Fortress Press, 1974).

17. Larry W. Hurtado, *One God, One Lord: Early Christian Devotion and Ancient Jewish Monotheism* (Philadelphia: Fortress Press, 1988).

18. Luke Timothy Johnson, *Among the Gentiles: Greco-Roman Religion and Christianity* (Anchor Yale Bible Reference Library; New Haven: Yale University Press, 2009), 129.

19. Michael Peppard, *The Son of God in the Roman World: Divine Sonship in its Social and Political Context* (New York: Oxford University Press, 2011); M. David Litwa, *Iesus Deus: The Early Christian Depiction of Jesus as a Mediterranean God* (Minneapolis: Fortress Press, 2014). Such approaches are not entirely new, of course. Adolf Deissmann's *Light from the Ancient East* was a seminal text in which attention to the interaction of early Christian theological conceptions with imperial cultic images and emperor worship was highlighted. See *Light from the Ancient East: The New Testament Illustrated by Recently Discovered Texts of the Greco-Roman World* (trans. L. R. M. Strachan; repr. of 1927 ed.; Peabody, Mass.: Hendrickson, 1995). Additionally, the earlier *Religionsgeschichtliche Schule* made connections between early Christianity and other Mediterranean religious themes, and the "myth and ritual" school, an anglophone phenomenon, was highly influential on this front as well.

20. Diane M. Segroves, "Racializing Jewish Difference: Wilhelm Bousset, the History of Religion(s) and the Discourse of Christian Origins" (Ph.D. diss., Vanderbilt University, 2012).

21. Vernon Robbins's use of "conceptual blending" to understand how early Christian discourse works is helpful here. Conceptual blending, as developed by theorists of cognition Gilles Fauconnier and Mark Turner, proposes that elements from various places are "blended" in a mental process that is largely subconscious and common to everyday language. See Vernon K. Robbins, *The Invention of Christian Discourse* (Rhetoric of Religious Antiquity Series 1; Blandford Forum, Dorset: Deo Publishing, 2009).

22. For a consideration of the methodological issues and questions at stake in maintaining distinctions between the categories of "politics" and "religion" in interpreting the New Testament, see Davina C. Lopez and Todd Penner, "Paul and Politics," in *The Oxford Handbook of Pauline Studies* (ed. R. B. Matlock; Oxford Handbooks; New York: Oxford University Press, 2015).

23. For further discussion on these issues from different angles, see Todd Penner, *In Praise of Christian Origins: Stephen and the Hellenists in Lukan Apologetic Historiography* (Emory Studies in Early Christianity; New York: T & T Clark, 2004), and Davina C. Lopez, *Apostle to the Conquered: Reimagining Paul's Mission* (Paul in Critical Contexts; Minneapolis: Fortress Press, 2008).

24. For a survey of this area of scholarship, whose main proponents are E. P. Sanders, James Dunn, Krister Stendahl, and N. T. Wright, see Kent Yinger, *The New Perspective on Paul: An Introduction* (Eugene, Or.: Wipf & Stock, 2011).

25. For a succinct overview of the New Perspective and the issues at stake in this interpretive trajectory in specific relation to Judaism, see Magnus Zetterholm, *Approaches to Paul: A Student's Guide to Recent Scholarship* (Minneapolis: Fortress Press, 2009).

26. Ronald Syme, *The Roman Revolution* (New York: Oxford University Press, 1939).

27. While the "revolutionary" pattern developed by Syme still persists in classical scholarship, a "cultural" approach that emphasizes gradual shifts from republic to principate has been deliberated for some time. Still, as with Christianity, the "break" between republic and empire and the emergence of the Augustan age as something completely different and unique in Roman history forms the basis of methodological negotiation in such studies. See Paul Zanker, *The Power of Images in the Age of Augustus* (Jerome Lectures; Ann Arbor: University of Michigan Press, 1988); Karl Galinsky, *Augustan Culture: An Interpretive Introduction* (Princeton: Princeton University Press, 1996); Ramsay MacMullen, *Romanization in the Time of Augustus* (New Haven: Yale University Press, 2000); and Andrew Wallace-Hadrill, *Rome's Cultural Revolution* (New York: Cambridge University Press, 2008).

28. The Vietnam War, the role of the United States in the Israeli-Palestinian conflict, the "Dirty Wars" of the 1980s, and the First Iraq War in the 1990s were also signal moments in terms of the North American development of empire-critical scholarship.

29. Such scholarship relies heavily on the concept of the "hidden transcript" developed by James C. Scott; see *Domination and the Arts of Resistance: Hidden Transcripts* (New Haven: Yale University Press, 1992). For an application to New Testament studies, see *Hidden Transcripts and the Arts of Resistance: Applying the Work of James C. Scott to Jesus and Paul* (ed. R. A. Horsley; Semeia Studies 48; Atlanta, Ga.: Society of Biblical Literature, 2004).

30. Indeed, Jesus is in some sense held up as the ideal in this respect – however he resisted or engaged with empire, he did so in some kind of nearly superhuman and transcendent manner. Conversely, in terms of the scholarly discussion, Paul evokes the incarnational aspect much more clearly – he is portrayed in ideal ways, but also, at times, in a more compromised manner. In the same vein we find post-colonial readings of compromised masculinity in the Gospels or "colonial mimicry" on the part of the Gospel writers. Despite differing accents, however, there is one fairly consistent position on which most scholars agree: the Roman Empire was oppressive and a force for the devaluation of human life in the ancient world, irrespective of whether early Christians were also implicated in that same system of power relations.

31. For an introductory discussion of the Roman Empire as a "macro" narrative in relation to the New Testament, and especially Paul's letters, see Bruce W. Longenecker and Todd D. Still, *Thinking Through Paul: A Survey of His Life, Letters, and Theology* (Grand Rapids, Mich.: Zondervan, 2014), 321–348.

32. At least, the early Christians are thought to have remained "image-less" until the third century. Scholars traditionally have positioned their adoption of images as a symptom of emergent alignment with imperial designs and the march toward state acceptability and the "triumph" of Christianity in the age of Constantine. For discussion, see *Picturing the Bible: The Earliest Christian Art* (ed. J. Spier; Kimbell Art Museum; New Haven: Yale University Press, 2007); and see especially Graydon F. Snyder, *Ante-Pacem: Archaeological Evidence of Church Life Before Constantine* (Macon, Ga.: Mercer University Press, 1985), which discusses how images develop in the post-Constantinian period, which is the time frame in which Christianity becomes "recognizable" to us.

33. S. G. F. Brandon, *Jesus and the Zealots: A Study of the Political Factor in Primitive Christianity* (New York: Scribners, 1967). See also Richard A. Horsley, *Jesus and the Spiral of Violence: Popular Jewish Resistance in Roman Palestine* (Facets; Minneapolis: Fortress Press, 1993).

34. See, however, Anathea Portier-Young, *Apocalypse against Empire: Theologies of Resistance in Early Judaism* (Grand Rapids, Mich.: Eerdmans, 2011).

35. For a survey of these approaches, see *Paul and the Philosophers* (ed. W. Blanton and H. de Vries; New York: Fordham University Press, 2013) and *Paul in the Grip of the Philosophers: The Apostle and Contemporary Continental Philosophy* (ed. P. Frick; Paul in Critical Contexts; Minneapolis: Fortress Press, 2013).

3

Objects, Objectives, and Objectivities
Material and Visual Culture and
New Testament Studies

Of Fragments and Forgeries

The fragile ancient papyrus fragment rather tantalizingly called the *Gospel of Jesus' Wife* is only 1.6 inches (4 cm) in height by 3.2 inches (8 cm) wide.[1] The text is in the Coptic language, and the fragment contains incomplete sentences on one side and barely legible writing on the other. The fragment is privately owned, and the owner has remained, as of this writing, anonymous. Although a recent purchase history is known, it is not exactly clear where and when the fragment was found, or by whom, or how it entered the market for sale in the first place.[2] The owner brought the fragment to Karen King, a scholar of the New Testament and early Christianity, ostensibly to help assess its value. King conducted initial tests on the papyrus to determine provenance and introduced the fragment to the world at an international conference in 2012. One of the lines – the one that gave this fragment its "name" – has been translated as "Jesus said to them, 'My wife...'" It is this line that has generated controversy about the fragment, prompting much discussion about its authenticity that is at times complemented by debate over whether such a text effectively challenges the narrative that Jesus was not, and could not ever have been, married or otherwise sexually engaged with a woman. Some have maintained that the fragment, like so many other "new finds" related to the ancient Christians that make their way to the marketplace, is a forgery, while King and the team of scientists who have

---

De-Introducing the New Testament: Texts, Worlds, Methods, Stories, First Edition.
Todd Penner and Davina C. Lopez.
© 2015 Todd Penner and Davina C. Lopez. Published 2015 by John Wiley & Sons, Ltd.

performed testing have proposed a date no later than the 8th century CE for the papyrus.[3] The implications of whether the *Gospel of Jesus' Wife* is "real" or not are fairly significant for contemporary narratives of how the history, ideas, and culture of early Christianity work. If the text is ancient, then it might contribute to a fuller, if more complex, picture of our understanding of early Christian conversations about gender and sexuality, not to mention raise questions about how this idea, and not others, was "lost" to us. And if it is not ancient, then all of these questions are part of some fanciful thinking, and by inference the traditional narrative is safe from alteration.

The *Gospel of Jesus' Wife*, along with the James ossuary that we discussed in Chapter 1 – text and stone – are but two of the myriad of extant ancient objects that are part of contemporary discourses describing ongoing efforts to delineate, explain, and understand the origins of Christianity through attending to the *realia* of its social world. While there is much investment by numerous parties in whether these items are forgeries or "for real," their representation and discussion, more than other areas of New Testament scholarship, both capture public attention and stimulate the imagination about the world of the early Christians, that is, the world that produced the texts that we now call the "New Testament," the world that produced the religious tradition we now call "Christianity." The contemporary academic study of the New Testament is concerned on some level with the distance between modern readers and ancient texts. If we accept that texts are responses to the world in which they are situated, then knowing as much as possible about a text's context and occasion – the world to which it responds – can only assist in efforts to make sense of that text today.

And yet these materials are probably far more interesting now, or at least interesting for different reasons, than they might have been to the ancients. While the content of the fragmentary *Gospel of Jesus' Wife* might be able to help make better sense of the various literary trajectories of early Christianity, including what kinds of social status questions such groups were entertaining in their time, its status as an ancient object enjoying contemporary fascination is of greater concern to us in this chapter. Making sense of ancient texts involves a certain measure of historical awareness and the deployment of modern categories. In our view, whether this papyrus fragment is a forgery or authentic is much less important for understanding the contours of modern scholarship than the suggestion that the papyrus, as an *object*, serves as a site where scholars might negotiate long-standing debates concerning narratives about Christian origins and early Christianity. Regardless of its purported contents, however, the *Gospel of Jesus' Wife* enjoys status as an artifact of ancient material culture. Much of what we can know about the world of the early Christians is to be found in attention to material culture, which takes modern readers beyond the boundaries of canon and text into what can be difficult terrain to navigate. How we relate to material culture, on what terms, and what difference it should make to do so is the location of ongoing debate and struggle in the discipline of New Testament studies, and it is to this topic and its attendant questions that we shall turn our attention in this chapter.

When introduced to the world of the New Testament as a means of investigating the connection between the texts and their contexts, material culture is often deployed as that which is completely ordinary and to be taken for granted as part of the landscape, on the one hand, and as completely sensational on the other. That we have a papyrus fragment or a bone-box, on its own, is in some sense completely unremarkable: thousands of ancient papyri have survived in the dry climate of Egypt, for example, and numerous ossuaries have been uncovered throughout Israel. It is when the material appears to provide a direct link to the New Testament texts that it garners both attention and suspicion regarding its authenticity and importance. Regardless of whether material culture is "authentic," however, the very idea that there *could* be such items is generally of great interest to a wide variety of people, from those who long for concrete proof of the historicity of the New Testament to those who are looking to undermine its claims. It is often an object such as a "newly discovered gospel" or that which is thought to have textual correlates in the New Testament (e.g., a synagogue or a sunken boat) that is highlighted as important for its ancient context, and thus for meaning-making in the present. As no one is neutral about the Bible, so no one is neutral about news concerning the Bible. Material culture – the "stuff" of the ancients – is camera-ready, and readily available for the spotlight.

The presence of objects in our studies of New Testament texts is by no means neutral, natural, or methodologically stable, even as such presences might seem to be "rock solid" on the surface. Objects, while at times touted as that which revolutionizes the study of the New Testament, often serve to reflect and to reify modern stories about ancient Christianity and ancient texts. In our view, this situation is methodologically accomplished through several interrelated uses of material culture: as illustrations for texts, as confirmation of textual historicity, and as illumination for theological concepts already thought to be in the texts. One need not delve too far into contemporary introductory New Testament textbooks, for example, to find lavish photographs of ancient sites such as Corinth or Ephesus, papyrus fragments, or various "daily life" objects that are labeled in captions as illustrating the "world" of the New Testament but not often discussed in the main body of the introductory text itself. In some sense, then, introducing the New Testament's milieu through material culture enables the texts to remain the focus of meaning-making attention, even as the rhetoric of the field might suggest otherwise. Material culture thus constitutes the most visually arresting, historically compelling, and yet least transparent area of New Testament studies.

As part of de-introducing the study of the New Testament, in this chapter we will discuss the use of material culture as a site where contemporary issues and questions of history and method are negotiated. Entering into a process of defamiliarizing the texts and objects themselves, as well as our narratives about the relationships among people, texts, and objects, in the past and in the present, involves locating and understanding several major operating assumptions about the intersections between ancient texts and material culture as performed in the field. Chief among these is the maintenance of the "text" – that is, the written word – as a primary means of engagement with the world of the early Christians, even when pictures are brought to the foreground. As such, we will herein examine the archaeological dimensions of New Testament studies, which we highlight as significant in two ways: disciplinarily and methodologically.

We are concerned with the contours of archaeology as a critical modern discipline that locates, analyzes, and interprets material culture in relation to the New Testament, as well as the historical and social contexts in which archaeology takes place. However, we also aim to understand narratives about material and visual culture in New Testament studies "archaeologically," in a Foucauldian sense of the term. That is, we aim to identify various strands of where we have been in the past so as to understand how we participate in writing a history of the present through the apparatus of our discipline. Finally, we will explore a possible realignment of the relationship between people and objects, and what that could mean for the study of the New Testament and material culture, which is ultimately about our relationship with ourselves in the present. To this end we will briefly trace and appraise an ancient visual trope, that of human subjugation, throughout the Roman imperial world of the early Christians. In so doing, we hope to problematize contemporary naturalized narratives about the relationship between ancient material culture and New Testament scholarship, as well as raise several further questions regarding who we are as students of the New Testament, what we do, and for whom we do it. Objects, like texts, are not fixed or transparent. They do not work on their own; we put them to work for us. Revealing something of the work we do with objects, and the work we make objects do for us, is thus our main focus below.

Archaeology and the Making of Objects

Any exploration, or excavation, of narratives concerning the relationship between ancient material culture and the study of the New Testament should begin with at least a cursory familiarity with, and deep appreciation for, the professional field and practice of archaeology, and the field of New

Testament archaeology in particular. That we have the material considered to be the "body of evidence" for the New Testament, Christian origins, and early Christianity – including manuscripts and papyri, remains of buildings, furniture, wall decor, everyday items, bones, and a myriad of other tangible evidence of the distant past – is due in large part to the discipline of archaeology. Archaeology of the New Testament includes the location, recovery, analysis, and interpretation of the material remains of ancient Mediterranean cultures. Although positioned as a field apart from New Testament scholarship in many ways, archaeology of the New Testament also understands that the material remains shed light on the world of the early Christians, a stance that is critical since understanding that world is thought to help us comprehend the texts of the New Testament.

While newer and somewhat different in orientation than the longer traditions of classical and biblical archaeology, New Testament archaeology nevertheless shares an epistemological heritage with those two modes of inquiry. Methodologically and rhetorically, New Testament archaeology functions both as a discipline on its own and in conversation with, and as an extension of, the study of the New Testament and Christian origins more broadly conceived. At the rhetorical core of archaeological approaches to the New Testament lie questions about historicity and veracity, social description, and the limits of what literary materials can tell us about the ancient world in an empirical manner. That said, as we shall explore throughout this chapter, non-literary objects are not as transparent or as self-evident as we might desire them to be, and although admirable in their empirical focus, archaeological discourses are no less historically located, epistemologically invested, or ideologically laden than other areas of New Testament scholarship.

In our view, archaeology is critically important for studying the New Testament today – no matter the "approach" or "method" one adopts or attempts to inhabit in the process of conducting scholarship. If in so doing our goal is to understand the figures of Jesus or Paul in their ancient context, for example, there is no way to do that in a comprehensive manner with the New Testament texts alone: Jesus left no writings of his own, and Paul's writings are letters to communities that give very little information on the apostle's life or world. The book of Acts narrates an "itinerary" of Paul, but is of limited assistance in historical reconstructive efforts. Despite considerable scholarly and popular efforts to the contrary, it is nearly impossible to understand the majority of the New Testament texts *as ancient texts* without some understanding of the culture they reflect. Regardless of the "background" we choose against which to read these texts – Greek, Jewish, Roman, or other – if our goal is to properly situate the texts in their historical milieu so as to aid exegetical analysis, archaeology is of essential importance. The texts themselves are partial in scope – the ancients were highly selective about what they wrote, to whom, and to what ends. A basic tenet of modern historical criticism emphasizes cultural and temporal distance between readers and texts. That is, historical criticism recognizes that the texts were not written directly for modern consumption but for ancient audiences, and this is an important step in interpretation. Thus, according to the logic of historical critical discourse, it behooves us to figure out something of what ancient audiences might have heard, read, and/or understood. Further, our New Testament texts represent not a complete record or reflection of the ancient world in which the first Christians may have found themselves, but a series of highly rhetorical choices made by ancient authors whose motivations and intentions are long lost to us. The archaeology of the New Testament supplies the data for the *realia* of the world in which the texts can be situated, providing an opportunity for a more robust set of options in the assessment of their rhetoric. In fact, there is hardly an area of New Testament scholarship that has not in some way been informed by archaeology.

Archaeology thus helps to produce the objects of interest for the study of the New Testament. In order to have ancient objects help us make sense of texts, they first must be located and made "fit" for consumption. Beyond extracting objects and places from the ground, archaeological efforts involve analyzing found materials, preferably those located *in situ* but also those from public and private collections and the considerable black market for antiquities. Such examination is done alongside that of specialists such as geologists, handwriting analysts, chemists, and other scientifically trained individuals who can help to determine, with some level of accuracy and precision, the provenance of the objects, the strata (historical layers in the ground) of which they are a part, and their potential relevance for Christian origins. Field and analytical archaeologists will often contribute site reports for scholarly review and appraisal. Some archaeologists participate in interpretive efforts through linking found objects and places with ancient texts in order to present possible scenarios about the New Testament world and the people in it. Each of these areas is distinct and overlapping. Especially valuable are archaeological finds, analyses, and interpretations that "provide a window onto the ancient Mediterranean world that will transform the reader's understanding of the New Testament"[4] by, for example, confirming via external evidence the existence of persons and places mentioned in the Gospels, Acts, or Pauline letters. A key term is "transform": that is, objects are thought to be things that can actually change someone's mind – even renew it! – about how the New Testament is to be understood.

New Testament archaeology has inherited scientific traditions and analysis associated with the rise of the philological disciplines in the post-Enlightenment era, coupled with the impulse to confirm the historicity of the biblical record of events, places, and people. And like all disciplines that deal with collecting and identifying the material remains of distant "other" cultures, New Testament archaeology has endured a long history of entanglement with the practices of antiquarian connoisseurship by cultural elites, for whom displaying such objects functioned as a means to exhibit wealth and accumulate social capital. It is thus in this broadest intellectual-historical context that the archaeology of the New Testament must be understood. Although archaeology as a mode of collection and analysis is a modern discipline, the display of "collections" of materials from other cultures dates to antiquity itself. For example, the Romans of the imperial period appear to have collected objects from the lands of the peoples they conquered in war, paraded these along with the foreign prisoners in triumphal processions, and displayed weapons, furniture, statues, and other objects in their homes and in public places such as Vespasian's Temple of Peace, which according to Josephus housed objects from the whole world including the riches from the Jerusalem Temple following its destruction in 70 CE.[5] The Temple of Peace, now lost, was hardly the only public place where objects from other lands were kept and displayed. One can still walk the streets of Rome today, for example, and gaze upon at least five ancient obelisks (themselves often inscribed with hieroglyphs detailing Egyptian conquests) that were "donated" by the Egyptians and transported via specially made ships from Egypt to Italy – a practice that was adopted in the 19th century as obelisks were transported to, and erected in, cities such as London and New York.

While for the Romans collecting the objects of others appears to have functioned as a means of affirming their status as cosmopolitan masters of the civilized (and uncivilized) world, one might ask if much had changed on this front by the time of the Renaissance. During that era, diggers for places like "ancient Rome" and "ancient Greece" mined the remnants of the past for works of art, inspiration for contemporary architectural projects, and other means of aesthetic appreciation. Of course, this was happening at the same time that materials from "ancient" buildings were being repurposed in places like Rome (and Jerusalem) and environs – places that had been continuously inhabited since antiquity. That is, stones from ancient structures might be used in buildings of later eras. Using ancient material culture as a means to understand something about the world that produced such items – that is, the consequences of a movement from "appreciation" to "archaeology" – developed in the 19th century along with the scientific philological disciplines in Germany and, to a lesser extent, England.[6] Herein a primary goal was to recognize ancient cultures as civilizations in their own right, and also to recognize that each ancient culture represents a particular stage, a "stratum," in a linear developmental model of human civilization writ large. The latter trajectory dovetailed with emergent Darwinian proposals concerning evolution that the humanistic sciences were in the process of embracing at that time. No longer, then, were the ancients a source for "art" – they were a source for historical science about human origins, development, and change over time. Thus the search for antiquities continued, but the way material culture was treated changed significantly, which in turn changed the way scholars (and the public) related to the ancient world and its texts. In conversation with the philological disciplines and as part of what the Germans called *Altertumswissenschaft* (the "sciences of antiquity"), archaeologists were able to historicize their objects and understand their "find-spots" as part of an overall system – both in terms of a site itself and also in terms of the site's relationship to a broader historical epoch and cultural worldview.

Perhaps the example par excellence of the effects of a shift from appreciation to archaeology is that of Pompeii, or the physical location of the ancient city of Pompeii along with the surrounding sites on the Bay of Naples (such as Herculaneum) that are often consolidated into a category termed "Pompeii." Pompeii is one of the oldest modern continuously excavated archaeological sites, and the layers of its modern investigation are almost as interesting as its ancient strata. To be sure, as a place and an idea, Pompeii had been just about forgotten long after it was buried under volcanic ash from Vesuvius in 79 CE. Similar to some other "ancient" places, it was "rediscovered" by accident in the 16th century when the digging for a civic works project to divert the Samo river hit some fresco-covered walls. Further work on the site revealed a larger complex with numerous images and objects, including, most (in)famously, those of a sexually explicit nature that were offensive to some Counter-Reformation eyes – and thus were collected and hidden from ordinary public view on a consistent basis until the National Museum of Naples opened its "secret cabinet" in 2000.[7] On account of the mid-19th-century transition from mining art wherever it might have landed to removing rubble, to injecting plaster into spaces in volcanic ash to reveal the shapes of Pompeii's ancient inhabitants in their "final forms," to drawing up maps of the ancient site, and to carefully exposing whole structures, alongside more precise examination of the locations where items such as frescoes and statues were found and looted, Pompeii re-emerged as an actual city and not just a rich art trove.[8] It is critical that Pompeii was long buried and not continuously inhabited, as the resultant "ancient" city appears more intact and thus authentic to modern viewing eyes. The excavations at Pompeii over time have revealed about two-thirds of a vibrant 1st-century Roman town, along with attendant objects of all kinds. Archaeological analysis of this material, coupled with ancient historical and art-historical interpretation, has provided scholars with enough data to construct something of a window onto the ancient Roman world. Pompeii has also served as a model for subsequent development of archaeological methods, and, indeed, as a model for how classical archaeology ought to be imagined as a discipline unto itself, as "more and more exact technique was a precondition for archaeology's emergence as a new, at least semi-independent field" among the sciences of antiquity.[9]

The development of classical archaeology as a discipline preoccupied with identifying and classifying the "civilized past" provided a systematically organized means by which to appreciate human ingenuity, aesthetics, and culture from distant times and places. While archaeology did much to generate intellectual interest in objects and material culture as that which can and should be studied in the same rigorous manner as literary materials, it is also the case that, at least for the study of the ancient world, the literary materials still held pride of place as purveyors of information about antiquity. The stones could talk and reveal things, but not as well as the books, and potential large-scale excavation sites were both identified through texts and "designed to bring to life the ancient world of the texts."[10] What if the texts, though, were not as "true" as was thought? What if Herodotus did not see all he said he did, or Pausanias did not describe Greece as it really was? What if the Trojan War, that etiological narrative for the ancient Greek world and thus for modern civilization more generally, never happened, or at least never occurred in the same way that the literary sources describe? What if Romulus did not found Rome as described by the ancient authors? The possibility that the texts did not uncomplicatedly represent reality as it really happened presented a conundrum for scientists of antiquity.

Throughout the 19th century, the development of the sciences of antiquity revealed the ancient world to scholars and the public, but also revealed some challenging paradigm shifts in how knowledge was generated and organized. These were manifest as historical skepticism and, by extension, a perceived undermining of claims to the authenticity of historical events and places as reported in ancient texts. Sometimes the *realia* of the sites and objects just did not match the words of the texts either. For example, much has been made of the German businessman Heinrich Schliemann's search, in the 1860s and 1870s, for the ancient Troy of the Homeric epics. Schliemann was not a trained archaeologist, but a businessman and dilettante, and along with archaeologist Frank Calvert (whose reputation Schliemann may have tarnished in order to steal the glory) he set out to locate prehistoric Greece in Turkey. Schliemann's "finds" at Troy – including a cache of objects that came to be known as "Priam's Treasure" – were sensationalized and very likely staged.[11] He is thought to have damaged the Trojan site at modern Hisarlik more than he preserved it for future analysis. Nevertheless, "Schliemann's archaeological interests were driven primarily by philological imperatives: his excavation of Troy was conducted to challenge the then-prevailing consensus among German scholars that the Homeric epics were works of fiction with no historical foundation."[12] For Schliemann, if some scholars thought the texts not to be true on account of the modern science of historiography, he would prove otherwise – through using the modern science of archaeology. If Troy was found, and thus was "real," then the texts must be telling the truth too. It should be noted, however, that regardless of whether Schliemann (and Calvert) in fact actually found the ancient city of Troy, excavations have continued unabated since the late 19th century as if they did.[13]

Ultimately, we cannot know whether Schliemann's Troy verifies the Homeric legends. We also cannot help but observe that Schliemann's interest in proving the "truth" of the Homeric epics through finding the physical remains of Troy, and in publicizing the results of that search as widely as was possible in his time, enjoys some parallels to the popular understandings about the archaeology of the Bible – both in the 19th century and since then. Schliemann's impulse regarding Troy in the face of skepticism about the truth of the Homeric epics, and impulses in biblical archaeology during the development of historical-critical biblical scholarship in Germany, do appear to be resonant with one another. But unlike studying Homer, studying the Bible as part of the sciences of antiquity had ecclesiastical authorities to negotiate, whose power regarding the role of sacred history in doctrinal positions and theological identities was profound. Confronted with mounting sentiments among "radical" biblical scholars that the Bible may not narrate history "as it happened," it is understandable that some scholars might have wanted to show otherwise – and thus in some way play out the supposed conflict between "science"/history and "faith"/religion.

Early "fathers" of archaeologically inclined biblical scholarship such as Edward Robinson or William Albright were more concerned with producing geographical surveys of the biblical cities of ancient Palestine and challenging the radical source theories regarding the Hebrew Bible through archaeological means than with explicitly verifying the historicity of biblical texts. Nevertheless, the biblical texts, and their value as historical records, served as a prerequisite for conducting such work in the "Bible lands." We would even propose that, in the case of biblical archaeology, locating objects that might confirm the historicity of the texts appears to have long been one of the operating assumptions of the discipline, regardless of church or theological involvement. In more recent history, aside from the "James ossuary," another famous example of an object that has served in this way is the ancient "Pilate inscription," which mentions Pilate and the prefecture he held in Judea. This inscription, found in 1962 at Caesarea Maritima, is thought to be just one of many artifacts that affirms claims that the New

Testament is historically accurate and, therefore, "true." While archaeology may proceed somewhat independently of biblical interpretation, it certainly assists in exegetical decision-making, especially when objects are thought to provide the "external confirmation" – that is, evidence beyond the pages of the New Testament or related literature like the writings of Josephus or Tacitus, both of whom mention Pilate[14] – that the places and people in the New Testament may actually have existed in antiquity.

While the field may have made significant advances over the last 150 years, and archaeology is no doubt integral to biblical scholarship, it is not conducted in an epistemological vacuum and is indebted to the complex legacy we have attempted to briefly sketch here. To be sure, biblical archaeology as a whole has a longer disciplinary history, and a longer ancient record with which to work, than New Testament archaeology. The archaeology of the Old Testament/Hebrew Bible was earlier concerned with mapping the Holy Land and determining the locations for the origins of the biblical narratives, as well as finding places like the location of the Genesis flood or Exodus route. The political boundaries of Solomon and David also received, and continue to receive, some archaeological attention. For the study of the New Testament and Christian origins, the discovery of the Dead Sea Scrolls in the 1940s, as well as the subsequent collection, classification, and translation of those texts, along with ongoing excavations at Qumran and environs that have produced objects from coins to lice-encrusted combs that are of importance to understanding the world of Second Temple Judaism and early Christianity, are likely the most spectacular archaeological events of the last century.[15] More than any other objects, these scrolls, which are thought to be contemporaneous with the life of Jesus and the writers of the Gospels, and include manuscripts of Hebrew Bible texts that are nearly a millennium older than the oldest manuscripts we had before, have propelled New Testament archaeology into the foreground of disciplinary consciousness. Since that time, archaeology has played a much more expansive role in New Testament studies.

The Dead Sea Scrolls comprise a critical area, textually and materially, where we can clearly trace the impact of archaeology on the study of the New Testament. Obviously, textual research such as translation work has been enhanced by this considerable corpus of Hebrew and Aramaic *comparanda*. While the texts are important, there has also been an increasing awareness that the data we use for historical reconstruction efforts must extend beyond texts, many of which, unlike most biblical manuscripts, date to roughly the same time period as that of Jesus and Paul. For example, analysis of the archaeological data about the Qumran community, which may or may not be linked to the Essenes mentioned in Pliny the Elder and Josephus,[16] bolsters a sense that contemporary readers of the New Testament can somehow access and imagine the 1st-century social, linguistic, and visual world and the events and people narrated as inhabiting it.[17] Similarly, the archaeology of the Galilean region asks us to imagine the everyday life of Jesus and his companions. It is not that every object might be that which Jesus actually touched or used, but rather that the artifacts, taken as a whole and examined as part of a larger framework in which questions about history, culture, and socio-economic relations in the 1st century can be posed, can help us imagine where, how, when, and perhaps even why Jesus "happened."[18] This is how we are asked to "excavate Jesus": not by hailing every new archaeological find as *his*, per se, but by reconstructing, as completely as we can, the world in which he and his companions, kinspeople, and antagonists lived. As a colossal find, the Dead Sea Scrolls and the Qumran site have contributed in no small way to this kind of interpretive work.

Again, it is difficult to overestimate the contemporary indispensability of archaeology as a way to "see" and understand the ancient contexts of the New Testament – and to make meaning in the present with those texts. Some scholars do not think that "excavating Jesus," as a way of reconstructing the world in which the early Christians lived, can be done with archaeology alone, or with exegesis alone, but rather that the fullest possible picture emerges when both stones and texts are used together. As John Dominic Crossan and Jonathan Reed note,

> Archaeology is not background for exegesis and neither is exegesis decoration for archaeology. Gospel and ground must each be read and interpreted in its own way and under its own discipline. An ancient mound has its dignity and integrity with or without Homer in hand. An ancient tell has its challenge and mystery with or without Bible in backpack. Words talk. Stones talk too. Neither talks from the past without interpretive dialogue with the present. But each talks and each demands to be heard in its own way. Only after archaeology and exegesis gets each its own full voice should they come together in doubled chorus and common report.[19]

Crossan and Reed's approach to the question of how archaeology might intersect with the study of the New Testament – "correlative stratigraphy" – asks how the related disciplines might inform one another in the reconstruction of the historical Jesus and his world, even as archaeology and exegesis might have distinct procedures. In attending to the archaeological strata, or layers of history built upon one another embedded in the ground, we might more fully appreciate exactly how many layers we have to dig through in order to access the 1st century on its own terrain and on its own terms. And, in turn, we might more fully understand how ancient texts like the canonical New Testament Gospels are stratigraphically oriented, peeling back the layers of text – traditions, translations, redactions, and so on – in order to reveal a more complete portrait of 1st-century historical figures like Jesus. One way to see the contribution of archaeology to the study of the New Testament, then, is that stones have much to teach us about texts – not just in terms of contents and historicity but also in terms of historical development. But this position assumes that there is something "in" the stones that is meaningful and must be extracted – which is structurally similar to a primary assumption of exegesis, that is, that meaning is located in ancient words and must be "drawn out" of them. Further, Crossan and Reed's conceptualization appears to grant material culture and literature equal weight in the study of the New Testament. However, it is worth asking if the basic presuppositions of studying the New Testament – that is, the existence of the events and people described in it at the oldest stratum, regardless of how many layers are piled on – could ever effectively be challenged by material culture. If not, then it could very well be the case that archaeology does, in fact, "illustrate" the texts or serve as the softer voice in the conversation between objects and literature.

Thus far we have been describing the broad contours of archaeology as a disciplinary configuration and as an important conversation partner in the study of the New Testament. Throughout the modern history of interaction with ancient places and objects, the archaeology of the New Testament has developed alongside of, and has interacted with, other areas of interest in the "sciences of antiquity." We observe that the interdependence of archaeology and textual study, at least as far as the New Testament and related literature are concerned, is fairly strong. It is also the case, though, that the New Testament texts are still a primary guide for how archaeology proceeds, and indeed provide the story of Christian origins that archaeological work implicitly appraises. We also note that shifts in approaches to backgrounds in New Testament scholarship do have an effect on archaeological work. For example, previous emphases on the "Hellenistic" qualities of Jesus and the early Christians resulted in archaeological work that suggested a Hellenized Palestine in the 1st century; a shift to a "Jewish" background for the New Testament, coupled with the finds at Qumran, has precipitated a wealth of archaeological data suggesting that Palestine might be more "Jewish" than was previously thought to be the case.

Words and stones might talk independently of one another, albeit through modern means. But that stones talk at all – and that stones speak the language of the New Testament in particular – is hardly a coincidence or an accident. Archaeology appears to provide and interpret the "raw data" of history, which can foster and naturalize what one might designate a "pictures or it did not happen" approach to the ancient world. It might very well be the case that, as Jonathan Reed notes, archaeology can only provide resources toward historicity and not meaning[20] – but the common expectations and disciplinary scaffolding around archaeology do not make it difficult to get to "meaning" from "historicity," or even to elide the two. If we have the stuff, then we can say something concrete about the world, which means we can say something definitive about the texts. Although this could be seen as an oversimplification of how both archaeology and New Testament studies might actually work, it also stands as a summary of a fairly standard narrative for how objects ought to be used in interpretive endeavors.

As part of de-introducing the study of the New Testament through drawing attention to how, and on what terms, the field interacts with objects, we highlight persistent tensions between the seeming ease with which we can use material culture to reconstruct narratives about an ancient world and what possibilities might open (and close) for readings of ancient texts and modern traditions as we do so. The practices of archaeology can both reveal and hide such tensions at the same time. As we have been exploring above, archaeology, as a distinct discipline, is involved in the process of uncovering and analyzing ancient artifacts and places, working through myriad layers of dirt, habitation, and history to find the stratigraphic areas appropriate to New Testament studies. Archaeology tends to seem more empirically oriented than textual studies, since it deals with things, which are thought to be solid and self-evident, rather than words, which are open to interpretation. However, things never "just are" but are made, and archaeology is far from neutral, objective, or free from operating assumptions or ideological inclinations. Archaeology tells stories too. For example, claiming that material culture has interpretive parity with biblical texts, and reconstructing a "context" in which the events of the New Testament might have taken place, does not actually have the effect of decentering literary texts from the core of New Testament studies, which in turn does not quite dislodge dominant narratives about how Christianity "happened" and "developed" over time. The texts still provide the overarching framework, questions, and in many cases impetus for archaeological work.

While archaeology contributes much to textual interpretation, the continued assumption that the New Testament texts are primarily theological or religious in orientation is hardly questioned or challenged through the use of material culture. While some archaeologists are honest in saying that we may never find definitive "proof" for the existence of Jesus or Paul, and archaeological data about Christianity in the 1st century is extremely scant, we hardly require that proof to continue to tell stories about Christian origins. Reconstructions of daily life in the time of Jesus or Paul, for example, are narrated in ways that prioritize religious practices and beliefs that largely cohere with modern conceptions of religious and theological thought and action. Even if we have no tangible evidence to suggest that the ancients viewed religion in the same way we do, religion still is a determinative category through which ancient material culture is viewed. The status of the New Testament as a set of documents that are ultimately about religion and theology, then, is affirmed; questions about that status are not generally asked, even when we are seemingly preoccupied with "daily life" issues through looking at archaeological finds. But determining whether a building or an object or a manuscript is "religious" or has theological weight (and therefore is of potential relevance to the New Testament) is a matter of *our* interests and investments rather than those of the ancients. That is, one of our main objectives in exploring the contours of archaeology is to suggest that objects do not speak for themselves, on their own terms, or naturally in relation to texts. People use stones to tell stories.

Archaeology may uncover objects and provide much to think with for the sake of analysis, exegesis, and story-telling. Yet it does not neutrally provide the raw material and data of history-writing for history-writing's sake, as it were. Excavation does not simply "discover" ancient objects and places – it produces them as products for consumption. And in so doing, it assists in the production of a series of relationships between people, objects, and places, across time and cultures. It also reifies the interpretive options available to render material culture intelligible, both as ancient artifact and contemporary evidence, the stuff of the ancient world and in this one. In that sense, method-ologically speaking the use of material culture in the study of the New Testament is more about our relationship with the past, and the story we want to tell about the present, than it is about the past as such. As it is with New Testament backgrounds, so it is with objects. When we excavate the ancients and their worlds, we are essentially excavating and negotiating our-selves and our worlds. To what extent we can tell a story about how stories in our field, such as those highlighting the relationship between material culture and the New Testament, get told is of methodological concern to us. Below, as part of our effort to call attention to that which we take for granted in the field concerning material culture, we turn to dynamics such as these at play at the intersection of ancient objects and the study of the New Testament.

Excavating Discourses that Produce Ancient Objects

For the last 250 years, ancient Pompeii has been the subject of archaeological interest. It was among the first large-scale excavations in modern archaeology, and it helped to hone the discipline's methods and techniques. It is in a remarkable state of preservation from being buried under volcanic ash, and thus lacks the multiple layers of subsequent habitation characteristic of other sites, which has enabled archaeologists to paint a relatively unadulterated portrait of an ancient town at a particular historical moment. Pompeii has been almost continuously excavated since its discovery and those results have shed much light on the Roman world. To be sure, this city has also captured the public imagination in no less thoroughgoing ways, and it has long been a tourist destination, inspiration for popular cultural phenomena, and money-making site for the Italian locals. In fact, the "archaeological park" of Pompeii is one of the most visited sites in all of Italy – more than two million people per year walk the streets of this ancient town in the modern world. While Pompeii might seem to be a solid old place that persists into the present, it is also a fundamentally unstable one. This is literally the case, as the buildings are crumbling due to poor upkeep, continued seismic shifts under their foundations, and heavy rainfall as the climate changes. Perhaps it is a peculiar irony that the exposure of the ancient world to modern elements and human neglect should result in a special challenge to keep that world safe from rapid decay.

We observe that Pompeii is similarly unstable as an interpretive site where the ancient world has "come alive" for our edification and consumption. The structure might seem "permanent," but the longevity of Pompeii as an archaeological and "cultural heritage" site where the ancient world has been rediscovered also shows that antiquity is revealed according to the desires, assumptions, cultural orientations, and imaginations of those doing the revealing, viewing, and examining. Scholars of the ancient world such as Ingrid Rowland have traced some of the numerous afterlives of Pompeii, showing the various reconstructions and configurations that have been made with the same stones and objects over time.[21] How people experience Pompeii, as a representative example of the ancient Roman world, is largely mediated by shifts in the cultural environment. Thus, there is not one Pompeii, but many Pompeiis that have been "excavated" according to the excavators' historical and social location and embeddedness in relations of power. There exists, all at once, the Pompeii of looters, the Pompeii of architectural inspiration, the Pompeii of sexual immorality, the Pompeii of Italian imperialism, the Pompeii of psychoanalysis, the Pompeii of archaeological science – and the list goes on.

We would agree, then, with classical archaeologist Alain Schnapp's sentiment that "each culture, each antiquary, creates its own antiquity"[22] – and each culture deploys objects and archaeological rhetoric to do so. This observation applies as well to the world of the New Testament and early Christianity as it does to Pompeii, Athens, Troy, or Rome. We create the tangible ancient world that suits us out of the assemblages of objects and places that are deemed relevant for that task. We can then write narratives of origins, historical development, and continuity to link the present with our distant ancient worlds. Archaeology might help us imagine an ancient world that is characterized by stability, unity, and universality, and yet that world is more reflective of our own circumstances and questions – or perhaps just our own desire for stability, unity, and universality – than those of the early Christians.

In addition to the disciplinary formation called "archaeology," another way to use archaeology is as a methodological tool for writing history that might help us appraise some of the issues at stake in using objects for interpretive purposes. In the Foucauldian sense, "archaeology," as a lens, signifies a multivalent way of thinking about and with the past that focuses on identifying discourses rather than truth. In this way, archaeology can assist us in examining the processes by which we write our relationships with, and understandings of, the present. To this end we might "excavate" not the past as it happened, but discourses about how, and on what terms, it happened. This kind of excavation examines past traces and residues in order to write a history of the present, or a means by which to ask how it is that we got to this place – in this case, the place wherein the New Testament is a collection of texts to be studied, a reflection of the historical reality of Christian origins, and a measuring stick for history and identity formation. What we excavate serves those ends, and is entangled with, and bounded by, discourses of knowledge as well of those of political and economic circumstances.

Even as there might be different modes of doing archaeology as a discipline, we emphasize that every act with material culture is interpretive, has political boundaries, has a history, and has a time at which it experiences a consolidation of disparate parts into a unity. In other words, archaeology can be seen as a way that, through objects, multiple pasts are channeled into a singular story about a singular past. Material culture is an especially valuable (and vulnerable) area where out of multiplicity such a singular past can very easily come into view and seem "natural." In our estimation, an expansive approach to archaeology as a methodological tool can help us make sense of how our narratives about Christian origins in the present affect our understanding of ourselves and the history of our own social positioning – which is always shaped by relations of power that are at once obvious and hidden. To help underscore this point, below we consider some of the conditions that make ancient objects, and contemporary narratives thereof, possible as products of antiquity. Modern science, the emergence of the modern nation-state, and the flow of capital have served as important influences on how we produce material culture and narratives about the ancient past. These are also spaces where the discipline of archaeology, as that which is concerned with finding and analyzing objects, is worked out as a discrete body of knowledge and epistemological framework, and where ancient objects are isolated and manufactured as discursive forms.

135

First, as a discipline, archaeology must be recognized as a modern phenomenon, and specifically as that which is linked to the rise of modern science. We have already touched on how archaeology is connected to the "sciences of antiquity" as they proliferated in the late 19th century. With the rise of modernism, the periodization of humanity and civilization became a central focus, along with the recognition that the past is necessarily different than the present. Humans, in effect, became the chief subjects of, and actors in, history. Objects, then, gained a new relevance by becoming a way to definitively differentiate chronological stages in human development, and archaeology assisted in such epoch-making endeavors. Archaeology is also wedded to the history of science and scientific discourses. In some way the identification of objects as "ancient" is not possible without science, which is itself a way to categorize and describe knowledge. Deploying the rhetoric of science gives the air of legitimacy and objectivity to archaeology, and in the process archaeologists emerge as disinterested researchers whose only pursuit is empirical knowledge. To be sure, there is much to be lauded about the scientific dimensions of contemporary archaeology, such as the capacity to use testing and technology to more accurately date materials. What we are concerned with is the rhetorical dimensions and effects of the link between archaeology and empiricism as manifested in scientific discourses. As archaeologist Julian Thomas observes,

> The growth of empiricism reflected a more general conviction that material things represented a legitimate course of understanding. For some while, antiquarians had been prone to point out that, unlike texts, artefacts could not lie. They thus formed a secure form of evidence. Now it began to be more widely recognized that objects were entities from which new knowledge could be drawn. This made interesting samples and specimens the effective equivalents of books, rather than simply illustrative examples of particular phenomena: they could be studied.[23]

Modern science has helped to render random ancient objects into a coherent and stable body of material culture. These objects are imbued with the assumption that they contain information that could assist in the production of knowledge about the stages of humanity they represent. In other words, modern science helps to reify narratives about objects wherein they function both as simple reflections of the past and as containers of data to be identified, sorted, and appraised. They are thus made available to examine by specialists, using specialized equipment and methods, for science grants that the generation of new knowledge is possible through such examination, and that the material world must be considered in some detail in order to learn new things.

With empiricism as a framework, science provides archaeology with a grammar of its own. Such language can be inaccessible to those outside of it – that is, there is a sense that scientific rhetoric takes the practices of archaeology out of the hands of the ordinary person and puts them into those of highly specialized experts. The rhetoric of science tends to help to hide the prejudice and historicity of discipline: if data is "scientific," it is not a matter of soft opinion, context, and meaning but hard facts, data, and truth. As part of its account of its efficacy, science insists that objects do not lie; if they do, it is much more difficult to catch them in the act than it is with texts. Modern science also contributes to a narrative of progress about the disciplinary configuration of archaeology that might go something like this: early in the development of the discipline we now know as archaeology, there were biblical archaeologists who were basically no different than dilettante antiquarians, roaming the so-called Bible lands in search of the ancients and the Bible. Now, the story might continue, we have learned and honed our techniques and methods, and the terms on which we discover and study the physical evidence for ancient civilizations are different and more advanced. This developmental narrative gives us a linear model through which we might extend the reach of archaeology into the future. What we *might* find and study is as important as what we have found and examined. This kind of scientific rhetoric pervades archaeological studies of the New Testament world: the objects are thought to contain information that, once unleashed through careful analysis, will help us to explain, for example, crucifixion in the ancient world, whether a town was Jewish or Gentile in population, where the apostle Paul walked, or where early Christians spent their time. Even if we know that we will likely never be able to answer questions of this type with any sort of certainty or accuracy, the rhetoric of science in archaeological discourses makes it seem otherwise. Through stabilizing objects as revealers of knowledge, providing a language and heuristic framework to describe the periodization of human civilizations, and incorporating empiricism into the fabric of the discipline, modern science contributes much to the articulation of a set of relationships between our present and the past via archaeology.

Second, despite its appearance of empiricism and disinterestedness, archaeology is linked to political processes and realities. Once ancient objects are isolated and classified as that which can contribute to knowledge production, they become wrapped up in the intricacies of the state, which is a political entity with its own story to tell. Although archaeology might possess and deploy the veneer of objectivity through its use of scientific rhetoric to stabilize and reify objects as uncomplicated reflections of distant realities, the development of archaeology as a discipline is intimately intertwined with emergence of the modern nation-state and the uses of material culture to demonstrate knowledge about, and appreciation for, the ancient past. This relationship is manifest on two main fronts of interest to our project. Most obvious is the persistent debate over who owns, and has the right to display and view, ancient objects and places: the state, the market, or someone else entirely. Ownership makes a difference in terms of discourses concerning the authenticity and accessibility of objects. For example, the anonymity of the owner of the *Gospel of Jesus' Wife* contributes to suspicion about its provenance and legitimacy. Perhaps less obvious, but no less relevant, are the ways in which ancient objects and places are used in constructions of etiological narratives about various nation-states, including their racial-ethnic origins. The State of Israel's deployment of ancient biblical sites as a means to lay claim to the land in the present is but one example of this entanglement of archaeology and nation-building in the present. Archaeologists have colluded with these political processes, even as they insist that their work is neutral, value-free, and conducted solely in the interest of curiosity and the search for knowledge.

Museums are institutions that have contributed to structural connections between archaeology and the nation-state. Modern museums might seem like nice places to visit as a tourist, as they conjure up images of entertaining, harmless houses for collections of visual representations, monuments to human ingenuity, and/or repositories for the "stuff" of knowledge. Linked to a legacy of displaying the private collections of wealthy elite travelers, connoisseurs, and institutions, the museum has in some way long been associated with the upper classes and the state. These elite collections often included materials from antiquity. Post-Enlightenment, museums became ways to display objects based on classification and comparison across cultures, genres, and time – and in displaying those objects, museums also began to serve as institutional centers where new knowledge could be generated. The discourses of modern science were implicated in this shift, including those discourses embedded in the emergent discipline of archaeology. As objects were transformed from "art" to "artifact," and treated accordingly as that which could assist in the production of knowledge, they became part of the state: "recontextualized in the museum, objects could be studied comparatively, and could serve as a means of instructing future bureaucrats and administrators."[24] In an age of colonial expansion, collections of foreign objects were important tools with which to articulate imperial selves and colonial others, stabilizing both identities in the process. Museums were often the first places where viewers could see other cultures, including antiquities, in person, and as such provided a site where visitors could obtain narratives about cultural development.

The display of foreign and ancient objects in museums became a tool by which a state could assert its national identity, culture, and history. This took the form of the "national museum" in the late 19th century, which was a place to cultivate European empires' interest in antiquities, and in particular taking antiquities from places such as Egypt, Turkey, and Greece to display at "home." The monumental Great Altar of Pergamon, for example, was moved to Berlin during this time as part of the "museum race" among empires to house and showcase antiquities as a means to showcase imperial splendor. The resulting display is arguably much less a reconstruction of the monument "as it was" but rather a product of the modern imagination about what an imposing, powerful ancient altar should look like *in Germany.* That is, how this monument would make Germany look was a factor in the decision-making about the Great Altar's "reconstruction" and exhibition.[25] A well-stocked museum could, and should, communicate national prowess and patriotism through its architecture and the layout of its objects.

Antiquities were not just harnessed for the narrative they could provide about the ancients – they were appropriated for national origin stories as well. The German interest in Greek antiquities was linked to discourses about German nationhood and its original ties to ancient Greece.[26] The British Museum serves no less a nationalistic purpose, and that it houses the Elgin Marbles from the Athenian Parthenon shows how Britons can be grafted on to a Greek past, even as the modern nation of Greece, where the ancient site from which the reliefs were taken is situated, also has a major and competing national stake in these objects. Thus, a state museum housing antiquities came to serve as a monument to the nation and a repository for its past. Therein the distance between ancients and moderns must be created and managed so that we might yearn to feel proximately connected with the objects on some level. In stabilizing the material culture of the ancients and claiming them as predecessors, we are able to stabilize our own narratives about ourselves, our histories, and our national identities.

Since the emergence of archaeology in the modern period, the nation-state has played a significant role in large-scale excavations, which serve as the events and sites that produce the raw material for national narratives. Herein, again, the creation of antiquity as something pure, distinct, bounded, and distantly related to us is part of the creation of modern discourse wherein we are linked to the past. The first modern large-scale excavations of Rome were conducted during the French occupation of 1809–1814, wherein the Forum Romanum, Forum of Trajan, and Coliseum were restored.[27] Napoleon I was an admirer of ancient Rome and looked to its antiquities, and particularly triumphal art such as arches and columns, as a template for the modern city of Paris and his own "emperorship."[28] An arresting example of this phenomenon lies in the modern excavation of ancient Rome commissioned by Benito Mussolini's 20-year regime.[29] That visitors to Rome now have access to what looks to be a relatively "pristine"

Roman Forum, Circus Maximus, Theatre of Marcellus, and Mausoleum of Augustus is due largely to Mussolini's excavation efforts – which often involved clearing inhabited neighborhoods and slums out of the way so that the ancient world could be exposed. For Mussolini, the Roman Empire was not simply an ancient civilization that long preceded the contemporary inhabitants of Italy. *Romanitas*, or "the idea of Rome," was that which provided the ideological anchorage for fascist discourses.[30] Ancient Rome, as excavated and imagined by Mussolini's archaeologists, architects, museum workers, and media, was constructed and deployed as a model for the modern fascist state and its inhabitants. Using the science of archaeology and the art of display, the "fascist man" emerged as a mirror-image of the Roman soldier, and the fascist state as the continuation of the pure-bred, unifying force of imperial Rome. Antiquity was "discovered" to contain exactly the right language, in words, symbols, and buildings, for the expression of modern fascist desires. Again, the material culture of our "ancient Rome" is intertwined with the history of modern politics.

The discourses of modern science and the modern nation-state have come together in the archaeology of Israel and Palestine, which for some of our readers will seem more relevant to this discussion as it is where the "biblical world" resides. Herein the distant past is systematically harnessed in the service of writing a contemporary national narrative, and this is an area where biblical archaeology and biblical scholarship have been participants. Although archaeological work in the region extends back in time much further than the Enlightenment, excavations in Israel and its environs have proliferated since the formation of the Israeli state in 1948. Far from an innocent search for the ancient Israelite and Jewish past, archaeology in Israel has become part of a set of nationalist traditions that have located objects and naturalized discourses concerning what exactly the history of the region is, which racial and ethnic groups were on the land, and who, then, could have legitimate claims to the land now. Using the rhetoric of empiricism, "homeland" and "race" are located in the strata of history as "proof" for Israel's national identity and actions in the present.[31] For its part, in the course of locating places and objects through which biblical texts can be authenticated, biblical archaeology privileges narratives about Israel's claim to the land as well, which has served colonial and nationalist purposes. In some sense, as with Mussolini's clearing of the slums to restore ancient Rome, the archaeology of ancient Israel has tended to downplay the significance of the "others" – in this case, Muslims – who also have a history with the land, and who may have inhabited that land longer than the ancient Israelites ever did.[32] Be that as it may, and regardless of the personal political convictions of archaeologists or biblical scholars, the State of Israel has benefited from the findings of the extensive excavations on the land,

and the state helps to decide which objects, places, and figures in its narrative about the ancient world are relevant for the present. Central to narratives such as these is the idea that ancient objects found within certain modern national boundaries must naturally belong to that nation, and must naturally be a part of its history, identity, and culture.

Third, and related to the discourses of modern science and the nation-state, the conditions under which archaeology can produce objects that can be part of narratives about the social world of the early Christians are determined in part by the modern flow of capital and the globalized, neoliberal market. It is the case that archaeological work is not an inexpensive form of research to conduct; without grants and other sources of funding, the cost of maintaining an archaeological site, not to mention paying the people who work in an excavation, can be prohibitive. Pompeii's crumbling edifice, for example, is as much due to a lack of secure funding for upkeep as it is a lack of human diligence. Archaeology, like all research, costs money. However, we mean to notice the flow of capital in a broader sense. That is, the marketplace of ideas about ancient objects is usually emphasized over the market as such; the market is invoked when an object's authenticity is questioned, and other than that, it remains largely invisible to ordinary viewers. But the monetary "value" of antiquities, including the capacity to make a profit from trading and trafficking in objects, is an integral and controversial component of how we have access to ancient material culture. Even as it is most helpful for archaeological and historical research if an object is examined *in situ* – in its find-spot or as close to it as possible – the reality is that most ancient objects of interest are not made available through those means, even after the UNESCO Convention of 1970 that aimed to curb illegal trafficking in antiquities, which it termed "cultural property."[33] The traffic in antiquities has posed a complex set of issues and questions for those who endeavor to examine ancient material culture. It also complicates the discourses that position artifacts as that which can provide some measure of stability, historicity, and meaning to an ancient social context.

Objects that are, or are thought to be, from the ancient world are also, for better or for worse, commodities that have a substantial, usually monied, consumer base. The so-called "black market" or "grey market" for antiquities persists. Thus, it is often the case that objects displayed in museums, held in private collections, and used in historical work are unprovenanced. That is, their archaeological and historical context is unknown because they have been removed from their find-spots and do not necessarily have traceable histories of changing hands. In these cases, literary materials may assist in filling out a material context for an object, but that strategy is often not enough to properly identify its origins, uses, legacies, and significance. This reality presents a persistent set of problems for researchers and others who

141

wish to extract meaning from ancient objects in order to deploy them in modern narratives about antiquity. As art historian Elizabeth Marlowe has pointed out, the reality that many of the "canonical" works of ancient art are unprovenanced is often downplayed in scholarly histories of visual representation.[34] In the case of discussions of Roman art (but applicable to research conducted with objects from other ancient cultures), this structure has resulted in the smoothing over of difficulties with identification and a persistent methodological focus on style and aesthetics rather than history and usage. The persistence of unprovenanced material culture highlights the reality that no matter how much we might want to know, and how much we might want a story that gives us certainty about the ancients, there are many things we do not, and cannot, know about the ancient world.

Furthermore, even passing attention to the extensive marketplace of antiquities reveals a long-standing, often deadlocked international debate among nations, museums, and archaeologists. At its core, this debate centers on whether antiquities are the property of the nation-state in which they have been found or are located, and, if so, what should then be done about the scores of objects located in museums and private collections around the world, not to mention those on the black market. Rhetorically, the market is configured as a prime locus of improper activity – that is, if objects were not looted or otherwise taken from the ground without proper excavation and documentation, then the market for antiquities would be dealt a severe blow, as museums would not have the option to purchase and display unprovenanced goods. Similarly, some archaeologists argue that looting contributes to the destruction of archaeological sites and the disappearance of the ancient record of material culture – only properly excavated items can have meaning and purpose, and everything else is just "stuff."[35] This dispute is manifest most publicly in calls for museums to return "improperly" acquired ancient objects to the nations from which they have been "stolen." Occasionally, high-profile cases of "plundering" for antiquities receive media attention, such as Greece's call for the return of the Elgin Marbles from England or Egypt's requests that the famous bust of Nefertiti be sent back from Germany to her "homeland." Herein museums are configured as villains and accomplices to looters and the market, the nations as victims, and archaeologists as conservators of culture. When a museum returns an object to the nation that has laid claim to it, as the Metropolitan Museum of Art did with the famous Euphronios Krater to Italy in 2008 (after more than three decades of debate with the government), it was hailed as a profoundly ethical move for the Met and a victory for the Italian state – and the object received a "hero's welcome."[36]

We observe that arguments about artifacts as cultural property constitute a complex arena where the discourses of science, the nation-state, and the market come together. Herein archaeology is presented as the guarantor of authenticity and legitimacy through its careful and empirical procedures. The nation-state claims to be the rightful owner of and heir to the cultural property located within its boundaries, as such objects are essential to the nation's identity and history and should remain in, or be returned to, their "home." And the market is positioned both as that which participates in the commodification of objects, thus conferring value on them, as well as that which encourages looting, forgery, and destruction of archaeological sites, therefore compromising our ability to learn about the ancient world. Of course, there is also an irony here in that, given the widespread destruction of ancient archaeological sites and antiquities during periods of war or as a result of repressive regimes, the black market and even looting itself might actually protect and preserve what otherwise would be destroyed and otherwise lost to us. In the end, then, there is no easy answer or resolution to these problems: should all objects be returned to nations who lay claim to them? What would happen to museums, which often are the conservators of antiquities and display them in the interest of knowledge and entertainment? Should archaeologists be the only people who are able to find, examine, and legitimate ancient objects? What does imposing limits and boundaries do to our objectives to generate knowledge as freely, and without determination of results from states or other entities, as possible?

The debate about the antiquities market extends much deeper than whether private citizens or museums can or should purchase such objects, and to be sure these questions are relevant to the study of the New Testament in so far as the field is linked to understanding the ancient world, and understanding ourselves, through objects. These are not simply arguments about identity politics, science, the disappearance of sites, things, and opportunities to generate more knowledge about the ancient world or the black market. The basic question, as art historian James Cuno has put it, is "who owns antiquity?"[37] Who owns these ancient objects and cultures? Can antiquity be "owned"? Are artifacts the property of a particular people, or people as such? Do archaeologists have the right to declare objects meaningless unless excavated according to their disciplinary standards? Are museums doing a public service, or disservice, by acquiring and displaying objects in the way they do? Are modern nations entitled to ancient objects found within their political boundaries? As Cuno has argued, it may very well be that the ancient world is not "ownable." It could be that antiquities are not the property of one certain group, be it ethnic, governmental, or scholarly, but of humanity as such. That is, it is worth noticing that our historical and cultural context – including the proliferation of modernism and the modern nation-state, global capitalism, and identity politics – has shaped the way we access and interpret objects from the ancient past. All of this is to say that the objects that we might take for granted as part of the world of the New Testament, the objects that we think tell us about the Jewish, Greek, and Roman worlds in which the early Christians lived, are anything but transparent or stable. Objects certainly have histories and stories to tell. But in the end, these stories might be of a modern construction rather than an ancient one, and whoever controls the discourse about objects controls the narratives that are written, and still to be written, about them.

For its part, archaeology is not distinguished by the objects it produces as such, but by its participation in the discursive creation of ancient objects themselves – as distinct from other things, and as distinct in that they can be examined as a source for knowledge production. In this section we have been concerned with various dimensions of archaeological discourse, as well as the archaeological dimensions of the study of the New Testament. Indeed, it is the case that the basic problem to which looting and unprovenanced objects point is the difficulty of aligning our narratives about ancient objects and culture: without "context," what we can say is limited. However, knowing where an object is found actually may not help us to determine its original use or context with much accuracy or certainty. In other words, where we might find something is not necessarily meaningful in its own right. This situation is especially the case with ancient objects that experienced multiple reuses and relocations in antiquity, such as weapons and household items. Stones were regularly reused and repurposed in building projects, and papyrus was recycled as well. Knowing a find-spot is only of limited assistance in many cases, then – and we would say that arguments insisting that an archaeological context is the only way to know something about an object rests on an assumption that ancient cultures are somehow stable and monolithic, that where objects were left in the ground somehow elucidates the totality of their significance.

Through excavating, thinking about, and thinking with some elements of the rhetoric of modern science, the nation-state, and the antiquities marketplace, we have attempted to reveal something of the complex set of issues that working with material culture presents. In so doing, we hope to have challenged the sentiment that objects are somehow "easy" to work with or that they provide indisputable proof and evidence for the claims we wish to make about the New Testament, Christian origins, early Christianity, or the ancient world more largely conceived. Objects are not as solid or simple as they seem to be, nor do they give us the window onto the ancient world that we might desire. That there is, or could be, unmediated access to objects and images is, in our view, part of the modern mythmaking about antiquity in which New Testament scholarship participates. With objects, what you see is never what you get. Material culture, and how and whether we access it, is created and managed for us as part of a history of the present, by numerous stakeholders and discourses. Objects may tell us more about ourselves and our own meaning-making processes than about the ancients and theirs. To this end, in the next section we will continue to explore what objects can do for us, and what we can do with objects, by turning our attention to some implications and methodological effects of working with material culture in the study of the New Testament.

What Do We Do with Ancient Objects?

Broadly speaking, our concern in this consideration of material culture is with how New Testament scholarship suggests certain structural relationships between people and things in the past. As we have been proposing throughout this book, though, our articulations of relationships in and with the past are really about our relationships in and with the present. There is certainly much to be done with ancient objects in the present. New items are found regularly; found objects await examination and categorization and, in the case of texts, translation; and of course various ancient items surface from private collections and modern workshops. And yet, although the archaeology of the New Testament has ignited the imaginations of many and the hopes of some, within the discipline of New Testament studies it still is the case that literary texts enjoy superiority. That people now engage the New Testament primarily through textual means, and not principally through objects, is itself a modern phenomenon that modern archaeological investigation and the discourses of archaeology do not quite challenge effectively, at least on a methodological level. Thus, in order to be a student of the New Testament, of the broader ancient world, and perhaps of religion generally, one must by necessity be a student of words and literary production. This is by no means a natural or inevitable position, as we will consider below: first, through clarifying some of the methodological issues and questions in the area of working with objects, and second, through examining a single ancient Roman visual trope in relation to the New Testament.

For all of the concentration on archaeological finds, their sensational status, and their utility for the study of the New Testament, the intersection of texts and objects is one of the most undertheorized aspects of the discipline as a whole. How to read and work with material culture is simply not a part of the discipline of New Testament studies in the same way that, say, learning languages or historical methods or details about backgrounds might be. This situation is partly a training problem and partly a larger methodological and theoretical problem. Some scholars, such as Robin Jensen, have suggested that working with ancient objects in relation to ancient texts, and especially working with objects and texts that are thought to be theologically or religiously oriented, requires learning the language of more than one disciplinary configuration (e.g. art history, archaeology, classics, theology, religious studies).[38] We would say that the issues are more basic than learning disciplinary rhetorics: while scholars appear to have a desire for ancient objects, we do not know what to do with them once we get ahold of them. While it may be the case that texts are easier to come by than objects, in our view the main problem is one of methodology – what matters most is what we want from ancient objects and what we want to make them do for us. As we have mentioned, scholars seem to use objects to supplement or otherwise illustrate the work that is done with texts. And in order to do so we participate in the stabilization of objects, fixing them in time and space and range of meanings, in order to bring greater stability and deeper understanding to literature.

Several main methodological assumptions within New Testament scholarship have contributed to a systemic lack of attention to the sorts of questions that working at the intersection of ancient texts and objects can raise for history, exegesis, and meaning-making in the present. Aside from the point that objects are not transparent or stable entities, a pervasive hierarchy between texts and objects remains. That is, structurally we have assumed that images are fundamentally different than texts in terms of language, function, and meaning-making possibilities. Texts are gateways to understanding and thus are elevated, whilst images are decorative and therefore controlled. But as art historian Michael Squire has argued, this configuration of a text–image hierarchy is more reflective of what he calls "Lutheran debts" that have extended from the Reformation era to the present than of the ancient situation itself.[39] That is, Martin Luther's prioritization of the word (and the Word) over the image as a critical component of his theological framework and "protest" against the Catholic hierarchy of the time has had much more of an impact in intellectual history than one would suppose; now it seems quite natural to us to relegate texts and objects to the proverbial opposite corners of the room. Squire, following theorists of object–text relationships such as W. J. T. Mitchell, proposes that reading texts as a completely separate procedure from encountering images is anachronistic when applied to the ancient Mediterranean world. An example would be the scholarly treatment of the ancient concept of *ekphrasis* – or the rhetorical dimensions of image-making – as a purely textual phenomenon. By concentrating on how texts generate images, and downplaying how images themselves are rhetorical, we may in fact deny the reality that text and object are far more interrelated in the ancient world than we might have imagined – that is, rhetorically speaking, images might generate texts in similar ways to how texts generate images. Maintaining a text–image hierarchy, then, obscures the possibility of an ancient interdependence and interplay between texts and objects.

A further, related, methodological issue facing the use of objects in the study of the New Testament is the assumption that there must be a one-to-one correspondence between texts and images in order for the latter to "work" properly as a correlate for literary materials. Because we tend to see images as illustrative and as that which must relate in some obvious, but subordinate, way to texts, we might assume that the Jews or the early Christians were not visually inclined or "had no art." Or the theological premise that God cannot be represented by an image is applied more widely to the assumption that there is no evidence for 1st-century Christians since they had no distinctive visual tradition or material culture of their own. This supposition affects how we identify objects as well as what kind of semantic range we ascribe to them. Scholars have tended to assume that ancient images, should they be tied to early Christian texts, needed to be of a religious or theological nature – since it is assumed that the New Testament is a set of texts expressing theology and reflective of religion. Thus we look for what we might consider to be religious themes and tropes in the search for viable images to examine alongside the New Testament – such as objects and images that feature ritual activity, biblical characters and stories, and/or theological symbolism.

Two considerations complicate the assumption that images and texts must align in a one-to-one, predominantly theological and/or religious, relationship in order for images to be useful in textual analysis. Steven Fine's work on Jewish art and archaeology suggests that Jews during the time of the New Testament were not as aniconic as has been assumed in the scholarly literature – that Jews in the Roman Empire, for example, may have negotiated the visual programming of the time by appropriating or manipulating familiar images. Such a proposition calls into question the extent to which we can determine what is "Jewish" and what is "Roman" about certain ancient objects and visual tropes, which in turn should help us rethink the assumption that ancient Jews and Christians prioritized words over objects.[40] Similarly, Jocelyn Penny Small's work on image–text relations in antiquity challenges scholarly assumptions that producers of visual representation were aiming to create literal illustrations of literary texts, that they were doing so "correctly" or "incorrectly," and that they were making images on account of the experience of having read texts.[41] This last point is especially important: while artists may be familiar with circulating stories and legends, there is no guarantee that they would have had access to those stories through reading texts – for one thing, as has been well documented, the ancient literacy rate was not high. For all of the modern privileging of texts as the primary communicative mode, it is anachronistic to map the same onto the ancients. While scholars of the ancient world have acknowledged the pervasiveness of the oral transmission of stories and ideas for some time, the idea that visual representation – for example, mythological or historical narrative relief sculpture in the Hellenistic and Roman periods – could also be a product of such transmission has rarely been recognized.

It is thus clear that there are some live and unsettled methodological issues regarding the use of material culture in the study of the New Testament, Christian origins, and early Christianity. We note that some scholars in the field perceive difficulties with approaches that continue to privilege the text alone. Indeed, moving beyond the text as a closed system of meaning unto itself has long been a preoccupation of critical biblical scholarship. Along with archaeological investigation, the proliferation of studies concerning ancient orality, literacy, memory, cognition, performance, and so on shows that there is a problem with relying on texts to the exclusion of all else for reconstructive and exegetical work. Further, the scholarly turn to theory and rhetoric in relation to the New Testament texts has precipitated a shift toward an understanding that texts do not reflect reality but participate in its construction through deploying the art of persuasion. For example, scholars might suggest through rhetorical criticism that Paul's letters do not simply reflect things as they were, but rather that in those epistles Paul is using specific vocabularies, tropes, and themes to convince his audience to think and act in specific ways. Likewise, rhetorically the Gospels are not literally biographies, but are stories about the life of Jesus, written long after his death, that are attempting to persuade specific audiences of particular details, contours, and implications of those stories. Even as scholars might make such overtures with texts, however, there still is less attention to how texts and images might be better realigned, whether they serve similar purposes rhetorically, and whether attention to objects might alter the questions we ask of texts.

Ultimately, images, like texts, are not neutral or merely to be relegated to the realm of appreciation. Objects have positions, stake claims, and are embedded in relations of power. Keeping this sentiment and the above-mentioned methodological issues in view, below we will explore the intersection of text and image using Roman imperial visual representation, which is part of the trajectory in New Testament scholarship that is concerned with the Roman Empire as the social, political, and theological context of the early Christians. To do this we will briefly think with a single trope, that of human subjugation, that is popularly represented in various media throughout the Roman Empire. What we are interested in raising here are some of the challenges of realigning texts and objects in the pursuit of new methodological questions. To this end, we aim to highlight that the instability of both images and texts can open up space for expansive questions about both the ancient world and the modern thrust and utility of examining our relationships with texts and objects.[42]

With a growing interest in ancient material culture, on the one hand, and the influence of a growing and rather complicated socio-rhetorical analysis of biblical texts focusing on the rhetoric and impact of images on the other, some scholars of early Christianity have turned to the use of Roman imperial visual representation as a means to more fully tease out the imperial ideological and power relationships that had previously been gleaned almost solely from textual sources. The visual representation established throughout the empire by the Romans is indeed stunning – and, in certain respects, celebrative of the violence and threats thereof that were necessary to maintain territories abroad. It is not a surprise that visual representation has become such a formative presence in contemporary scholarship on empire and early Christianity in the last few decades – although we note that late 19th- and early 20th-century scholars such as Adolf Deissmann, William Ramsay, and J. M. C. Toynbee already noted illuminating and intriguing parallels between Roman imperial iconography, inscriptions, and other objects and the New Testament.[43]

As we have been attempting to illustrate throughout this chapter, working with visual representation alongside textual materials offers an immediate and daunting presence and methodological challenge to the study of the New Testament. Images are not simply evidence of a reality or history in an unproblematic way – they are, as texts are, highly rhetorical. That is, images make arguments and attempt to persuade audiences of a particular version of events and reality. As Aristotle noted with respect to the narrative technique of *ekphrasis*, the visual was understood to have the power to cut through the rational processes and go straight to the emotions. This is one of the reasons it was considered to be such a highly effective rhetorical tool, as it is in our own time too. We would also suggest that just as texts may conjure images that may not necessarily be "real" such as the depiction of Achilles' shield in the *Iliad* or Virgil's description of Aeneas's shield in his *Aeneid*, visual representation may also narrate images and objects and realities that may not be "real" but may nonetheless still be persuasive. To explore what types of questions can be posed when we consider objects and texts alongside one another, we will focus on one particular aspect of Roman visual representation as manifest in the world of the early Christians: images of human subjugation, or images that communicate relations of domination between human beings. Such images appear to have been extremely common throughout the Roman imperial world, and thus serve as a potentially effective means by which we might realign objects and texts. And these images have also been used in recent "empire-critical" New Testament scholarship to illustrate and affirm readings that position the early Christians as resistant to Roman rule and thus empire more generally.

As the contemporary advertising industry well knows, repeating an image over and over is an effective means to naturalize it as an unproblematic reflection of reality. Such naturalization can lead us to accept the world "as it is" and shape our responses to it. Let us provide an example of how this can work in our world. Few of our readers (at least, those of a certain age) will likely forget the endless looping of the images of New York's World Trade Center towers collapsing on September 11, 2001 – one could make the argument that without that image, played day after day, it might be harder to explain the ramping up of American military forces placed in service of securing the dangerous places in the world, of constructing, and then ferreting out, the enemies. It is "just an image" – but that should not minimize the dramatic and irrevocable impact that images have on us as humans. We likely do not need to reprint an image of the towers falling in this book for it to come into view for you. That said, what that image looks like and what it represents are not stable in terms of the possible ranges of signification – and while the image may be easy to recall, the meaning may not be. In fact, it very well may be that the image we are describing to you now never had any inherent meaning – two very tall buildings collapsed under the impact of two passenger planes. The image and its representative meaning, however, immediately became bound up with a diversity of power relationships that transfigured the image into a bold representation, which of course shifted depending on one's previous political and social commitments. We would do well to bear this process in mind as we begin to turn to the use of Roman imperial images in the interpretation of early Christian social realities and literary representations.

War is an event, or a series of events, and is highly localized and occasional. And the Romans appear to have been good at narrating the events of war to their populace visually, in the service of breaking the news and feeding it into a distinctive, if complex, ideological program. In fact, as Katherine Welch has proposed, perhaps what makes Roman art distinctively "Roman" is the depiction of violence, war, and conquest that span media, geographical location, and time periods.[44] Certainly, readers of the New Testament ought to be familiar with one monument in particular, the Arch of Titus, standing in what has been excavated and packaged to us as the Roman Forum. On this arch, dedicated after the conquest of Jerusalem and the destruction of the Temple in 70 CE, there are two famous friezes thought to depict and commemorate what happened after the people of Judea were defeated. On one side, the south panel, a procession of people carries the booty from the temple in Jerusalem, including the menorah, table of showbread, and trumpets, through the gates of the city (Figure 3.1). On the other, the north panel, the Emperor Titus is led in a quadriga, being crowned by Victory herself. This monument, used in the study of the New Testament as a

Figure 3.1 Arch of Titus, Rome. Interior narrative relief depicting a parade, possibly of Judean captives, carrying Jerusalem temple objects through a triumphal arch. Photo by Davina C. Lopez.

visual illustration of the humiliation of Israel at Roman hands, is often complemented by smaller images like the Judaea Capta coin types featuring ethnic prisoners flanking a date palm tree. The message here is clear: Jerusalem was destroyed, Judea was defeated, and, by extension, the New Testament texts refer to these historical events. Since there is external confirmation of its referents, the study of the New Testament, it is assumed, must be anchored, at least to a degree, in ancient historical realities.

Far from the only monument concerned with Roman military conquest and assimilation of ethnic enemies, the Arch of Titus can be read as part of a long and pervasive pattern of communicating success in specific battles as a means of communicating the eternal victory of empire, or what might be called images of triumph and glory. For example, the trophy monument is itself a trace of a local event. The erection of a trophy made of weapons and armor on the site of battle to mark its completion is thought to be a custom with a history going back to the Greeks, who would use actual armor. From the surviving visual representation, it appears that the Romans took this practice and made it sculptural, and therefore portable. Citizens of towns and cities, and not just soldiers on a battlefield, could see a trophy, and this visibility

Figure 3.2 Trajan's Column, Rome. The base of this monumental column is decorated with reliefs of piles of weapons and armor of the conquered Dacians. Photo by Davina C. Lopez.

helped to transform a local and singular event into part of a grammar of universal victory. The trophy takes several forms in Roman art – from a rather simple representation of foreign weapons and armor hung on a post, which was thought to be true to what was erected on battlefields, to a pile of weapons carved in relief like that which decorates the bottom of Trajan's Column (Figure 3.2). Often foreign prisoners are shown bound to the trophy. And sometimes, a personification of Victory accompanies the trophy, such as on reliefs from the Sebasteion at Aphrodisias, where a female figure, perhaps a goddess, places a trophy near a captured barbarian at its base. Victory poses similarly on Trajan's Column (Figure 3.3), where she is shown "writing" on a shield between two trophy monuments, signifying what is thought to be the end of one Dacian war and the beginning of another. Victory need not be present at a trophy monument; for example, on a 1st-century frieze thought to be from the reign of Domitian (not pictured), two large captives, male and female, the latter in a mourning pose and perhaps the personification of Germany, are bound with a trophy. Sometimes, the captives and trophy are given a fuller range of significations by being shown with the Romans, such as in the famous Gemma Augustea,[45] which is divided into two registers, the

Figure 3.3 Trajan's Column, Rome. A large winged Victory inscribes a shield and is flanked by two trophy monuments. This image is thought to signal the end of the first Dacian war, the story of which wraps around the column from the bottom to this point, and the beginning of the second Dacian war, which extends to the top. Most of the detail would likely not be visible to viewers on the ground. Photo by Davina C. Lopez.

upper showing the imperial family and the lower showing conquered others sitting near the erection of a trophy monument. This theme is repeated on the Grand Cameo of France in three registers, with sitting captives at the bottom and the Julio-Claudian victors, flanked by family dead and alive, at the top. The message seems to be that Roman peace, fertility, and divinity, if we can call it that, are predicated on the defeat and subjugation of the others. Repetition of these images in different media, geographical locations, and time periods confers their status as natural and inevitable.

Victory, for the Romans, appears to signify the conclusion of a war and the statement that a battle has taken place, is over, and the Romans have won. Victory imagery is common in surviving Roman visual representation from all over the empire, at center and periphery, in public places and in private homes, on monuments large and small, whether find-spots are known or not. In fact, the bound, anonymous barbarian is one of the most common images in all of Roman art, and bound female figures are especially numerous.[46] The wars themselves, though, are also at times narrated visually,

153

giving another layer of "natural" reality to the representation. The columns of Trajan and Marcus Aurelius in Rome, for example, appear to be comprehensive narrative depictions of wars that happened in, and over, the northern hinterlands. These columns, which may or may not be meant to be read in order up the spiraled shafts, appear to be overwhelming, and overwhelmingly detailed, depictions of actual events, characters, places, and outcomes. A main theme on both columns is the encounter between Romans and others, where the Romans are orderly and the barbarian enemies are depicted in all manner of ethnically appropriate chaos. As in mythological battle reliefs of the Hellenistic period, here the gods fight on the side of Rome, as Jove does in one scene on Trajan's Column. And usually the barbarians are routed, thwarted, captured, killed, and enslaved, as multiple scenes on the column depict. In the Column of Marcus Aurelius, which is thought to tell the story of the Marcomannic wars against the Quadi and Sarmatians, the violence between the Romans and others is heightened and the battle scenes more messy, with more foreign women being stabbed, pulled by their hair, begging for mercy, and so on (Figure 3.4). When the emperor

Figure 3.4 Column of Marcus Aurelius, Rome. Battle scenes between the Romans and Quadi. In the middle register of this image foreign women and children are forcibly being taken hostage, with one woman being pulled by her hair. The "rain god" scene is located on the bottom right. Photo by Davina C. Lopez.

receives the conquered, he does so in the middle of battle scenes, which are, again, more extensive than those on Trajan's Column.[47] And as on Aurelius's columnal predecessor, the Romans have the help of the divine in their efforts, or at least the rain, as is represented in one scene by a hairy-looking winged male figure who helps to rout the barbarian enemy.[48]

So far what we have seen of Roman imperial ideology expressed visually fits very well with the idea that we are looking rather transparently at the violent, death-dealing world that some would hold the non-violence of the Jesus movement, Gospel traditions, and early Christians more broadly sought to subvert. Images of human subjugation and war-making permeated the Roman visual landscape during the time of the New Testament and Christian origins, from Augustus to Marcus Aurelius. It would be easy to conclude from this brief engagement thus far that the Romans clearly represent violence, and the New Testament represents resistance to violence. Herein Caesar is the self, and the enemies are the "other," and the task here is to let the subaltern speak, to do history and theology from the point of view of the conquered, where the New Testament could serve as the residue of such voices. And if we reconstruct the occasion for the New Testament writings in that way, then perhaps we can have some ammunition for subaltern struggles in the present – which, to some, might be a worthy or necessary task. However, the success of such a project depends upon representation – literary or visual – being the same as reality in both the ancient and modern contexts, a conflation that we have attempted to problematize throughout this chapter and in this book as a whole.

In working with depictions of human subjugation through Roman war and victory, it is incredibly tempting to resort to an interpretation that boils down to "what you see is what you get." To be sure, as attractive as it is, such a reading would be indebted to the modern distinction between images and texts wherein images are more transparently real than literature. The narrative wherein images convey historical events in a transparent or literal manner is challenged by the objects themselves – for example, in scenes that seem reminiscent of the great mythological battles but with historical characters. Such is the case with the friezes of the Great Altar of Pergamon in Berlin or the so-called Parthian monument, found in Ephesus and currently housed at Vienna's state museum. The use of mythological themes and symbolism confounds our efforts to read visual narratives as straightforwardly and literally "historical." And further complicating the picture is the Romans' pervasive use of allegorical personifications along with mythological tropes in order to communicate something of a universal, eternal, natural victory and vertical hierarchy. Images of victory and apotheosis are not filled only with historical personages but also are usually chock full of personified places such as the Earth, sun, and sea. Victory and ascension to heaven rest on dominion over the world, which is less a declaration of "what happened" and more an argument for "the way it is and ought to be."

Indeed, the Roman use of personifications in visual media to express ideas about land, virtues, and so on is highly ideological, and enables a blurring of the boundaries between reality and representation. It is the case, for example, that a female personification of the city of Rome, Roma, might stand on top of a sitting female personification of the Earth, perhaps Gaia, as is the case in one relief from Aphrodisias Sebasteion. Female barbarians make widespread appearance as part of a series of "conquered nations" depicted in Aphrodisias and also in reliefs of the Hadrianeum in Rome, some of which currently adorn an outdoor grotto at the Capitoline Museum. Conquered nations are highly stereotypical representations of women in "native" dress, holding attributes that would perhaps be recognizable representations of their land. Their standing, rather than crouching, pose may signify their willing assimilation and cooperation as provinces into the Roman imperial structure; Hadrianic visual representation in particular tends to be careful in its visual characterization of conquest as "friendship" with foreigners. It is not just the women who come to represent ideas central to Roman victory and victimhood, though – some male bodies were deployed to represent certain virtues associated with war. Honos and Virtus, the temples to whom were built with spoils from a war with the Gauls, represent Roman Honor and Roman Virtue, and are often represented with what we might call hypermasculine military imagery. Virtus, in particular, is often dressed in armor, shown with his foot on either the planet or a helmet, and holding a staff in one hand and a dagger rather suggestively in the other.

The variety of visual grammatical elements in representations of Roman war and victory is a site where we would suggest that commemorations of local battles are transformed into a broader message of Roman victory and power that is easy to miss when one is focused on one-to-one correspondences between text and object, the rhetorical transparency of images, or the singularity of meaning that can be extracted from an object. Readings of the Judaea Capta coin type in New Testament studies, for example, have not until recently paid full attention to the broad semantic range here. It is common to read the female figure as a personification of Judea, and the male figure as the Roman soldier responsible for her defeat. That may be the case, but the male figure here is also standing in the pose characteristic of Virtus, which would arguably be obvious in a context where his image was popular. The question then is: is the defeat of Judea a matter of Roman virtue? A just war? For the record, just to return to an image we thought we knew earlier, it is thought to be Virtus heading up the quadriga in the Arch of Titus as well, which would suggest that this image was used in connection with the Jewish War. In terms of a visual argument, both readings of the image are possible; what we do not know is whether ancient audiences preferred one over the other, or held both options, in addition to others we have not identified or considered, in tension with each other.

The pervasive presence of personifications in depictions of Roman victory marks these images as not necessarily only about "what happened," but also about deploying "what happened" as a means to construct a certain kind of reality. In the noisy fray of what seem like endless battle scenes and piles of weapons and collections of conquered nations, there is a visual language of war and conquest that marks what art historian Tonio Hölscher has called the transformation of event into structure, that is to say, the transformation of specific conquest into universal political statement, of victory into power.[49] If one looks more closely at these Roman visual victory narratives, it becomes clearer that stock scenes and ideas are used to knit together a portrait of the world and its intended natural order. These stock scenes are often focused on an interaction between Romans and their so-called enemies before, during, and after a battle or series of them, and on monuments like Trajan's Column (if we accept that the column is to be "read" vertically) follow a basic structure of departure from the city, sacrifice, speeches to troops, surrender of enemies, installation of client kings, arrival back in Rome, triumphal entry and procession, more sacrifice, collection of slaves, and distribution of resources. Each of these actions is the signifier for certain virtues and other ideals, rather than an eyewitness report of what happened. Triumph is linked to victory, sacrifice to piety, surrender to clemency, and so on. Whether these events occurred in the way the images say they did is irrelevant – what matters is that the images are mounting an argument, using rhetorical strategies that might be familiar to those who work on texts.

All of this is to say that working with the visual language of conquest and victory in relation to the New Testament is not so simple as to display pictures to illustrate the world in which the texts were written and to which early Christians may have responded – if such images are even consulted as part of a project that takes the Roman Empire seriously as that which the writers of the New Testament negotiated. And when they are taken seriously, images like the ones we have been encountering during our brief discussion here are used in several ways: as part of a background against which New Testament literature is illuminated, as that which affirms concepts and ideas already thought to be present in literary texts, and/or as illustrative of Roman imperial ideology thought to be in the texts on which we desire to perform politically inclined exegesis. For example, images such as the ones we have been discussing can quite easily be used to illustrate the brutality of the Roman Empire, which would then account for the New Testament's supposed stance against Roman rule. They can also be used to affirm the idea that the early Christians were victims of an endless cycle of violence that resulted in the destruction of the city of Jerusalem, the religious and political center of Jews, in Judea. Images such as these become a way to talk about hierarchies, to help make Jesus and the early Christians political, to say things about violence that words cannot or do not say as well. Images illustrate empire, which illustrates the imperial dimensions of New Testament texts. The images can thus serve to "prove" that thinking about the Roman Empire in relation to the New Testament is a productive exercise.

This last observation brings us to a critical question that attention to Roman imperial visual representation might obscure: what is the precise ideological function of empire discourse in the first place? What comes into existence as a result? What vanishes from existence (so to speak) as a result? The stability of an imperial Roman material propaganda machine, especially through its images, does important work for modern New Testament scholars. The more recent turn to images, moreover, serves these aims even more vividly and potently, for the sense that is acquired of their objective status reifies the existing categories established for Roman imperial theopolitics. Images are thus particularly attractive to modern scholars because they vivify an objective apparatus constructed through texts and archaeology, with the major accent falling on the former. They make things real – or appear to be so. In this way, the various entities that they invoke also take on the appearance of the real in the process. So whether we are talking about early Christian groups or particular theological concepts that need an explicitly traceable "background" in order to bring them into existence and imbue them with meaning, in all cases, when images of empire are deployed, it is done with the aim of producing an immutable background against which the New Testament texts can be read. In this respect, Christians and Christian theology are imaged (and perhaps also imagined) into existence.

We contend that creating stability through attention to Roman imperial images is not enough to address the serious methodological questions that are complicated when material culture is taken seriously as a source for doing New Testament studies and early Christian history. That there is still a wide division between texts and objects in such studies, and that there is an implicit hierarchy where texts remain superior, betrays more about modern methods and legacies than it does about ancient proclivities. The particular uses of Roman images we have just described rest on assumptions about what pictures do – namely, that they comprise a reflection of reality, that they are statements of facts, that the commemoration of events like battles and wars is to be taken at face value in all of its detail, down to the very last facial expression and ethnically specific garment and weapon. And while images might betray what Roland Barthes called "the reality effect," wherein details upon details serve as a means to produce "realism" itself, it is also the case that responsible historical analysis should question all narratives that present themselves as "what happened." To do otherwise risks the perpetuation of an elision between representation and that which is represented, between narrative and reality.

In other words, images like the ones we have been describing are not simply a reflection of reality – even as they might be "realistic." They are constructions of a particular reality that was considered to be persuasive, and need not correspond in a one-to-one ratio with literary accounts of any kind, including those of the New Testament. It very well could be the case that these images developed in a tradition completely separate from textual accounts of war and violence, or that the images were responding to the texts, or vice versa, or some of both. It could also be the case that, due to our own legacies of putting images second to texts, we are not quite recognizing some critical ways in which these objects and texts are playing off of one another or are dependent on each other. Regardless, in our view these images serve to articulate particular sets of power relationships that, while perhaps not "real," are hard to ignore. Roman images of war and victory invite the viewer to move from the specific, local battle to the universal political statement, from the commemoration of what happened to the articulation of ideas about the order of things, from the events to the structure in which the events must be seen as natural and inevitable. As constructions of reality, images must be seen not as mere statements of facts, but as critical components of discourses of power. In that sense, the monuments do not just display pictures of weapons. The monuments *are* weapons, which transform historical record into programmatic statements, controlling what it is a population can, and should, desire to see and to experience, in themselves and others, constructing an entire world in the process.

More fundamentally, we observe that material culture is unstable in terms of its range of meanings, which suggests that we need to make it stable in order to stabilize our ancient texts, worlds, and theologies. This is, again, a modern task and not an ancient one, and reveals more about us than about the New Testament or the ancient world. To insist that there is one reading of ancient images, that there is a narrow semantic range that must align perfectly with texts in order for our exegesis to work, to discard images as useless or irrelevant unless we can locate find-spots or perfect literary correlates, or to ignore that images may challenge texts is to deny a fuller set of interpretive options. It also denies a wide range of interplay and interdependence between objects and texts. This is not just the case with Roman art, but with material culture more broadly. We propose that a task for using images and objects in conversation with the New Testament, then, is to move beyond the background/illustration approach, beyond the simple utility of objects for reconstruction and proof, beyond seeing images as stable – beyond the idea that what and how we see is determined by dominant discourses in the first place. The task, in short, is to think about, with, and through images as reflections not of reality, but of struggles over power, authority, and agency.

What Do We Want with Ancient Objects?

Ancient objects, and perhaps especially those that can be linked to biblical texts and worlds, make for sensational media coverage. The "new find" can generate much controversy and spectacle: will this thing be the one that proves the Bible is true? That it is not true? Once and for all? And this question is usually followed by: how do we know this thing is real? Who gets to decide? The scientists who do the testing on the object? The scholars who do handwriting analysis? Biblical scholars who have had no contact with the material? The private collectors who have the money to spend on such objects? The public? In the case of the *Gospel of Jesus' Wife*, it is worth noting that discussion about this ancient papyrus fragment has largely taken place in "real time," in blogs and other online media sources. This approach has its strengths and its drawbacks. The immediacy of the information and opinions available through blogging platforms lends an "open-source" quality to the scholarly discussion. Information seems to be transparent, and updates can be provided quickly. However, the downside of this real-time approach is that opinions can be shared before they are fully formed, misinformation can spread with the same speed as information, and misunderstandings can proliferate rapidly. In this case, though, we highlight that the discussion of issues related to the contents of the *Gospel of Jesus' Wife* – notably, issues of gender and sexuality, from the sexuality of Jesus to the gender of the scholar who is studying it – have very easily turned toward the personal.[50] This shift is not surprising: we do acknowledge that the scholarly is often deeply personal, which also underscores the point that ancient objects serve as sites where modern issues might be mapped onto the world of the early Christians, where identities might be constructed and constricted, and where questions and possibilities might be explored or denied.

We do grant that the New Testament is, first and foremost, a collection of texts, and so we understand how textual analysis might have become that which is foregrounded in the field. However, this orientation is not as methodologically natural, inevitable, or universal as we might like to think. As we have noted and as archaeologists have forcefully demonstrated, in order to understand something of the "big picture" about Christian origins and early Christianity we ought not to limit ourselves to texts. However, what exactly to do with objects is not easy to determine, and is embedded in controversies and relations of power, as we have endeavored to demonstrate in this chapter. Basically, to use material culture in the study of the New Testament is to deploy objects in the service of constructing modern narratives about the texts, their authors and subjects, their theological inclinations, and their continuing relevance in the present. These narratives, while seemingly ancient and historically accurate, more precisely reflect our own sensibilities and orientations to the world, even as these might be (often unintentionally) hidden from view. As such, the use of material culture in the study of the New Testament is ultimately about constructing narratives about our own relationship with the texts and the worlds that produced them.

In our view, arguments for a more expansive set of relationships between texts and images, as well as the observation that images need not be literal illustrations of texts to be relevant, have important applications in the study of the New Testament and early Christian literature. Simply put, ancient images may serve a purpose similar to texts: they respond to stories, and narrate new stories in the process of doing so. As such, they construct worlds as much as texts do. As much as we might want objects to reflect ancient realities to us, we may need to concede that what is actually revealed therein is our modern attempts to stabilize and naturalize both objects and texts. By contrast, it is possible that images can be taken every bit as seriously as texts in terms of communicative power, and in so doing we might foreground the instability of both texts and objects.

We have attempted in this chapter to de-introduce the deployment and role of material culture in the study of the New Testament, Christian origins, and early Christianity. The archaeology of the New Testament, as a disciplinary formation that locates, examines, and interprets ancient objects for study, has cultivated interest in what real and ordinary people's lives might have been like in the ancient world – how the people who followed Jesus or received letters from Paul might have lived, what their daily lives would have consisted of, and so on. Objects are essential to this task. The use of objects seems straightforward in historical reconstruction, exegesis, and other kinds of interpretive work, but that is not the case. Far from transparent, objects are used in various ways to tell stories about the field, the Bible, and the world. They are not neutral, but entangled in discourses about modern science, religious and national identities, and the flow of capital.

These last points should not be downplayed or ignored in working with objects in the study of the New Testament. In particular, the persistence of the market for private collecting and ownership of antiquities plays a much larger role in controlling access to ancient objects, and thus to narratives about those objects and their positioning in history and culture, than many scholars are willing to admit. One rather high-profile recent example of these dynamics is the Green Collection, established by arts-and-crafts chain store Hobby Lobby founder Steve Green. Green is an American billionaire who has amassed a sizable collection of biblically related antiquities – more than 40,000 pieces between 2009 and 2012 and still growing, making this one of the largest private collections of biblical antiquities in the world. The Green Collection has a considerable media presence and has secured a building in Washington, D.C. to house it as part of the planned Museum of the Bible. Green has also assembled an international team of biblical scholars tasked with studying the materials (many of which, including 1,000 papyri, have never been translated or published) as well as to tell a particular (and particularly linear and developmental) story about the history, and historicity, of the Bible. In fact, as Green has readily admitted in an interview, "We are story-tellers first, and these items tell a story … We're buyers of items to tell the story. We pass on more than we buy because it doesn't fit what we are trying to tell."[51]

Green's sentiment expresses rather clearly the point that objects might be used to tell a particular story, according to the desires, assumptions, proclivities, and in this case wealth of the storytellers. But the narrative is already there before the materials are even bought, and what does not fit that story is set aside. Whether one agrees with the specific story being told is less relevant, in our view, than the reality that the issue at stake is who controls the narrative, and for what purpose. In this case, capitalism has created the conditions possible for a wealthy private collector to control access to ancient objects, which is a means to control the narrative and "own antiquity." It is not only what ancient objects can do for us, but what we do and want with ancient objects, that matters. Herein are embedded significant power relationships that are important to foreground as we conduct our work as students of the New Testament.

Notes

1. The *Gospel of Jesus' Wife* has its own website, housed at Harvard Divinity School, where visitors may read press releases, consult the scientific results of the tests, view photos (including photos of the scientists examining the fragment with their equipment), and explore basic questions of provenance and meaning. See Harvard Divinity School, "The Gospel of Jesus' Wife," http://gospelofjesusswife.hds.harvard.edu/home (accessed November 27, 2014).
2. Karen L. King, "'Jesus said to them, "My wife…"': A New Coptic Papyrus Fragment," *Harvard Theological Review* 107.2 (2014): 153–154.
3. Noreen Tuross, "Accelerated Mass Spectrometry Radiocarbon Determination of Papyrus Samples," *Harvard Theological Review* 107.2 (2014): 170–171.
4. Jonathan L. Reed, *The HarperCollins Visual Guide to the New Testament: What Archaeology Reveals about the First Christians* (San Francisco: HarperOne, 2007), 3.

5. For ancient references see Josephus, *Jewish War*, 7.5.7; Pliny, *Natural History*, 34.84, 36.20. For the larger framework of these Roman staging events, see Ida Östenberg, *Staging the World: Spoils, Captives, and Representations in the Roman Triumphal Procession* (Oxford Studies in Ancient Culture and Representation; New York: Oxford University Press, 2009), and Steven H. Rutledge, *Ancient Rome as a Museum: Power, Identity, and the Culture of Collecting* (Oxford Studies in Ancient Culture and Representation; New York: Oxford University Press, 2012).

6. James Turner, *Philology: The Forgotten Origins of the Modern Humanities* (Princeton: Princeton University Press, 2014), 167–209.

7. The "secret cabinet" was a source of considerable controversy. Women were not allowed to enter the cabinet until the 1970s. The materials are now housed in a separate room at the Naples museum. The "erotic" frescoes that were not removed from the walls of the Pompeii site were surrounded by locked metal cabinets that were opened only for select male individuals, and often for a fee. See Michael Grant et al., *Eros in Pompeii: The Secret Rooms of the National Museums of Naples* (New York: William Morrow, 1975); John Clarke, *Roman Sex: 100 B.C. to 250 A.D.* (New York: Harry Abrams, 2003); Mary Beard, *The Fires of Vesuvius: Pompeii Lost and Found* (Cambridge, Mass.: Belknap Press, 2010).

8. Turner, *Philology*, 185.

9. Turner, *Philology*, 185. See also Stephen Dyson, *In Search of Ancient Pasts: A History of Classical Archaeology in the Nineteenth and Twentieth Centuries* (New Haven: Yale University Press, 2006), 45, and Suzanne Marchand, *Down from Olympus: Archaeology and Philhellenism in Germany, 1750–1970* (Princeton: Princeton University Press, 1996), 36–74.

10. Jonathan M. Hall, *Artifact and Artifice: Classical Archaeology and the Ancient Historian* (Chicago: University of Chicago Press, 2014), 10.

11. Hall, *Artifact and Artifice*, 10. For an overview of the legacy of Schliemann in classical archaeology, see Anthony Snodgrass, "Greek Archaeology," in *Classical Archaeology* (ed. S. E. Alcock and R. Osborne; Blackwell Studies in Global Archaeology 10; Malden, Mass.: Wiley-Blackwell, 2007), 13–29. For an examination of the role of trained archaeologist Frank Calvert in Schliemann's archaeological efforts, see Susan Hueck Allen, *Finding the Walls of Troy: Frank Calvert and Heinrich Schliemann at Hisarlik* (Berkeley: University of California Press, 1999).

12. Hall, *Artifact and Artifice*, 11.

13. For a survey of the excavations and attendant literature, see Charles Brian Rose, *The Archaeology of Greek and Roman Troy* (New York: Cambridge University Press, 2013).

14. Josephus: *Antiquities of the Jews*, 18.89. Tacitus: *Annals*, 15.44. See also Philo, *Embassy to Gaius*, 38.299–305. For scholarly discussion of the historical and rhetorical evidence for Pilate see Helen Bond, *Pontius Pilate in History and Interpretation* (Society for New Testament Studies Monograph Series 100; New York: Cambridge University Press, 2004).

15. For an accessible summary of the considerable impact that the discovery of the Dead Sea Scrolls has made in the study of the New Testament, see J. H. Charlesworth, ed., *Jesus and Archaeology* (Grand Rapids, Mich.: Eerdmans, 2006); Jodi Magness, *The Archaeology of Qumran and the Dead Sea Scrolls* (Studies in the Dead

Sea Scrolls and Related Literature; Grand Rapids, Mich.: Eerdmans, 2003); and James VanderKam and Peter Flint, *The Meaning of the Dead Sea Scrolls* (San Francisco: HarperOne, 2004).

16. Pliny, *Natural History*, 5.17; Josephus, *Jewish War*, 2.119.

17. For a contemporary extrapolation of finds at Qumran to reconstructions of daily life in Palestine at the time of Jesus, see Jodi Magness, *Stone and Dung, Oil and Spit: Jewish Daily Life in the Time of Jesus* (Grand Rapids, Mich.: Eerdmans, 2011).

18. The main debate in the history of scholarship on the archaeology of Galilee has been the extent to which we can call the region "Hellenistic/Greco-Roman" or "Jewish" in terms of culture. Both options, of course, influence the way a portrait of Jesus and the 1st-century world of the New Testament might look. Recent archaeological work has suggested a shift from a predominantly "Gentile" Galilee to a "Jewish" Galilee. For discussion see Mark A. Chancey, *The Myth of a Gentile Galilee* (Society for New Testament Studies Monograph Series 118; New York: Cambridge University Press, 2004), and *Greco-Roman Culture and the Galilee of Jesus* (Society for New Testament Studies Monograph Series 196; New York: Cambridge University Press, 2008). See also Eric M. Meyers and Mark A. Chancey, *Alexander to Constantine: Archaeology of the Land of the Bible*, vol. 3 (Anchor Yale Bible Reference Library; New Haven: Yale University Press, 2012).

19. John Dominic Crossan and Jonathan L. Reed, *Excavating Jesus: Beneath the Stones, Behind the Texts. The Key Discoveries for Understanding Jesus in His World* (San Francisco: HarperOne, 2003), xv.

20. Reed, *Visual Guide to the New Testament*, 3–9.

21. Ingrid D. Rowland, *From Pompeii: The Afterlife of a Roman Town* (Cambridge, Mass.: Belknap/Harvard University Press, 2014). On Pompeii's afterlives see also Judith Harris, *Pompeii Awakened: A Story of Discovery* (New York: I. B. Tauris, 1997), and S. Hales and J. Paul, eds., *Pompeii in the Public Imagination from Its Rediscovery to Today* (New York: Oxford University Press, 2011).

22. Alain Schnapp, "The Antiquarian Culture of Eighteenth-Century Naples as a Laboratory of New Ideas," in *Rediscovering the Ancient World on the Bay of Naples, 1710–1890* (ed. C. C. Mattusch; Studies in the History of Art 79; Washington, D.C.: National Gallery of Art, 2013), 11–46: 14.

23. Julian Thomas, *Archaeology and Modernity* (New York: Routledge, 2004), 13.

24. Thomas, *Archaeology and Modernity*, 16.

25. For discussion see Can Bilsel, *Antiquity on Display: Regimes of the Authentic in Berlin's Pergamon Museum* (Classical Presences; New York: Oxford University Press, 2012).

26. Marchand, *Down from Olympus*, especially 152–227.

27. For a history of the French excavations in Rome, see Ronald T. Ridley, *The Eagle and the Spade: Archaeology in Rome during the Napoleonic Era* (New York: Cambridge University Press, 2009).

28. Diana Rowell, *Paris: The "New Rome" of Napoleon I* (New York: Bloomsbury Academic, 2014).

29. See Borden W. Painter, Jr., *Mussolini's Rome: Rebuilding the Eternal City* (Italian and Italian American Studies; New York: Palgrave, 2005).

30. Scholars have often argued that Mussolini's deployment of ancient Rome for fascist purposes was not much more than pomp and circumstance. There is much evidence to suggest that the appropriation of classical antiquity, and the Roman Empire in particular, was critical to the articulation of Italian fascism, both internally and among European countries. For an appraisal of the centrality of ancient Rome to modern Italy, see Joshua Arthurs, *Excavating Modernity: The Roman Past in Fascist Italy* (Ithaca, N.Y.: Cornell University Press, 2012).

31. Nadia Abu El-Haj, *Facts on the Ground: Archaeological Practice and Territorial Self-Fashioning in Israeli Society* (Chicago: University of Chicago Press, 2001), 3. See also Shlomo Sand, *The Words and the Land: Israeli Intellectuals and the Nationalist Myth* (Active Agents; Los Angeles: Semiotext(e), 2011).

32. Nur Masalha, *The Bible and Zionism: Invented Traditions, Archaeology and Post-colonialism in Israel-Palestine* (New York: Zed Books, 2007), 240ff.

33. The 1970 United Nations Educational, Scientific, and Cultural Organization (UNESCO) Convention on the Means of Prohibiting and Preventing the Illicit Import, Export and Transfer of Ownership of Cultural Property served to define antiquities as cultural property, and specifically as the property of the nation-state that claims it as important, on religious or secular grounds, to the archaeology, art, literature, and history of that territory. Under this act nations are asked to prohibit the sale and transfer of antiquities unless proper documentation is produced.

34. Elizabeth Marlowe, *Shaky Ground: Context, Connoisseurship, and the History of Roman Art* (Debates in Archaeology; London: Bristol Classical Press, 2013); see also Colin Renfrew, *Loot, Legitimacy, and Ownership: The Ethical Crisis in Archaeology* (Duckworth Debates in Archaeology; London: Duckworth Press, 2000).

35. Refrew, *Loot, Legitimacy, and Ownership, passim*; for a different set of views see J. Cuno, ed., *Whose Culture? The Promise of Museums and the Debate over Antiquities* (Princeton: Princeton University Press, 2009).

36. Elisabetta Polovedo, "Ancient Vase Comes Home to a Hero's Welcome," *The New York Times*, 19 January 2008. http://www.nytimes.com/2008/01/19/arts/design/19bowl.html (accessed November 27, 2014).

37. James Cuno, *Who Owns Antiquity? Museums and the Battle over Our Ancient Heritage* (Princeton: Princeton University Press, 2008).

38. In an introductory text on early Christian art, Robin Jensen argues that students of religion need to learn the language of art history in order to work with objects, and students of art history need a basic understanding of theology in order to work with Christian art. See Robin Jensen, *Understanding Early Christian Art* (New York: Routledge, 2000).

39. Michael Squire, *Image and Text in Graeco-Roman Antiquity* (New York: Cambridge University Press, 2009), 1–86.

40. For a review and appraisal of the modern scholarship that constructs ancient Jews as predominantly, if not exclusively, aniconic, see Steven Fine, *Art and Judaism in the Greco-Roman World: Toward a New Jewish Archaeology* (New York: Cambridge University Press, 2005), 1–56.

41. Jocelyn Penny Small, *The Parallel Worlds of Classical Art and Text* (New York: Cambridge University Press, 2003), 9.
42. For further consideration, see Davina C. Lopez, "Visual Perspectives: Toward Imag(in)ing the Big Pauline Picture," in *Studying Paul's Letters: Contemporary Perspectives and Methods* (ed. J. Marchal; Minneapolis: Fortress Press, 2012), 93–116.
43. Adolf Deissmann famously called archaeological remains, and particularly inscriptions – objects in their own right – from the Roman east a matter of "polemical parallelism" with the New Testament; see *Light from the Ancient East: The New Testament Illustrated by Recently Discovered Texts of the Greco-Roman World* (trans. L. R. M. Strachan; repr. of 1927 ed.; Peabody, Mass.: Hendrickson, 1995). Ramsay was trained in the Tübingen school of F. C. Baur and initially doubted the historicity of the New Testament. It was the archaeology of Asia Minor that "converted" him to the historical veracity of the New Testament's people, places, and events. See, for example, William M. Ramsay, *The Bearing of Recent Discovery on the Trustworthiness of the New Testament* (London: Hodder & Stoughton, 1915). We would suggest that many contemporary New Testament scholars have followed the "Ramsay trajectory," using archaeology to confirm the historicity of the New Testament and even in some cases to date the literature to the 1st century (as Ramsay did with the Acts of the Apostles, which he previously had thought was a 2nd-century document). Jocelyn M. C. Toynbee, an art historian, noted the "coincidence" between honorific titles for Hadrian, in image and text, and those attributed to Jesus in the Gospels; see *The Hadrianic School: A Chapter in the History of Greek Art* (Cambridge: Cambridge University Press, 1934), especially 120–121.
44. Katherine Welch, "Introduction," in *Representations of War in Ancient Rome* (ed. K. Welch and S. Dillon; New York: Cambridge University Press, 2006), 1–26.
45. For an extensive and critical reading of the Gemma Augustea's role in legitimating Roman dynastic power through the conquest of others, see John Pollini, "The Gemma Augustea: Ideology, Rhetorical Imagery, and the Construction of a Dynastic Narrative," in *Narrative and Event in Ancient Art* (ed. P. Holladay; New York: Cambridge University Press, 1994), 258–298, and Pollini, *From Republic to Empire: Rhetoric, Religion, and Power in the Visual Culture of the Roman Empire* (Oklahoma Series in Classical Culture 48; Norman: University of Oklahoma Press, 2013), especially 204–270.
46. See Iain Ferris, *Enemies of Rome: Barbarians through Roman Eyes* (London: Sutton Publishing, 2000).
47. The Column of Marcus Aurelius is underexamined in Roman art history and archaeology. The column itself, while one of the best-preserved Roman monuments, is also currently in poor shape due to wear by the elements and an earthquake that caused a shift in its registers. For discussion of the monument see Martin Beckmann, *The Column of Marcus Aurelius: The Genesis and Meaning of a Roman Imperial Monument* (Studies in Greece and Rome; Chapel Hill: University of North Carolina Press, 2011), and Iain Ferris, *Hate and War: The Column of Marcus Aurelius* (Stroud: The History Press, 2009).

48. For a discussion of the "rain miracle" on the Column of Marcus Aurelius and in ancient literature, see Davina C. Lopez, "Miraculous Methodologies: Critical Reflections on 'Ancient Miracle Discourse' Discourse," in *Miracle Discourse in the New Testament* (ed. D. F. Watson; Early Christianity and Its Literature; Atlanta: Society of Biblical Literature, 2012), 225–248.

49. Tonio Hölscher, "The Transformation of Victory into Power: From Event to Structure," in *Representations of War in Ancient Rome* (ed. K. Welch and S. Dillon; New York: Cambridge University Press, 2006), 27–48.

50. For an appraisal of the gendered discourse surrounding the *Gospel of Jesus' Wife*, see Eva Mroczek, "'Gospel of Jesus' Wife' Less Durable than Sexism Surrounding It," *Religion Dispatches*, May 6, 2014. http://religiondispatches.org/gospel-of-jesus-wife-less-durable-than-sexism-surrounding-it/ (accessed November 27, 2014).

51. Interview with Steve Green, *Les Enluminures*, Autumn 2013. Quoted from Roberta Mazza, "A Trip to Rome (with a detour on eBay): A Review of Verbum Domini II," *Faces and Voices: People, Artefacts, Ancient History*, April 29, 2014. http://facesandvoices.wordpress.com/2014/04/29/a-trip-to-rome-with-a-detour-on-ebay-a-review-of-verbum-domini-ii/ (accessed November 27, 2014).

4

Brand(ish)ing Biblical Scholars(hip)
New Testament Studies and Neoliberal Subjectivity

Who Can Be a "New Testament Scholar?"

During the summer of 2013, a short video rapidly made the rounds on social media and other internet outlets. The terms on which this video went "viral" – the "headline" – in Facebook and Twitter news feeds and in email subject lines was "Is This the Most Embarrassing Interview Fox News Has Ever Done?"[1] In what has been termed the "digital age," that a video goes viral is hardly news. However, the subject of this particular clip, as well as its reception, turned some public media attention to the academic study of the New Testament – or, at least, to those who claim to study the New Testament professionally. This "most embarrassing" video featured Reza Aslan, a professor of creative writing in California and author of a then recently released Random House book *Zealot: The Life and Times of Jesus of Nazareth*. In the video, Lauren Green, a religion correspondent for Fox News, conducted the interview with Aslan. Green hosts an online show, *Spirited Debate*, at FoxNews.com. The video, then, was not aired on broadcast or "analog" television, but was produced for online consumption only. The "most embarrassing" part? Not Aslan's scholarship, or what the public should and should not expect from a "new" popular book about Jesus, but Green's repetition of a single question to her interview subject: how is it that Aslan, who claims to be a Muslim, could write a whole book about

De-Introducing the New Testament: Texts, Worlds, Methods, Stories, First Edition.
Todd Penner and Davina C. Lopez.
© 2015 Todd Penner and Davina C. Lopez. Published 2015 by John Wiley & Sons, Ltd.

Jesus? How does that work? Should he have done that? Is the book a fair portrait of Jesus, or is it a Muslim-inflected one?

Aslan's personal performance as a "scholar of religion" included claims that he had spent "more than two decades" reading and thinking about Jesus. According to the author's note at the beginning of *Zealot*, Aslan is an Iranian American immigrant to the United States and "a kid raised in a motley family of lukewarm Muslims and exuberant atheists,"[2] had converted to evangelical Christianity whilst in high school, questioned that position in college, has reaffiliated with some Islamic roots, and now claims the stance that "today, I can confidently say that two decades of rigorous academic research into the origins of Christianity has made me a more genuinely committed disciple of Jesus of Nazareth than I ever was of Jesus Christ."[3] Despite Aslan's insistence that he was trained and that his work was "historical," Green persisted in her demands that her Muslim interviewee account for his interest in the founder of Christianity. To his credit, Aslan seemed to remain collected for the duration of the interview. However, his repetition of his position (i.e. that he was allowed to be interested in Jesus) and scholarly authority (i.e. that he was a "historian of religions" with a Ph.D.), whilst cogent and, some might posit, convincing, did not dissuade his interviewer-turned-"opponent" from maintaining that Aslan's Muslim identity be the focus of their interaction.

As a video and cultural production, Reza Aslan's interview with Lauren Green was just short and pointed enough to rapidly become the internet sensation it did. The video exhibited enough stereotypically uninformed statements about religion and the New Testament that it was likely very easy to read it as an example of media ignorance. Moreover, as Jeffrey Scholes has noted, the reality that "a different scrutiny is applied to the work of religious studies academics" because "almost everyone they meet is an expert in religion" made the video's content an easy target for online criticism.[4] It was quickly enlisted in a number of editorial quarters as a quick-flash justification for a number of already circulating hot issues in American discourse (at least, online discourse) about religion, politics, and the media. The interview was cited as another example of how Fox News chooses to air anti-Muslim sentiments in its "fair and balanced" reporting, it was yet another piece of evidence pointing to the reality that Christianity has lost its moral center, it was proof that Aslan was not a "real" Muslim, and so on. For some, Aslan vs. Fox News signified an ongoing battle between "left-wing" intellectuals and "right-wing" pundits. Green in particular was the target of much vitriol for her behavior toward Aslan. Such dynamics were thought to betray what Elizabeth Castelli, in her assessment of this exchange in *The Nation*, called a "familiar misunderstanding" – that is, the "conflation of the academic study of religion with personal religious identification."[5] Others defended Green's right – indeed, perhaps her duty – to get to the bottom of this "Muslim question" via pressing Aslan "on the issues."

The "debate" about whether one who identifies as a Muslim can write a book about Jesus proved to be highly effective for book sales. In the days following Aslan's appearance on Green's show, *Zealot* shot up in sales to the number 1 position on Amazon.com, about which Aslan stated "you can't buy this kind of publicity." According to an article that appeared in the *New York Times* (on whose bestseller list *Zealot* also appeared) following the infamous Fox interview, Aslan was "eager" to promote his book with that network – apparently his agent attempted to secure an appearance on *Fox and Friends*, a morning talk show, with no results.[6] Aslan, the founder and owner of his own eponymous media company, is no stranger to self-promotion. The publicity for *Zealot* came not from his participation in the Society of Biblical Literature or other presentations to those who would be – according to his own self-narrative – his scholarly peers in "history of religions" or "origins of Christianity" at academic conferences or other public venues. His "new biography of Jesus" became a sensation due at least in part to an extensive personal performance for the public via internet links and social media platforms. Thus, the rise of Reza Aslan's book in the public consciousness could be seen as an effort to generate attention and publicity for Reza Aslan – and not necessarily to contribute to current scholarly debates about Jesus as a historical figure with massive cultural import, or discussions about the evidence for the ancient settings that form the background(s) for portraits of the historical Jesus as a "zealot" or any other type of character, or conversations about the utility of another book about Jesus for today's world. Rather, the attention is given to the figure, the persona, of Aslan and his world, albeit through the figure of Jesus and his.

Following Aslan's sudden high-profile public appearance as a "scholar of religions" who was seeking to contribute a "new" biography of Jesus, several biblical scholars weighed in publicly via various online and print media outlets. Dale Martin reviewed *Zealot* for the *New York Times*, noting that, while Aslan exhibited the qualities of a decent creative writing professor, his scholarship on the historical Jesus was outdated, his conclusions rather tame, and the book otherwise found wanting.[7] At the *Huffington Post*, Greg Carey attempted to engage Aslan's work on its own terms, as a biblical scholar, and remarked that while the argument about Aslan's Muslim identity "had no place in public discourse," the book itself had some fairly serious "glitches" in terms of some of its historical claims, glitches that are notable enough to warrant a response from biblical scholars.[8] And Craig Evans engaged Aslan's work for *Christianity Today*, stating that, while *Zealot* was well written, the author's project "resurrected" outmoded scholarship – specifically, the 1960s thesis of S. G. F. Brandon about Jesus and zealotry – and was "riddled with errors" about which readers should be aware.[9] Other scholars and commentators engaged with Aslan's credentials and qualifications to either affirm or discredit his work as presented in *Zealot*.[10]

In our view, the criticisms of Aslan's work on Jesus have been well covered. Further, regardless of his own qualifications, the public conversation about Aslan's work on Jesus suggests that there remains a desire for investigation and debate about "the historical Jesus," his world, and how that matters in our world. However, there is another set of issues raised by "the Aslan debate" that is of concern to our project as a whole, and to this chapter in particular. As public engagements with the New Testament and early Christian literature tend to be mediated through people, the personae and performances of those people can matter a great deal. There are no unmediated, non-human introductions to or encounters with the New Testament, regardless of the media form in which such encounters take place. Ultimately, then, it is the public performance of Aslan himself, as an expert in the study of Jesus and the New Testament, and not the content of what he actually says or does not say about Jesus, that seems to have mattered the most in the so-called controversy over *Zealot*. It is, in our view, the contours of Aslan's public performance – that it was so easy to construct such a persona as a scholar of the historical Jesus via the publishing industry and social media – and particularly what that performance betrays about the particular aspects of the context in which contemporary New Testament studies takes place, that is most significant to us. In fact, it is the "branding" of Aslan, as public persona, which can tell us the most, not about Jesus, but about ourselves as scholars of the New Testament and early Christian literature. Thus, "Reza Aslan" serves as a site from which we might think critically about the study of the New Testament, and in particular appraise what is at stake for us in identifying as "scholars of the New Testament" in the first place.

We are concerned with how self-proclaimed "public" and "scholarly" figures such as Reza Aslan, and the performance of professional New Testament scholarship more broadly, serves as a signifier for an important complex of methodological issues regarding scholarly comportment and image construction in the field as a whole. The politics, procedures, and power relations inherent in constructing ourselves as "brands," as a means of constructing, managing, and performing individual and social identities, is a critical, and critically underdiscussed, aspect of how the methodological landscape of New Testament studies looks in our late-capitalist economic context. Branding functions as the means of producing what we might call a "neoliberal subjectivity" in biblical scholarship, and is, in our view, an important, if underrecognized and undertheorized, part of the methodological landscape of the field. While in other chapters we have focused on various aspects of methodological predilection, in this chapter we turn the focus onto the New Testament scholar him/herself, as "brand," which we would suggest is a critical component of "method" overall. That is to say, any discussion of method with regard to the ancient world ultimately is a reflection of, and must come back to, us. In some respect, as we do our work on texts, we are actually working on ourselves – branding ourselves, managing ourselves, and constructing ourselves in relation to others. Thus, the methods we use are reflections and extensions of, if not outright symptoms of, our self-constructions in particular historical and social contexts.

In this chapter, then, we will explore "branding" as a critical means of performing a type of neoliberal subjectivity in New Testament scholarship wherein scholars construct and promote themselves as "brands," "sellers," and "consumers" in relation to intellectual currents and content. In this schema, it is the scholarly persona, more than scholarship itself, which functions as a "product" manufactured and promoted for consumption by an "audience," construed at various moments as the "public," in the so-called marketplace of ideas. Branding and brand culture, as a mode of identity-making, is a cultural phenomenon closely associated with the development of neoliberal, late-capitalist economic discourses and cultural practices during the 20th century. Such discourses and concomitant power relationships shape us as human beings, not to mention "us" as scholars of the New Testament. To this end, we will outline neoliberalism as the broadest possible context in which identities are constructed and in which contemporary New Testament scholarship takes place, locating branding and brand culture as symptoms and expressions of neoliberal economic relationships. As this chapter concerns the construction of scholarly persona and identity, we will locate such practices in relation to branding strategies. We will also consider constructions of the "public" as an important element in constructions of the New Testament scholar. Finally, we will reflect on some of the implications of branding for de-introducing the study of the New Testament, offering questions for further consideration as part of the methodological interventions offered in this book as a whole.

Neoliberalism and the Politics of Identity

Far from being natural, universal, and timeless, ideas – and the people who create, discuss, and disseminate them – are located in time and space. They are also affected by the world(s) in which they are situated – even, one might say, produced by such world(s). This is as much the case for modern scholars and scholarship as it is for the ancient texts of the New Testament, and part of the task of biblical scholarship, at least as we see it, is to interrogate and denaturalize that which appears to be unquestionable or taken for granted as "the way it is." We understand, and aim to deploy, denaturalization as much with contemporary contexts as with ancient texts. "Context" means environment, history, and culture, broadly construed, and also includes ideological systems and material conditions. The contexts in which we live and do our work change over time. Thus, the history of New Testament scholarship has changed and "evolved," not just in terms of ideas proposed and theories and evidence used, but also in relation to ideological and material structures. The scholar, as personality, has changed over time as well, as have the audiences for which scholars produce their work.

For the purposes of furthering an understanding of the types of scholarly identity construction and performance we aim to discuss herein, we characterize the contemporary context in which the study of the New Testament takes place with the term "neoliberalism."[11] In the broadest possible sense, "neoliberalism" is helpful in that it is a descriptor denoting complex and interrelated aspects of our material circumstances, including economic, political, cultural, and social dimensions. That said, we understand "neoliberalism" to be a notoriously slippery, often ill-defined concept in contemporary discourses, both inside and outside of the academy, and particularly within the study of the New Testament. Below we attempt to provide a cursory outline of some of the key themes of neoliberalism as we understand it, followed by a discussion of some of its cultural effects that we highlight as germane to our discussion of identity and scholarly performance in New Testament studies.

"Neoliberalism" is in some sense a catch-all term, a signifier for developing socio-economic dynamics since the mid-20th century that has gained some traction as a category in academic and public discourses during the last several decades in particular. Since the mid-1970s neoliberalism, as theory and practice, has been tied fairly closely to *laissez-faire* economic policy-making across the world, contributing to the rapid global expansion of capitalism under the banner of "globalization." Such political and economic activities have been coupled with the rhetoric of democracy and freedom, especially market freedom and, ultimately, individual freedom.[12] According to geographer and social theorist David Harvey, who has attempted to define and historicize this concept, long discussed primarily by economists and political scientists, neoliberalism is "in the first instance a theory of political economic practices that proposes that human well-being can best be advanced by liberating individual entrepreneurial freedoms and skills within an institutional framework characterized by strong private property rights, free markets, and free trade."[13] In other words, neoliberalism denotes a phase in the capitalist global political economy in which the world's wealth is redistributed in such a manner as to be frequently concentrated in the hands of a few, whilst often eroding state-sponsored activities that benefit the general populace.

The discourses of neoliberalism maintain that society and its members will reach their full potential for well-being and freedom if the capitalist marketplace flourishes without restrictions or reservations. Thus, it is important that the public/state role in human activity decreases, whilst the private/corporate role increases. For example, proponents of neoliberalism work to challenge, reconfigure, and diminish the state's role in managing and regulating such institutions as education, healthcare, "welfare"/public assistance, and housing. This situation is particularly the case in the United States, where the last several decades have witnessed a systemic scaling down of state "interference" in economic activities and a palpable increase in private corporate agency and involvement in civic affairs – indeed, it now even seems "natural" that private corporations, as "people" with "voices," are heavily represented in public discourse and decision-making practices (e.g. political elections, legal discussions). A visible example of how neoliberalism might look "on the ground" lies in the proliferation of privately funded public works projects in cities. Neoliberalism cuts across partisan lines; that is, it reflects a tendency that so-called "social liberals" and "social conservatives" have in common. Harvey has designated this pattern of institutional realignment with corporate interests and attendant wealth redistribution as "accumulation by dispossession," whereby public assets (land, schools) are privatized, financialized, and managed by corporations instead of governments.[14] Those entities thought to impede the unfettered progress and reach of the market become a target for eradication. As a result, the boundaries between "public" and "private" are eroded, and the market functions as that which has a profound impact on shaping human actions and interactions. In fact, an important aspect of neoliberalism is its tendency to bring as much of human action as possible into the realm of the market. This includes basic articulations of human identity – who we are, how we narrate ourselves as socially located in time and space, and how we relate to each other and the world around us.

A critical aspect of neoliberalism is to be found in its integration into, and equation with, cultural norms. This facet is manifested chiefly by pervasive rhetoric about freedom, progress, and choice that closely aligns, in the United States at least, with the discourse of personal freedom and choice that has long been a vital part of public engagement. That is, in a neoliberal framework the eradication of state control is justified by appeals to maximizing individual freedom in, and through, the freedom of the market. The progression of the market into every part of life is presented as that which is the logical and most beneficial development of economic relationships under capitalism. And the reduction of state control in favor of market proliferation

175

is articulated as that which offers maximum choice for consumers, which in turn precipitates maximum well-being of individual bodies and the social "body." At the same time, neoliberalism seems especially difficult to describe and critique, perhaps as a result of its appearance as a totalizing system – what Jason Hickel and Arsalan Khan, following Jim McGuigan, have called a "cosmology" that is assumed to be natural, inevitable, and universal, as well as that in which we are asked to have "faith" as "sovereign consumers."[15] That is, in hiding its human dimensions, neoliberalism appears to be that which is beyond human control. In neoliberalism, consumption is part of the logic that "posits market solutions for political and economic problems, celebrates the 'consumer' as the supreme agent of change, and obscures the coercive dimensions of capitalism that generate the very problems that these forms of consumer activism aim to remedy."[16] The maintenance of neoliberalism is dependent upon rhetoric insisting that the present world order is "the way it is and should be;" that there is not, and should not be, an alternative to this order; and that this order is the sole option for the world as a whole.

Thus, we are shaped by neoliberal rhetoric and values, which appear to be simply a part of the natural landscape of our lives. However, neoliberalism did not become "the way it is and should be" overnight. Following World War II, and especially since the 1970s, the rhetoric of neoliberalism circulated throughout social institutions – what Louis Althusser would have termed "ideological apparatuses" – such as the media, religious organizations, and higher education. The proliferation of neoliberal ways of thinking and knowing in multiple arenas of social life fostered a "climate of opinion in support of neoliberalism as the exclusive guarantor of freedom"[17] that resulted in the reification of neoliberal "cosmology" and the disappearance of the human element in its articulation. Herein the rhetoric of guaranteeing individual freedoms through reducing state control and suppressing non-market institutions was very effective in masking shifts in class dynamics. As we have noted, this rhetoric was not so much about economic activity per se, but rather took on moral overtones regarding such values as freedom and choice – values that are central to contemporary identity construction. Such rhetoric functioned in part both to allay fears about capitalism and to cultivate anxiety about its possible alternatives, thus limiting the imagination concerning what might be possible in human social, economic, and political activity to the range of options offered under capitalism. It also has functioned to remake human constructions of identity and performance in the image of the corporation, and vice versa, using ever-improving technological tools to commodify, assimilate, repackage, and profit from human identities and interactions. We are most concerned with this particular effect and set of dynamics for our discussion of performances of scholarly identity in New Testament studies, and we turn to these issues below.

Identity and the market are inextricably linked under neoliberal capitalist discourses and practices. The market's reach extends to personal and collective identity, which renders identity and culture as products that can be created, bought, sold, and traded according to market values and processes. As John and Jean Comaroff have argued, one of the effects of the spread of neoliberalism across the world has been its transformation of culture and identity into marketable commodities, in what they have termed an "identity industry" called "Ethnicity, Inc."[18] From the branding of "Scottishness" (for example), to the marketing of "traditional" Amazonian healing practices to visitors, to the production of "native" and/or "ancestral" African objects and spaces as authentic cultural attractions for consumption by tourists and other "outsiders," Ethnicity, Inc. arises out of a complicated and multivalent dialectic between the incorporation of identity and the commodification of culture.[19] Herein "authentic" cultures can reclaim and repackage their "own" elements that render cultural differences visible, desirable, and consumable, whilst remaining faithful to the market as well. Neoliberal subjectivity, focused on freedom of expression through performances of authenticity and difference, is constructed through the manufacturing and distribution of cultural objects, practices, and places that are fetishized and "trademarked" as belonging to certain groups. In fact, the selling of culture and identity-markers as commodities is a critical means by which to participate in the marketplace, which in turn appears as that which celebrates "heritage" and "diversity." Humans become entrepreneurs and advertisers for their own identities and cultures, which insiders and outsiders both consume under the rubrics of freedom of cultural expression, authentic cultural experience, and cultural tourism.

The buying and selling of identity and culture points to the reach of the market into that which is intangible, such as experience, knowledge, and ways of producing and performing the self. In this "identity economy," the differences between production and consumption are made smaller. In order to construct an identity and subjectivity that is intelligible, one must consume the appropriate cultural objects, clothing, food, and so on, all of which are readily available in the marketplace, and are at times produced by the consumer her/himself. Thus, African peoples who are related, however tangentially, to the Zulu can participate in consolidating, packaging, and marketing various indigenous worldviews and lifeways under a minted and trademarked concept called the "Zulu Kingdom," which signifies an intelligible bounded place with people and objects visible and readable to others as "Zulu," and is complete with its own advertising campaign and tagline: "The Zulu Kingdom Awaits You."[20] We note in this slogan the explicit appeal to outsiders, "You," who will ostensibly function as the consumers of "Zulu Kingdom" as a place – and product. Under neoliberalism, the "Zulu Kingdom" can open for business, as can other cultural configurations across the world such as regions of Spain, China, and Canada.

We also note that the commodification of cultural identity is not by any means limited to "exotic" peoples. The linking of culture to tourism and consumption also takes place, for example, in the packaging of particular regions of the United States as cultural destinations. "I Love NY" sells the heritage and culture of New York State (beyond New York City, which has its own "brand"), and features largely defunct glass and ceramic production, winemaking, and American history, including the history of historically underrepresented people such as women, African Americans, and LGBT people. "From mountains to museums," New York "has it all," with the emphasis that the state is especially welcoming of LGBT visitors.[21] The repackaging of Texas as a tourist destination features the slogan "It's Like a Whole Other Country," which plays on both Texas's history and contemporary cultural differences from the rest of the United States. "Texas" is commodified as the land of cowboys, livestock, and rich American historical sites, not to mention "over 300 miles of beaches, some without a single bootprint."[22] In the case of both New York® and Texas®, the states are populated with stable populations of "authentic" New Yorkers and Texans, the "things to do" are narrated as authentically belonging to the identity of that state, and the unique objects indigenous to the landscape (wine, barbecue) are highlighted as "only here" items. The complex contours of culture, identity, and history are consolidated and naturalized into an easily recognizable and consumable packaged product, which in turn informs how culture, identity, and history are configured. One purchases and consumes the experience of culture and identity, which shapes both the identity and culture being consumed and that of the consumer. Of course, hidden from view in all of this celebration and consumption of authentic, homespun regionalism is another palpable effect of global capitalism: the ubiquitous chain stores and restaurants that are everywhere the same and dot the landscape of even the quaintest, most "real" tourist destinations.

To be sure, the dialectical relationship between identity, culture, and the market that produces neoliberal subjectivity is neither wholly "positive" nor wholly "negative," and can be seen as both appealing and disconcerting. Through alignment with neoliberal discourses of individual (rather than communal) agency, responsibility, and freedom via the promise of the market, neoliberal subjectivity presents both an opportunity to locate new forms of empowerment and recognition and a challenge to collective mobilization. Neoliberal subjectivity, such as that of Ethnicity, Inc., "has *both* insurgent possibility *and* a tendency to deepen prevailing lines of inequality, the capacity *both* to enable *and* to disable, the power *both* to animate *and* annihilate."[23] That is, late-capitalist neoliberal subjectivity is a complex endeavor: on the one hand, so-called "non-dominant" identities can become visible and consumable in the marketplace, which can function to enhance affective and identitarian organization. On the other, the market can "handle," and even participates in the manufacturing of, such "dissenting" identities that seem, on the surface, to challenge neoliberal values but are actually easily assimilated into their framework.

Comaroff and Comaroff extend their analysis of Ethnicity, Inc. to wider contexts such as "Nationality, Inc." and "Divinity, Inc.," which denote the commodification of national and religious identities under neoliberalism. Again, assimilation and resistance are part of the same process of identity formation in an age of neoliberalism. We would also extend this analysis to include other categories of identity such as "Gender, Inc.," "Sexual Orientation, Inc.," and "New Testament Scholars, Inc." While it might seem as though the recent history of social movements and "dissent" has effectively challenged gendered, racialized, heterosexist status quo hierarchies under neoliberal capitalism, it is also the case that such identities, alongside their visible configurations and their attendant accouterments, are in some respect possible due to capitalism and are produced as that which is available for consumption.

Neoliberal capitalism, with its expansive market reach and discursive power, has maintained a structure wherein the construction and performance of identities and culture are at once collectively homogenous and intensely "individual." As discourse and practice, neoliberalism did not create the varieties of human identities and cultures, but its discourses have taken them up and redeployed them to further the reach of the market.[24] And there is no imaginable alternative in view, as it has been shown to be difficult, if not impossible, to mount effective resistance to neoliberal logics, discourses, and impulses. This situation is due, at least in part, to neoliberalism being as much a war of ideas as a material reality; neoliberalism's utopian promise of endless prosperity, progress, and freedom is, in fact, difficult to resist. That said, the privatization of human services and the eradication of state power have precipitated a shift from structural analysis to individual responsibility. In other words, as Angela Davis has noted, neoliberal discourse highlights individual acts of racism (for example) as the problem of those particular situations and those people's particular performances of identity and culture, rather than understanding racism as a complex of institutional and structural issues that might shape those situations in decisive ways.[25] Thus, it is the individuals, and not the issues, that are addressed. Individuals are highlighted for their attitudes and behaviors, for which they must "take responsibility," whilst the broader institutional

179

dynamics that may have given permission for such attitudes and behaviors go largely unaddressed. So, in the United States at least, while some people of color are highlighted for their achievements and advancement, and some white people are singled out for their poor behavior in relationship to minority groups, "racism," as a historically potent category that denotes deeply rooted structural relations of power and privilege, is reconfigured as an identity issue. Similarly, what used to be called "women's liberation" is now part of discourses about women's individual capacities and responsibilities; meanwhile, patriarchy and misogyny as pervasive structural issues are forgotten or configured as "over." And the rhetoric about the how the poor have created their own poverty by not taking responsibility for cultivating their own upward class mobility and prosperity has deepened under neoliberalism. As the neoliberal age exists at the so-called "end of history," it has effectively mystified, if not obscured, the historical contingencies of identity formation, power relationships, and patterns of domination and oppression.

As the main venue for public and social interaction is the market, social struggles in a neoliberal age are framed as that which concerns adequate visibility and representation of certain identities and/or categories of persons, rather than a redistribution of material wealth or a restructuring of economic relationships. As Nancy Fraser has argued, the struggles to change culture via representation of non-dominant identities in a framework of "diversity," rather than change the political economy as a whole, in what she calls the "turn to recognition" have "dovetailed all too neatly with a rising neoliberalism that wanted nothing more than to repress all memory of social egalitarianism."[26] Writing about feminist organizing in particular, Fraser notes that the subordination of struggles for redistribution to struggles for recognition has hurt, rather than helped, feminist organizing – and has even unwittingly served to bolster neoliberal capitalist expansion. That is, the rise of second-wave feminism, in theory and in practice, coincided with shifts in the capitalist political economy that wound up accommodating and enabling the consolidation of "women's issues and struggles" into a visible, intelligible discourse. These shifts also encouraged a decoupling of feminist claims to recognition for women from claims to justice via restructuring the economic landscape. This separation of cultural and identity-based claims from economic ones resulted in the resignification of "feminism" under neoliberalism. Thus, a critique of patriarchy and androcentrism *without* a critique of the capitalist social order in which patriarchy and androcentrism are embedded was made possible. As such, women could make strides toward equality in a separate "cultural" sphere, infusing all of cultural life and identity with visibility about women and gender, while in the "economic" sphere the rising influence of the market and structural inequalities between rich and poor continued to proceed in a relatively uninterrupted manner.

Further, "feminist" became an important identity-marker that, in some of its public manifestations, provides a slight critique that capitalism could then absorb and adapt to include. For example, criticism concerning the lack of women's presence and advancement in the workplace is easily incorporated into a neoliberal framework. The increase of women's visibility on the job as wage-earners effectively ties "feminism" to capitalism without addressing the underlying issues about economic structure. Companies who employ women, in turn, are able to deploy the discourse of equality and fairness in the service of attracting more consumers and accumulating yet more capital.

For Fraser, as for Davis, social organizing in the present must take structural concerns into account. Yet such organizing also must contend with the ways in which categories that are already culturally and historically contingent, such as those related to race, class, gender, and a whole host of other markers of identity and social hierarchy, have taken on different significations in neoliberal capitalism. For both, as well, sustained neoliberal financial crisis also indicates that struggles solely for recognition lack the force needed to contend with economic transformation. Effective critique of neoliberal discourses and practices could include, to use Fraser's terms, recognition *and* redistribution, or cultural *and* economic dimensions, whilst recognizing the largely false boundaries between those spheres. While it is clear that it would be futile to wax nostalgic about the effectiveness of struggles for civil rights or social justice in the past, it is also not the case that searches for viable alternatives to the neoliberal status quo ought to be abandoned.

We would extend Davis's analysis of racism, and Fraser's analysis of feminism, under neoliberalism to notice a pattern of identity construction that is certainly relevant to the production and performance of scholarly personae in New Testament studies. First, we note that the politics of identity formation are linked to, and even dovetail with, neoliberal capitalism. This is the case whether one is explicitly discussing "class," calls oneself a "Marxist," uses "ideological criticism" to discuss ancient texts, or denies that economic realities have anything to do with identity formation at all, in the past or the present. In our view, it is worth considering that the ways we articulate our own performances of identity as scholars, while imbued with elements of authenticity and authority, to be sure, are also always expressions of power relationships under neoliberal capitalism and its apparatuses. Further, attempts to separate out discourses of "culture" – and, by extension, "religion" – from neoliberalism serve, in our view, to hide, and extend, a naturalizing and totalizing system that has religious dimensions of its own and incorporates its own forms of dissent and critique. It is also worth considering how cultural or identitarian arguments about the contours of the field, its history, and its future do not fully address the neoliberal capitalist dimensions of the discipline itself. Additionally, it is worth considering how we, as scholars of the ancient world and modern interpretation, participate as producers and consumers of identity and knowledge in an age of neoliberalism, as well as what kinds of identity and knowledge we produce and consume, how we do so, and to what ends.

Thus far we have aimed to notice and describe the constructions and performances of identity under neoliberalism, broadly conceived. We understand that, rhetorically, the terms "neoliberalism," "identity," and "culture" all enjoy a complicated and convoluted semantic range. The term "neoliberalism," in particular, is often used in a derogatory manner and signifies an implicit dissatisfaction with, and criticism of, capitalism. Whether we liken neoliberalism to "capitalism with the gloves off," as Robert McChesney would have it,[27] or see it as a – or even *the* – positive force for prosperity, progress, and freedom in an era of globalization, or perhaps as something in between, it is critical, in our view, to attempt to understand the power relationships and economic structures that shape our work and lives as scholars of the New Testament. For the last several decades, those power relationships and economic structures have been defined by neoliberalism. We concur with Noam Chomsky that neoliberalism is not by any means "new" in that historically the gap between those who "have" and those who "have not" has rarely, if ever, been narrowed or closed.[28] However, we note that at the so-called end of history it is critically important to consider the historical contingencies and exigencies of relations of power that shape how human beings articulate notions of self, agency, and community. The logic of the neoliberal market hides persistent hierarchies and inequalities while claiming to address and alleviate discrepancies in status through identity-based consumerism.

While we have only scratched the surface of neoliberal subjectivity, we want to highlight, again, the relationship between constructions of identity and the market, or the construction of identity through production and consumption. In an age of neoliberalism, the boundaries between cultural production and capitalist business practices are blurred dramatically. Cultures and human bodies are commodities, and are treated as such; humans, as individuals with "something to sell," engage in self-articulation in large and small ways, through mounting advertising campaigns and participating in technologically advanced communicative platforms such as social media in order to "get the word out." These strategies serve as means of performing, and promoting, the self as a "brand" to which consuming audiences are hailed into loyalty. We submit that New Testament scholars, as branded "experts" and "intellectuals," are participants in such constructions of identity. Branding is a critical, if also ambivalent, lens through which we might understand and appraise how performances of the study of the New Testament are currently configured in relationship to scholars, audiences, and subject matter. We turn to these issues in the section that follows.

Branding as a Practice of Neoliberal Subjectivity

As we have been describing above, "neoliberalism" denotes the broadest possible material context in which the study of the New Testament takes place. With its emphasis on the deregulation of corporations, the privatization of human services, endless competition, and personal and collective entrepreneurship, neoliberalism enables the rhetoric and logic of the market to infuse the myriad of social interactions and relationships that comprise everyday life. Within neoliberalism, human subjectivity takes on forms that are deeply imbricated with consumer capitalist discourses and practices. Technological advancements such as the internet and social media render it ever easier to perform identity in ways that are congruent with the commodification of the self. Under these rubrics the self, as product, is conveyed through marketing and branding strategies. In this section we will explore the contours of branding as a means of articulating neoliberal subjectivity. The *branded* neoliberal self is a significant site from which we can think about performances of scholarly identity in New Testament studies.

Neoliberal practices and rhetoric are not enforced solely "from above," but, like all cosmologies, are naturalized largely by consent and participation "from below." The reach of the market into everyday life enables a myriad of small acts that serve to both inform subjectivity and affirm neoliberalism. Coupled with the rhetoric of freedom and progress in neoliberalism is the rhetoric of unlimited access to, and participation in, such small acts in the marketplace – especially through the flow of information in many directions. This flow is made easier through advancements in information technology that enable users to conduct their business with ever more speed, style, and seamless interconnectivity. Indeed, bringing all of human activity into the domain of the market necessitates "technologies of information creation and capacities to accumulate, store, transfer, analyze, and use massive databases to guide decisions in the global marketplace."[29] To this end, neoliberalism has been extremely friendly to the pursuit of information technologies – the predominance of Silicon Valley entrepreneurs and internet startups is only one symptom of the compatibility of information technology with consumer capitalism. The congruence between networked communication and the procedures of the market provides neoliberalism with a technological infrastructure that enables both endless communication and endless wealth accumulation.

Neoliberal subjectivity is expressed in part through such "communicative capitalism,"[30] wherein the self is constructed through communication and networking with others. The proliferation of information technology has imbued neoliberal capitalism with communicative dimensions that make it easier for everyone to be a producer and a consumer at the same time, which points, again, to the blurring of the boundaries between culture and economics. Another important eroded boundary is that which is thought to exist between the consumer and the citizen. As we have explored above, contemporary identity construction is in part predicated not necessarily on what one *is* or *does*, but on what one *sells* and *buys*. In neoliberal capitalism, the market provides ample opportunity to perform what Roopali Mukherjee and Sarah Banet-Weiser have termed "commodity activism," wherein consumers can participate in market activity that functions to mark identity.[31] One's consumer choices – be they Apple technology products, organic produce, rainbow flags, sweatshop-free clothing, hybrid cars, or "pink" breast-cancer awareness objects – comprise expressions of identity that can be shared with, and approved by, other like-minded consumers. ("I share that I shop at Whole Foods, and thus I am someone who cares about the environment." Or: "I share that I am familiar with N. T. Wright's books, and thus I am someone who is an educated, theologically engaged student of the New Testament." Or: "I share that I have read *In Memory of Her*, and thus I am someone who is committed to feminist New Testament scholarship.") Likewise, in neoliberal communicative capitalism it is easy to express infinite political views and opinions through regular participation in, and sharing of, surveys, online petitions, blog posts, news articles, and other bits of information that consumers can customize and consolidate to fit an expression of the self as an "engaged" citizen. Jodi Dean has observed that such online expressions have taken the place of collective organizing and political activity in the "offline" sphere and contribute to the "fantasy" that one is actually participating in an unprecedented freedom and abundance of information and democratic process when one is actually letting the technology do the work.[32] Robert McChesney has noted that digital technologies constitute a site where democracy and capitalism are in tension.[33] It is clear that a hallmark of communicative capitalism lies in its dovetailing with the processes by which identities are constructed and advertised for public consumption.

Commodity activism is but one example of how neoliberal subjectivity depends more upon the construction of an image that exudes an individual's authentic engagement with issues, experiences, and objects than upon substantive content or social interaction. In this framework it is enough to shop, and more importantly, to share one's consumer choices – to display the accouterments of identity – via communicative platforms. Expressions of consumption of, and loyalty to, certain things, ways of life, and political views in turn bolster authenticity and credibility and, importantly, contribute to the self as "brand." In the language of advertising, a "brand" is a complex of symbols, terms, and other features comprising a discourse that aims to stabilize and to naturalize associations of feelings, experiences, attitudes, and ways of life with a certain product, which then sets that product apart from others and renders it easily readable and accessible to consuming audiences. The brand is one of the most elemental signifiers in the rhetorics of advertising and marketing – a brand is as much about a story as it is about an object. Brand stories transform objects into commodities, and transform ordinary experiences into brand identification. Consumers' resonance with these stories results in making a brand successful. Successful brands exhibit consistency, cultivate loyalty, and accumulate cultural and economic capital. They are immediately recognizable to their audience by their visual rhetoric (logos, colors), slogans, and packaging. Brands are memorable: consumers need not have an advertisement for the brand in front of them to remember the story and recognize the brand's presence in the marketplace. Consumption of brands bolsters those brands' reputations and affirms the story. And in the neoliberal era where social media is paramount to brand management, consumers are critical to the success of the story, as brands are explicitly linked to their audiences through visibility on Facebook postings, blog entries, YouTube videos, and other means of sharing consumer practices. In fact, in a neoliberal era companies use "brand ambassadors" – who tend to be bloggers or other heavy users of social media – as a means to bolster their brand; in exchange for free access to the products, brand ambassadors weave the products into their blog posts, share their consumption of said products in their Twitter feeds or Facebook statuses, and otherwise promote the products as an integrated part of life. This form of marketing acknowledges the power of the consumer in making and breaking a brand by contributing to its story. Brands, then, are not only successful stories in their own right – consumers become part of the stories of beloved brands, and brands become part of the narratives that consumers construct about their own lives.

Thus, "branding" is an especially significant aspect of subject formation in neoliberal culture, where it not only applies to objects but also to people, principally by means of self-construction and presentation to others and publics via technologically advanced communicative platforms. Branding is a cultural phenomenon more than an economic strategy, although admittedly in a neoliberal framework the line separating culture and economics is blurry. Branding denotes the process of creating and managing relationships between brands, producers, and consumers through the development and dissemination of rhetoric concerning brands. These relationships are predicated upon constructions of reality that feature connections and resonances with, and desires for, brand experiences. Branding establishes the affective terms on which brands are experienced – ultimately, what is appealing about brands is not the commodities as such, but what those commodities signify about identity, and especially how those commodities fit into performances of identity. For example, consuming Starbucks coffee is much less about the coffee product than it is about the desire to consume a middle-class, environmentally thoughtful and somewhat "hip" experience, identity, and lifestyle associated with the coffee, as Starbucks participates in a highly effective branding campaign that features narratives about what consuming this particular brand of coffee "does" affectively.[34] Whether or not Starbucks actually does what its narrative says it will is not the main issue, as the affective reality narrated by its branding practices is persuasive enough to generate customer desire, resonance, and loyalty. As a rhetorical strategy, branding provides the persuasive narratives that generate the affect and experience of brands, which cultivates bonds with consumers, which in turn informs the narratives that consumers tell about themselves. If we take branding seriously, then we also must take seriously that part of its power in neoliberal culture lies in loosening the boundaries between what is "real" and what is "unreal" in the making of such stories.

Branding – as a powerful form of rhetoric, as storytelling and mythmaking with an especially broad reach – should not be underestimated. Brand narratives provide a lens through which consumers can see themselves in relation to the brands they use, and these narratives take place in as many places as the market can reach. According to Sarah Banet-Weiser, branding "impacts the way we understand who we are, how we organize ourselves in the world, what stories we tell ourselves about ourselves."[35] Branding provides a primary context for meaning-making and identity formation in neoliberal culture: "brand cultures are spaces in which politics are practiced, identities are made, art is created, and cultural value is deliberated."[36] The reach of the market into every sphere of life has shaped the spaces in which meaning-making and identity formation take place in contemporary culture. While spaces where consumption happens – coffee shops, restaurants, supermarkets, and bookstores – have taken on narratives about meaning and purpose, branding has also entered spaces where meaning-making traditionally has taken place that are not ordinarily associated with capitalist business practices. As mentioned above, ethnic groups, nations, and regions of the United States participate in identity consolidation and construction through branding. However, colleges, museums, and religious and political institutions are also branded spaces, and in many cases branding strategies have helped to secure visibility and market share for such places that have not necessarily been easily intelligible in the neoliberal imagination.[37] Consumers of education, art, religion, and politics are in effect participating in narratives about those institutions, and are adding experiences of those brands to their own narratives of self and world.

Increasingly, also, "private" spaces such as homes are sites where branding can take place, and the human subject itself is a rich site for branding in the neoliberal era. Self-branding, or "personal branding," is the application of branding principles and strategies to constructions and presentations of personal identity. Often associated with image-building for career purposes, branding the person is critically important as a means of constructing and performing neoliberal subjectivity. Branding the self involves creating an image and narrative of the self, as subject, that creates and manages perception, affect, and desire for the self as product and commodity. As a business strategy, personal branding has a substantial history over the last century.[38] And as with neoliberalism as a whole, the present manner in which all of life can be reached by the market and branded accordingly has a genealogical relationship to marketing and advertising as well as the emergence of identity politics. The branding of identity in its contemporary forms is linked both to the crystallization of identitarian discourses tied to social movements since the mid-twentieth century, on the one hand, and niche marketing, on the other, as "[t]he double mobilization that characterized US counterculture, where difference was an important part of politicization and resistance cultures while simultaneously mobilized by consumer capitalism for individuated markets, also made possible niche marketing in the later part of the century."[39] Niche marketing concentrates on narrating brands through the involvement of so-called real people. Focused on difference, particularity, and the specificity of social location as opposed to a universal human subject, niche marketing acknowledges that consumers can be divided into individual groups based on race, class, ethnicity, gender, geographical location, age, sexual orientation, and so on.

In terms of branding, identity-based niches are located and articulated through distinction from each other as well as from the "white, middle-class" mass consumer of the pre-identity-politics era. In her discussion of the history of the "authentic" branded self, Banet-Weiser observes that

> though consumer culture was often positioned as part of the white, male establishment against which so many groups protested, it was also consumer culture that provided the context – albeit in a reimagined way – for identity-based movements to articulate political and cultural aims. A politicized notion of "difference" – especially in response to what some saw as the stifling conformity of mass production and consumption – was, in fact, doubly mobilized. The counterculture, civil rights movement, second-wave feminist movement, and others mobilized politicized difference in protest, but advertisers also recognized its flexibility and profitability in the marketplace.[40]

That is, while in the past advertising would narrate as broad an audience as possible into the story of the brand, niche marketing links the broad, mass consumer to the "dominant social position" against which the particular identities embedded in niches are positioned. Moreover, the principles claimed by countercultural social movements – freedom, equality, progress – have also been claimed by the market and commodified under neoliberalism. Thus, niche marketing pursues the discourses of recognition, freedom, diversity, and visibility. Minority groups – women, Hispanic Americans, LGBT people – who might experience underrepresentation and invisibility in the broader culture are invited to feel at home, and to feel "visible" and "equal" and "free" and "progressive," with niche brands. Whatever is "resistant" about countercultural claims is "resistant" according to the logic of the market – which may or may not be "resistant" at all. The articulation of identity politics and the honing of niche markets and branding strategies work in tandem; the recognition of minority communities and underrepresented groups in the public sphere translates well into market categories.

The dovetailing of identity politics with branding strategies resonates with Fredric Jameson's contention that postmodernism is more appropriately named "the cultural logic of late capitalism."[41] That is, changes in culture are linked to changes in the market that have produced an increased emphasis on the image or simulacrum rather than that which is represented, a tenuous relationship with historical contingencies and realities, and the alignment with technological advancement and connectivity that stands in for globalized late capitalism. In terms of neoliberal cultural logic, it appears natural that branding would extend even further than social identities to personal and individual subjects. Thus the branded self is a site where identity politics plays out in the marketplace. Herein the boundaries between the self as part of culture and the self as part of the market are not so clear. In terms of narrative, the authenticity and consistency of the self – through the communication of the self's affective relationships with other people, brands, places, and ideas – becomes part of a personal branding strategy.

As a brand, the self is an entrepreneur, producer, and consumer at the same time. Branding in the neoliberal era is not so much about delivering content as it is about promotion of various relational aspects of self via content-delivery platforms. Branding the self becomes a way to make a profit (whether in financial or cultural capital) and, especially, to serve as a means to deliver more capital to corporations and keep the flow of money moving into the hands of the wealthy. Using the same rhetorical strategies as branding on a broader scale, the branded self tells a story that cultivates relationships as a means of commodification. At the same time, the representation of people as "entrepreneurs of the self" naturalizes and hides the material circumstances that necessitate branding in the first place.

Within neoliberal communicative capitalism, technology and social media represent a primary locus of self-branding strategies that are used for marketing the experience of self, ideas, and world. Herein branding is a means to manage and "care for" the self. Alice Marwick assesses the uses of social media to articulate identities in our neoliberal era, and argues that the free market serves as a form of governmentality in the Foucauldian sense.[42] For Michel Foucault, governmentality includes "the totality of practices, by which one can constitute, define, organize, [and] instrumentalize the strategies which individuals in their liberty can have in regard to each other."[43] Governmentality is a means to govern people through providing available technological options that they might use to express themselves and their relationships, thus imbuing personal action with political power. For Foucault, a "technology" (from the Greek *technē*) is a practice that is governed by an aim or goal. In the case of capitalism, technologies make it possible for people to express themselves in categories that are aligned with business ideals. In this framework governmentality is a means by which people are able to willingly perform, manage, and regulate their own behaviors according to the technological options available. As Marwick notes, while in earlier eras public schooling was a way to regulate children so that they might work in factories, thus aligning their behavior with industrial capitalism, the proliferation and use of Web 2.0 technologies "function similarly, teaching their users to be good corporate citizens in the post-industrial, post-union world by harnessing marketing techniques to boost attention and visibility."[44] While the contours of labor have shifted dramatically with the rise and dominance of the technology industry, requiring a mobile, flexible, and self-sufficient workforce that is attuned to, and willing to learn with, rapid change, performances of the self have altered accordingly. Again, how identity "works" is linked to capitalist discourses and practices.

Branding the self through the use of social media is a means by which the neoliberal subject is brought to life. Branding is a highly effective "technology of the self," which, according to Foucault, constitutes the practices people use to help govern themselves according to certain idealized forms circulating in culture. Technologies of the self are ways of self-regulation "from below," rather than capitulation to regulation "from above." Through willing and comfortable participation in bringing the logic of the market into as many areas of life as possible, the ideal neoliberal subject is a self-governing one, performing self-centeredness, entrepreneurialism, visibility, and availability for consumption by other similarly branded selves. The narratives of self that are expressed through, for example, online shopping (and sharing what one purchases), Facebook status updates, Twitter entries, blog posts, and other visible online writings (e.g. *Huffington Post* columns) render the neoliberal subject intelligible and consumable along these lines. Online expressions of opinion through blogging on recent developments in parenting tools or the archaeology of the Galilee region serve the same purpose: such declarations become part of an overall narrative of self as brand. We also note that the neoliberal subject is defined by their use *or nonuse* of Web 2.0 technologies, exemplified by such exchanges as "Do you have a blog? What is the address?" or "What do you mean, you're not on Facebook? How will anyone find you?" or "You don't use Twitter? I didn't get it at first but now I can't live without it."[45] Students, undergraduate and graduate alike, are urged to brand themselves online for greater visibility on the job market, which places the responsibility for getting a job on how well they construct and promote themselves as a product (through, e.g., Linkedin or Academia.edu). Social media has become a naturalized technology of the self and a conversation topic in the offline world (e.g. "Did you see what so-and-so said on Facebook/that blog/Twitter?"). As a way to brand the self it is ubiquitous; it creates and manages personae and embeds an ideal neoliberal subject even when people are not actively engaged with it.

We want to assure our readers, at this point, that by discussing the ideas and issues in this chapter we are not making a case "for" or "against" neoliberalism, identity politics, branding, and/or social media. Rather, we want to make the case for paying at least some attention to these issues and ideas in our disciplinary configuration. All of our scholarly work is now conducted within this framework of neoliberalism and its attendant technologies of the self. That is to say, despite what some who promote "resistance" hermeneutics might insist, there is no means of doing biblical scholarship that is not in some way informed by neoliberalism, except through trying to imagine how biblical scholarship might look from another framework or standpoint. Our reason for drawing attention to branding as a means of inhabiting neoliberal subjectivity is precisely that we need to become aware of, reflect upon, and make connections between the current conditions under which we produce our scholarship and ourselves.

In our view, the point of thinking about neoliberalism in relation to the construction of one's scholarly persona in New Testament scholarship is not to decide that it is "good" or "bad." In exploring some of the contours of our context as we have attempted to do here, however, we do observe that neoliberalism is "contradictory" in the Marxist sense of that understanding. That is to say, neoliberalism contains within it a proliferation of wealth and status and extreme poverty at the same time; it promises "diversity" and recognition of multiple identities while creating the market options by which such diversity can be achieved; it also ensures social and cultural status and freedom through branding "individualism" while managing and surveilling the communicative means by which such standing can be reached. And rhetorically, all of this is presented as natural, as the way it is and should be, with no desirable or possible alternatives. De-introducing, as a means of denaturalizing and defamiliarizing that which we take for granted or think is unquestionable, for us emphasizes the cultivation of a critical awareness concerning these dynamics as we conduct our own work as students of the New Testament, Christian origins, and early Christianity.

Branding New Testament Scholars(hip)

It is critical to remember that branding, as a rhetorical strategy, is much more about narrative representation than reality – and when branding is effective, representation and reality appear to be, and are reified as, one and the same. As part of fostering a critical awareness about the larger conditions that intersect with the work of New Testament studies, we note three interrelated aspects of branding, as means of constructing and expressing neoliberal subjectivity, that we think are important to keep in mind as we consider the contours of scholarly identity in the field. In other words, we want to highlight here the rhetorics of scholarly persona as framed and shaped by neoliberalism. First, neoliberal subjectivity emphasizes self-centeredness and self-promotion in the "attention economy." As with branding of all commodities, what matters is that the narrative of self is constructed in such a way as to nurture a relationship of some sort with an audience. The audience, as co-branded participants in this relationship of production and consumption, serves to affirm self-promotional strategies as effective. Second, and building on this point, neoliberal subjectivity, particularly in a Web 2.0 world, constructs the authority of the self in direct relationship to the popularity of the representation. In this respect the content of the narrative matters less than how many views, "likes," and/or "retweets" the story (and storyteller) can accumulate, which in turn affirms the story's veracity and value. Third, and importantly, branding is an important conduit for the construction, stabilization, and performance of authentic identities that are narrated as informing how a neoliberal subject sees, and consumes, the world. As students of the New Testament, we, too, inhabit and perform neoliberal subjectivity. Below we explore the ways in which we see this manifested in the field, concentrating on three interrelated areas of the contemporary methodological landscape of the discipline: negotiations of identity politics and social location in scholarship, methodological identitarianism, and scholarship for "public" audiences. Far from being isolable, these three areas come together in various ways as scholars narrate themselves and their work in the neoliberal era.

Branding in – and of – the study of the New Testament is an important part of constructing and experiencing the world in a neoliberal framework. In this respect our selection and performance of personal and communal identities in New Testament scholarship, whether through ethnic or otherwise "minoritized" hermeneutics and exegesis, methodological identitarianism, or "public" engagements, dovetail with the cultural power and prowess of the market. None of the ways that we articulate self and world are "just there" or beyond defense. "De-introducing" in this respect is about identifying the larger conditions that inform the categories we use in our work, and not necessarily about taking a stance one way or another. While we cannot claim to be "neutral" or "objective" about these larger conditions, we also do not see it as our task to judge, for it is precisely in "taking a stance" that one is fully operating under a neoliberal paradigm. As we understand it, neoliberal capitalist discourses and practices both contain the technologies for resistance and have the capacity to assimilate, and adapt in response to, resistance and dissent. Neoliberalism already provides the options to produce the "counter" in counterculture, the "resistance" to dominant culture. Positioning oneself as either "pro-" or "anti-" certain discourses within and about neoliberalism serves only to hide this particular dynamic and, in the discourse of the market, feeds a narrative about countercultural branding. That said, we also would caution against taking a stance that there is no "hope" or imagination concerning social change vis-à-vis neoliberalism, for that, too, only serves to reify the idea that there is nothing "beyond" the framework in which we are situated.

Identity and social location: Ethnic exegesis and beyond

One predominant example of where scholarly persona in the field of New Testament studies is branded, and thus presents a persuasive narrative that is expressive of neoliberal subjectivity, lies in the turn to identity and social location as a means by which to conduct biblical scholarship. It is undeniable that the last several decades have been characterized by major shifts in the field in terms of methodological orientation and outlook. Identitarian modes of biblical scholarship, often characterized by specific affinity and alignment with expressions of identity along the lines of race, class, gender, sexual orientation, ethnic location, colonial status, religious affiliation, and so on, have privileged the articulation of social location as a primary means by which biblical texts are encountered. Herein the persona of the scholar, as a "flesh and blood" reader with a specific social location informed and shaped by identity markers, is positioned as that which is as important as, if not more important than, the text under consideration.[46] Scholarship that articulates the identity politics of interpreters in New Testament studies – consolidated and called "feminist," "African American," "Asian American," "LGBT(QIA)," "postcolonial," "evangelical," and the list goes on – has been used to negotiate methodological departures from what has been called "traditional" New Testament studies, wherein the scholarly persona is thought to be "invisible." Reading from a particular place, as particular people or "ethnos," has been a way to use difference to narrate the experience of self, field, and world as distinct and distinctive. As products, such articulations of difference and distinctiveness comprise a form of participation in the branding of scholarly image and identity.

Identitarian work in New Testament studies constructs scholarly personae and the relationship between those and the larger scholarly body in specific ways that are aligned with the emergence of social movements and politics of identity since the middle of the 20th century. As with movements that emphasized the politics of recognition (rather than the politics of redistribution), "reading from this place" – no matter what that place might be – has been defined through claims to difference between groups within a social and cultural hierarchy. Proponents of identitarian modes of doing biblical scholarship have defined these perspectives over and against what they name as a hegemonic disciplinary configuration, often simply called "traditional scholarship," "dominant scholarship," or "historical criticism," wherein, as we discussed in the Introduction, a universal subject is assumed and historically dominated groups are invisible. This invisibility takes on two prominent forms in the rhetoric of identitarian scholarship: the lack of attention to how particular people might read and experience texts from those biblical scholars in dominant positions and the lack of non-dominant voices among those who occupy the position of "biblical scholar." Articulations of difference in this way propose methodological movement away from historical criticism and the universal subject toward "cultural criticism" and the particularities of identity. Herein historical criticism is positioned as that which is "neutral, scientific, and objective," is undertheorized, and is univocal, as opposed to identitarian modes which are subjective, self-consciously aligned with theory, and pluralistic. Historical criticism is further characterized as being solely interested in "antiquarian" matters, and as representing attempts to understand the meaning of a text in its own context whilst denying the embeddedness of the reader. By contrast, identitarian modes privilege contemporary contexts and acknowledge that a reader's embeddedness in culture will change how he or she reads a biblical text, regardless of how the ancient context is utilized.

Identitarian modes of conducting New Testament studies tend to construct an oppositional framework that pits historical criticism, as that which is "traditional" and "hegemonic" and concerned only with "texts," over and against the plurality and diversity and innovation of "resistant" readings that are possible should one take the social location of the reader and interpreter seriously. The arc of such critique usually charges historical

193

criticism, in positioning itself as "method" (and thus representing a universal human experience), with not being aimed at "real" and particular people, in the past or in the present. As a result historical criticism, since it was performed mostly by European (read: German) "white" men and represented their interests, became a predominantly exclusionary, patriarchal, racist, homophobic, and neocolonial enterprise. The "others" of history (historically dominated or underrepresented groups) can then adopt a linear, progressive model to explain developments in relation to the beginnings of the field, relating that the presence or absence of women (for example) as professional interpreters in the guild makes a difference for how we might understand both the presence and absence of women in ancient texts and in the contemporary field itself. There is no doubt that on some level this is true – the "landscape" of New Testament studies looks very different with different sorts of bodies in the room, so to speak. However, an important assumption lies in the background of claims for particularity and recognition of identities, that is, claims about how simply including the "others" and their perspectives changes the field: namely, that there is something "authentic" and essential about "women's perspectives" (or those of any other "other") that is quantitatively and qualitatively different than the "dominant white male" perspective, and that people who inhabit those bodies automatically should resonate with narratives about how those identities work. Rhetorically, then, particularity becomes an important opposition to, and weapon that should undo, universalism. Structurally, we observe that this is the case whether the articulation of scholarly persona emphasizes racial dimensions, gender performance, or confessional or denominational affiliation: there is something that the particulars and pluralities of social location and identity "add" to interpretation that universal and univocal traditional scholarship is "missing."

Further, in constructing opposition as a means to argue for the politics of recognition, identitarian modes of conducting New Testament studies participate in the consolidation, homogenization, and stabilization of both dominant and minoritized identities as they might be present in or absent from ancient texts, the history of the field, and the contemporary landscape. Such a strategy not only deposits the complex history of historical criticism into one box called "traditional, hegemonic scholarship," but it also shapes how minoritized voices ought to sound in order to be considered authentic. That is, in identitarian scholarship we detect a methodological move from treating the text as something fixed and stable to treating the scholarly persona as fixed and stable, and thus as that which stands outside of historical contingencies and exigencies.

Attempts to stabilize identity and scholarly persona in the name of "difference" are congruent with strategies of articulating neoliberal subjectivity as we have outlined them above. Essentialist and social constructionist debates about the construction of identity notwithstanding, we observe that these conversations and conflicts over the identity of the reader and scholar in New Testament studies are themselves a product of late-capitalist discourses, and thus are themselves expressions of neoliberal subjectivity. Declarations of identity and affinity, via personal narratives about who a scholar might be and what her or his relationship with biblical texts and biblical scholarship has been like, can often serve, then, as a prerequisite and prelude for engaging texts – which are then seen through the "lens" or "optic" of identity. Within neoliberalism, identitarian scholarship uses the rhetoric of difference, otherness, and authenticity to seek recognition by a dominant culture. While much has been contributed from these perspectives, however, questions about whether the politics of recognition alone actually change scholarly culture or the hierarchies embedded within it are rarely asked. To this end, one might inquire if justice for minoritized biblical scholars is truly served by an exclusively identity-based framework where inclusion and recognition of voices of those thought to be unrecognized by historical-critical scholars and methods is the primary goal.

The recognition that minoritized voices are authentic, that they are different, and that they represent something pure and essential that traditional historical criticism has corrupted or ignored – that historical criticism represents a "false consciousness" of sorts or is a stand-in for dominant culture itself – is to us a curious phenomenon that is more than slightly resonant with the narratives comprising niche marketing and branding within neoliberalism. Our economic context permits and encourages the articulation of these differences as a part of constructing scholarly personae while, at the same time, assimilating those differences into the marketplace and configuring them into market categories. In the neoliberal marketplace of New Testament studies, narratives of authentic scholarly identities function as a means of branding and point to a series of "boutique brands" unto themselves. These brands, which are packaged and promoted in intelligible ways, are that with which interested consumer-citizens are invited to forge affective and loyal relationships. Hailed as "new methods" for biblical interpretation and "new readings" of texts, such scholarly brands are at once reflective of individual experiences with biblical texts and marketed as that which can be duplicated by consumers who desire to read from similar places, regardless of their own experiences or identities.

Methodological Identitarianism

The social location of the New Testament scholar, as highlighted here through the example of identitarian or minoritized scholarship, is only one area in which scholarly persona is bounded by, and functions in alignment with, neoliberal subjectivity. Closely related to the articulation of authentic identities and social locations is the isolation and proliferation of different methods for reading and interpreting biblical texts. Similar to identitarian discourses, these methods and approaches have their own stories and histories, are often positioned in opposition to "traditional" historical-critical scholarship, and are packaged for consumption as departures from business as usual, as something "new," something "different," and so on, with the expectation that there is a consuming audience for such newness and difference. In the process of branding a "new method," it is important to ensure that it is both linked to the identity and persona of its "founder(s)" and that it is applicable beyond its historical contingency. Indeed, a cursory review of the Society of Biblical Literature's list of program units alone betrays an impressively large range of groups claiming circumscribed scholarly space around a particular methodological approach or issue.

We denote efforts to develop and market narratives that cultivate brand allegiance to scholarly methodologies as "methodological identitarianism." In some respect, one no longer can simply identify with biblical scholarship, or with New Testament studies as such. Instead, one is hailed to express alignment with particular methods as distinct brands, which in turn function as another means to claim particularity, identity, and subjectivity. In the discourses of methodological identitarianism, choices in method are narrativized as that which reveals something about the scholar's personal and political proclivities, much as shopping at Whole Foods serves as a signifier for those consumers who care about "the environment." To be sure, the publishing industry in some way helps with the branding of method: making sales and profits, after all, is a priority there, and advertising methods as discrete products does assist in that regard. However, we are concerned with the ways in which scholars themselves participate in the branding of method.

As with ethnic-exegetical and other identitarian modes of doing New Testament studies, methodological identitarianism is predicated on narratives that circumscribe the methods under consideration, marketing those methods as desirable and useable to consumers. Whether one favors cultural theory, systematic theology, cognitive science, or political philosophy as a conversation partner in the development of distinct reading strategies and criticisms, declarations of such proclivities and preferences contribute to the commodification of methodology itself. That is, while the preponderance of methods as products available for consumption is narrated as part of a linear progression of ideas beyond traditional scholarship, such diversity of perspectives also signifies alignment with neoliberal tendencies. As the "society" of biblical scholarship, broadly conceived, relaxes the "regulation" or "hegemony" that historical criticism has had over the field, the marketplace can open itself up to multiple avenues toward progress and freedom. Narrating the field in this manner – that is, as experiencing a shift away from dominant scholarship toward multiple methods – places the field at the end of its own "history" and naturalizes the idea that what scholars are doing somehow represents a logical progression in a linear developmental model of ideas. The commodification and branding of scholarly identity and method in the present enables scholars to create and manage appropriate and inalienable "traditional" pasts from which present trends emerge. Identifying with particular modern methods in the study of the New Testament, then, becomes another way to construct a self in relation to others.

We submit that methodological identitarianism, like ethnic and minoritized exegesis, mirrors observable patterns in our larger cultural and economic framework. This structure can be seen in how the origins of different methodological innovations are delineated, as well as how methods as such are narrated and reified as stable products from which interested consumers can expect predictable, universal results. The reification of a method is complete when it has a critical mass of consumers devoted to it who keep the narrative going over time and across social locations. In fact, we would argue that the rush among scholars to identify and "try out" the latest fads in theory and method in the service of developing a distinctive approach to the New Testament that can be marketed to other like-minded individuals constitutes a means of fetishizing method. That is, representing certain modes of interpretation as methods unto themselves – as commodity fetishes – manages perceptions about how knowledge is made and what ends it serves. Such representation hides the economic relationships of production and consumption and encourages self-promotion of method as a way to cultivate and affirm its efficacy among its proponents.

As a fetish object, a particular method is assumed to have its own inherent value separate from others, which is thought to satisfy the desires of its adherents and practitioners. Methodological identitarianism features practices that help to render methods as brands. For example, the multiple turns to theory in the study of the New Testament – literary, feminist, queer, trauma, Marxist, and "affect," to name but a few – feature scholars who function as "missionaries" for those theories, bringing those branded discourses into conversation with biblical texts. These scholars align with the vocabularies, precepts, and presuppositions of the chosen theories, imbuing those rhetorics with some kind of power to help interpreters both rescue texts from the stranglehold of historical criticism and articulate aspects of their own identity in the process. These methods are marketed as distinctive and as the guarantors of recognition and "prosperity," narrated as both different from traditional scholarship and as that which should move the field as a whole forward in some way. And, of course, every method, as brand, has its own associated ambassadors who serve as the spokespeople for the product, as scholars whose personae are partially predicated on what kind of method they "do" in the study of the New Testament. Those who develop methods engage in self-promotional strategies to the extent that they might stand apart from others, and often can achieve "celebrity" status in the guild – especially in the age of Web 2.0 branding and publicity strategies.

It is at this juncture that ethnic exegesis and methodological identitarianism align both with each other and with neoliberal market logic, and particularly with branding strategies and effects such as self-promotion, authenticity, and popularity with consumers. Both processes are as concerned with the identities and inclinations of those doing biblical scholarship as they are with the content of the scholarship. In some way, the identification with a special brand of New Testament scholarship – whether through social location or affinity with a method, or some combination of both – takes priority over structural concerns about how such forms of scholarship may reflect broader power dynamics precipitated by the reach of the market into all areas of life under neoliberalism. For example, one might promote "secularism" in biblical studies, or attempt to render a method out of examining the interplay between secularism and the politics of interpretation.[47] To do so, one might first identify as a secularist, and then identify elements of secularism that would contribute to a methodological complex worth reifying as a brand. The same could be said of "Jewish interpretation" or "Christian theological interpretation" in so far as these ways of reading are codified as methodological orientations; in these schematics, practitioners would first identify themselves as belonging to a certain social location, and then designate and deploy reading strategies toward the construction of a distinctive methodological framework. While "secular" and "Jewish/Christian theological" might appear to be radically different from one another, and while branding strategies associated with these methods might be predicated on their difference from each other and from "traditional" scholarship, structurally they are not all that distinct. As brand narratives, both utilize similar technologies of the self to achieve similar aims. Different scholarly identities, personae, and methods might be portrayed as "opposites," but in the end they are constructed, stabilized, and packaged for dissemination within a neoliberal paradigm in similar ways.

"Public" scholarship

Alongside ethnic exegesis and methodological identitarianism, New Testament studies designed for, and presented to, non-specialist or "public" audiences affords a rich site from which to explore performances of scholarly

198

persona as reflective of neoliberal subjectivity. By "public" scholarship, we mean books (including introductory New Testament textbooks), lectures and seminars, videos, online writings for outlets aimed at a "general" audience such as *Huffington Post* or other websites, and other products of the field designed to explain the New Testament, Christian origins, and early Christianity to non-specialists in what is thought to be "plain language." This type of scholarship constitutes a brand unto itself. It might seem as though "public" New Testament scholarship is the most closely aligned with market capitalism, since this type of scholarship makes explicit use of the popular media and enjoys a long-standing relationship with major for-profit publishing houses, and as such is marked as different from the other two examples we have discussed so far. However, what we are more interested in here is how public New Testament scholarship is narrated and branded as something distinctive from "traditional" scholarship, how scholarly persona is constructed and performed therein, and how relationships between readers, texts, and audiences are created and managed. Publicly inclined New Testament scholarship constructs scholarly and audience personae in specific ways that mutually inform one another, reflecting a certain interdependence. Moreover, in our view, public New Testament scholarship, particularly as performed in the United States, reinforces certain stereotypes about scholarly identities and the field as a whole that, as operating in a neoliberal framework, are consonant with both ethnic exegesis and methodological identitarianism.

Biblical scholarship, and perhaps New Testament studies in particular, has multiple audiences for its work. As a means of producing, sharing, and consuming knowledge about biblical texts, contexts, and histories of interpretation and deployment, the study of the New Testament has a scholarly audience. The Bible, of course, is also a "live" sacred text, used in a myriad of ways as an authoritative set of scriptures by multiple communities who may (or may not) consider themselves a part of long-standing institutionalized religious bodies and hierarchies. Biblical scholarship's main object of analysis, while fully a product of the ancient world, is also different from other ancient texts of its milieu in that it enjoys ongoing status as "sacred." It is also difficult to overestimate the influence of the Bible, and especially the New Testament, in world cultures. By means of its history of interpretation and reception, the New Testament has endured innumerable afterlives beyond the ancient worlds that produced it. The Bible has shaped (and been shaped by) our cultures of origin indelibly, whether we acknowledge it or not, inside and outside of organized religion. An understanding of the Bible enhances a comprehension of religion as a cultural phenomenon, particularly in the contemporary United States. However, engaging the Bible also enriches understandings of the paintings of masters such as Rembrandt

199

and Caravaggio, the music of the likes of Bach and Mozart, the works of Shakespeare and Darwin, the circumstances around scientific discoveries like those of Copernicus, Galileo, and Mendel, the architecture of some of the world's great buildings, histories of major wars and patterns of colonialism, and so on.

Thus, it is important for specialists and non-specialists alike, regardless of theological orientation or religious commitment, to engage the Bible. Major aspects of world cultures and histories, for example, are even more comprehensible if we try to understand how uses of the Bible might be implicated therein. The idea that the New Testament is solely to be read and interpreted by certain groups, and has only one correct option in terms of meaning-making, denies the complexity of the contents, legacies, and meanings of these texts. In addition to being acknowledged as scripture, then, the New Testament must also be recognized as a monumentally significant document, a response to the worlds in which it was written and compiled, which, in turn, the world has been interacting with and responding to for much of the last two millennia. Simply put, the New Testament's production and interpretation have been an integral part of how we got to this place, and it continues to play a critical role in the production of narratives about humanity and the cosmos. Even if the questions asked are shaped by contemporary political debates and media controversies rather than church engagements, they are questions that New Testament scholarship attempts to address on some level.

While New Testament scholars might acknowledge the Bible's legacies and importance in culture, and may attempt to engage the public on such matters, how exactly the guild has constructed the "public," "authentic," and "non-specialist" audiences reflects certain assumptions and stereotypes that, in turn, inform constructions and performances of scholarly persona. In order to render ideas about the New Testament fit for public consumption, the public needs to be constructed, stabilized, and managed as a relatable consumer category. In order for public New Testament scholarship to work as a brand, a narrative about who the people of the public are, what questions they have about the New Testament, and how they might relate to such scholarship, must be articulated and promoted. This orientation, of course, is intended to sell the scholarship as a product to the greatest number of people, and need not necessarily reflect any sort of reality about who the public actually are or what their questions might actually be. That said, one need not search very far in New Testament scholarship for evidence of how a non-specialist audience is constructed. For example, it is not uncommon for introductory New Testament textbooks, ostensibly aimed at undergraduates taking a biblical studies course, to contain a preface or other introductory material that delineates why the Bible ought to be examined in the context of an academic course, why it ought to be understood beyond ecclesiastical walls, and why it matters in culture. Such statements serve to circumscribe and to identify the audience, homogenizing and consolidating its character into something called a "public."

In the front matter in popular scholarly books on the New Testament and Christian origins, a scholar might narrate his or her own faith journey and religious commitment in relation to the New Testament, implying that a public audience is interested in such stories and commitments, or that they somehow lend more credibility to the scholar as publicly engaged author. Such narrative elements contribute to constructions of both author and public audiences as people who have religious and theological relationships with and interest in New Testament literature, which in turn serves to naturalize the idea that the New Testament is primarily or solely a "religious" text. In public discourse about the New Testament, the audience is construed as knowing both something and nothing about the literature of the New Testament, and if they do know something, they know it through being "churched" and thus learning through the lens of a rather uncritical faith – rather than through the critical lens of historical understanding, which is structurally opposed to faith. This sentiment betrays an implied assumption that a public audience is rather uncritical about religion even as they might be (in some cases, deeply) religious. Bolstering this presupposition is the discourse concerning the public's relationship with scientism, empiricism, and historical veracity. That is, public New Testament scholarship tends to construe its audience as people interested in the "truth" of the New Testament by entertaining questions about whether and how Jesus and/or Paul did things in the ancient world, what they said and did not say, and whether we have original ancient texts to verify what they did and did not say and do. Thus, public New Testament scholarship attempts to catch the attention of its audience with titles that express questions such as "Who was Paul, *really*?" and "What is the *real* story of Jesus?"

Public New Testament scholarship, as a consumable product, maps desires and questions such as these onto its audiences. At the same time, embedded in the discourse of public New Testament scholarship are the exact opposite assumptions about its audience. This is how stereotypes work: they bring together opposites to distance the self (scholar) from the other (audience), and are often couched in terms of contradictions. In the case of public New Testament scholarship, the audience is characterized as at once capable of reading data and arguments about the New Testament and yet intellectually inept. As far as language is concerned, public New Testament scholarship should come in "frustration-free" packaging – that is, scholars should explain the content in a jargon-free manner, as plainly as possible, so as to guarantee that the public will "understand." New Testament scholarship for public consumption should also be practical, which not only implies that scholarship is impractical or serves no purpose in its specialized forms, but also positions the audience as not interested in intellectual pursuits for their own sake, or capable of making meaning with texts on their own. Such practical understanding is desirable in part because of an implicit claim that the public has been misled and misinformed about the New Testament by the church and by other authoritative bodies, and may not be able to "handle" some of the more "trenchant" claims of biblical scholarship. Public New Testament scholarship, then, must display a heightened sensitivity to those who may have been churched and give practical advice about the material and questions. On the other hand, by insisting on an implicit opposition to the church, public New Testament scholarship often tends to embed an aim to transform public understanding away from religious commitment. These assumptions and contradictions may or may not be true about the public; they nevertheless connect to narratives that inform how the "public" is to be addressed as a group by the scholar, which in turn shapes the former's identification as a market category.

Constructions of the audience in public New Testament scholarship, along with constructions of scholarly persona through attention to the public as a category, serve as a site where identities are negotiated and branded. To be sure, these constructions are also where important relations of power in the guild are articulated. Debates over audience and persona point to live and unsettled questions in the guild about scholars, audiences, and modes of interpretation. As with ethnic exegesis and methodological identitarianism, characterizations of scholars and publics function as indicators of long-standing uncomfortable relationships between the study of the New Testament as it is conducted in the academy and in non-academic contexts. Again, in relying on oppositions between what is labeled as "traditional" scholarship and public work, public New Testament studies is positioned as that which concerns authentic people on their terms, rather than the "view from nowhere," the inward-looking focus of traditional historical criticism. Again, branding a public audience is predicated on its difference and distinction from so-called dominant, academic readers. In public New Testament scholarship, then, the scholar is someone who, as an expert who engages the public, is performing a service that is more important, and less elitist, than producing knowledge for other scholars. Whether relaying complex historical data about Christianity's origins or revealing through the news media the latest papyrological discoveries and whether they change anything about the canon, public New Testament scholarship brings affirmation and popularity (and, ultimately, profits) to the scholars who participate in such endeavors and the publishing houses that back them.

Branding one's scholarly persona as authentically "fit for public consumption" and promoting it as such through public scholarly output and
use of social media can bring celebrity to a New Testament scholar, which
reifies her or his status within a framework of neoliberal subjectivity.
Branding religion, religious texts, and the people who can explain such
matters to the "public" with intelligible and exciting rhetoric is another way
in which the market has moved into our lives. Such scholars also build a
following by using the discourse of care and interest in the lives and concerns of the public, as well as explicitly attempting to allay an audience's
fears that reading the New Testament is bad or automatically marks one out
as "religious" by repackaging New Testament scholarship as a safe product
to consume, no matter one's religious identification. Achieving popularity
through cultivating an affective relationship with the public is important in
terms of the market, for celebrity status (that is, a scholar with a proven
"following") leads to speaking invitations, more high-profile and large-
advance publishing contracts, and an increase in profits. In an era when
faculty wages at institutions of higher education are stagnant, an influx of
capital can be highly desirable. Within the neoliberal marketplace, network
culture and communicative capitalism have made it all the easier for New
Testament scholars to "get out there" and construct themselves publicly –
via "biblioblogs," Facebook, Twitter, and other online means – and for the
market to monitor popularity and brand desirability.

Sentiments about audience and scholarly persona in public New
Testament scholarship are often supported by the for-profit publishing
industry; books are, after all, commodities. In the writing of books, which is
and has been the primary form and genre of New Testament scholarship,
the audience can become a concern: will the book "appeal" to its audience?
Will the audience buy a lot of these books? To this end the audience for New
Testament scholarship is constructed and deployed by publishing houses
as part of efforts to control the shape, scope, and flow of revenue-producing
information. The audience, then, can serve as a weapon: asking scholars to
use "plain language" that appeals to the "average layperson," for example,
can function as a way to manage and contain some of the more uncomfortable claims of scholarship. When publishers ask scholars for accountability,
what they might actually mean to ask is how a scholarly product will make
money, where the market and marketability will lie, and what kind of consumers, and how many, will be attracted to the work. The public, after all,
is a consuming public; most scholarship is thought to be "irrelevant" to the
lives of ordinary people – and ordinary people may not spend money on
that with which they do not resonate. Through purchasing and consuming
books and other media, through paying to attend gatherings, through seeking graduate programs where they might study with "stars," the public

matters to the material conditions of New Testament studies. The publishing industry, then, contributes to debates about the personae of New Testament scholars, demanding branding as a "way to connect" with an audience, particularly if that audience consists of non-specialists and ordinary people with disposable income to spend on books about the New Testament.

It is not the case that public New Testament scholarship is a recent innovation in the field – in some ways questions about audience and public consumption are perennial in biblical scholarship, given the profile of the Bible as something that is regularly read and engaged outside of the academy. Concerns about the audience have in some sense always been with the field, since the Bible occupies a particularly important place in the consciousness of culture. A cursory glance at the history of New Testament textbooks in the United States, for example, shows a number of volumes that are concerned with presenting information in ways that are easy for non-scholars to understand, thus perhaps betraying earlier anxieties about the intelligibility of biblical scholarship. That said, the discipline of biblical studies as a means of producing knowledge with and about the Bible is a relative latecomer to the scene of scripturalizing practices, compared to the numerous ways that the Bible has been appropriated, read, and otherwise engaged by communities throughout time and across cultures. New Testament scholarship has always had multiple audiences, and has always had to manage a "public." The audience is, and likely always has been, unstable and polyvalent in composition. However, the terms under which public New Testament scholarship is conducted have changed in concert with broader cultural and economic shifts under neoliberalism, and perhaps are more obviously capitalist in nature at this juncture. Since scholarly personae are branded in certain ways that might change over time in relation to the market, the contours of the scholarship we do for the public, or for whichever audiences we imagine, necessarily must change as well.

In our view, the complex interplay of biblical scholarship and the media and publishing industries, coupled with the persistence of the Bible as a useful authoritative text, construct audiences, methods, and readers as a convenient cipher for larger and more thoroughgoing disciplinary issues. Struggles over audiences, authorial social location, and alignment with methods in the present reflect similar struggles that go all the way back to the beginnings of historical criticism: namely, struggles over who and what a biblical scholar is, what she or he is supposed to do, and to what ends. New Testament scholarship, far from being monolithic even at its "origins," has created a narrative about tradition, innovation, and responsibility to non-specialists that has helped to brand the field as something different from other ways of producing knowledge. We cannot blame people for wanting to write to and for the public – whomever the public includes.

We also are not "anti-social media," and we think social location and methods matter in the work we do. However, in so far as the work we do with the ancient world, and how we do that work, is ultimately a reflection of our world, we can use such critical moments and spaces as scholars to make observations about the world around us, and how our field may in fact be colluding with dominant cultural interests at the very same moment that we celebrate authenticity, accessibility, individualism, methodological innovation, and recognition of identity politics. Simply put, that we are concerned with the shaping and branding of the reader, the methods, the audience, and our interactions with all of those elements as part of constructing the scholarly persona is itself symptomatic of late-capitalist, neoliberal culture. In this culture, our scholarly output and products, methods, and personae are formed by, and at times in response to, these economic and cultural realities.

The One-Dimensional New Testament Scholar?

In the aftermath of the high-profile attention and massive surge in book sales given to *Zealot* through the "controversy" over its Muslim author, Reza Aslan continued to build and promote his own brand, in part through discussing the affair as symptomatic of how scholarship is perceived in public. Along these lines, Aslan made several statements about the task and shape of academic research and writing as well as scholarly persona in the social media age. At an appearance at Harvard Divinity School, from which he earned a master's degree, he discussed the *Zealot* affair, and focused on the contours of scholars' public performances. He also offered some advice to those academics who might want to make their work more "accessible" to the public: "Learn how to embed your research," he said. In academia, proof is often emphasized above the argument itself. Though methodology should be present, he said, it belongs in the back of the book, as supplementary information for interested readers. His own book offers two versions of the central argument: one directed toward lay readers interested in the overall narrative, and one for those who want to follow the academic back-and-forth. Secondly, he urged his colleagues to simplify: "Your grandmother doesn't care about your methodology or your research. She just wants to get to your conclusion." Finally, "Learn how to write … [w]e have such a specialized writing style in academia, with our own secret language that no one can decipher, and that only we ourselves understand … You have to get past that."[48]

In providing this advice, Aslan constructs the public, the scholarship, and the scholar in ways that our readers should now recognize as consonant with his own branding strategy and articulation of neoliberal subjectivity. In this view, the public, such as it is, is interested not in complexity, or in thinking, but in "narratives." Scholarship is too complicated and must be "simplified" in terms of methodology, which "your grandmother" does not care for anyway. And scholars themselves cannot write for the public, for they are so insular that they use a "secret language." Elsewhere, Aslan was clearer about his sentiments about the irrelevance of academics and the importance of branding for a scholar's persona. In a *Chronicle of Higher Education* article about the "promise and peril" of online identity construction by scholars across the disciplines, Aslan offered his view on why branding is a good idea: "[w]e as academics spend far too much time talking to ourselves in our dusty basement offices, and far too little time reaching out to the public with our ideas ... [b]uilding an online brand won't break that mold entirely, but it's a start."[49] Aside from ignoring the vast public output from numerous biblical scholars, that Aslan takes criticism of any sort – about his work, qualifications, or persona – and incorporates it into his brand narrative is especially telling about how his performance aligns with neoliberal capitalism.

While some of us have never had a "dusty basement office," and it is patently not true that New Testament scholarship, in particular, spends "far too little time reaching out to the public," we observe that Aslan's statements say less about the public, methods, or scholars than they do about his own rather blatant participation in the technologies of the self associated with neoliberal subjectivity. Aslan's statements about scholars being irrelevant to the public rely quite heavily on already-circulating stereotypes about academics and intellectualism, at least in the United States. Aslan's deployment of these stereotypes in his rhetoric about scholarship serves mostly to justify his own public performances and his own missteps in scholarly methodology and research concerning the historical Jesus. In so doing he is also performing an act of self-promotion as an academic who knows better, who is friendlier to non-specialists through his performances of authenticity and simplicity, and who collects pageviews, followers, and profits as a result. In fine neoliberal fashion, Reza Aslan has used the historical Jesus as a means to draw attention to himself, to create and manage an affective relationship with "fans," and to at once promote himself as a "scholar of religion" and denigrate the rest of the guild as irrelevant to the public due to a chronic inability to engage with anyone but other scholars properly.

It is worth reiterating that the drama over *Zealot* played out in the media and in the marketplace – but not in the guild, among the biblical scholars and other historians of religion among whom Aslan counted himself. For all of his insistence that he spent "more than two decades" researching the historical Jesus, Aslan is suspiciously absent from the scholarly conversations and institutions – some of them, like the Westar Institute, itself heavily invested in the "public" – where the "historical Jesus" is vigorously researched and debated. A cursory glance at the Society of Biblical Literature (the national scholarly guild for biblical scholars) annual meeting programs over the last decade shows that Aslan was not a participant or a member. This observation, on its own, means very little – non-participation in the Society of Biblical Literature's programs and meetings surely does not disqualify one from researching or writing about Jesus. The problem is that Aslan has made "biblical scholarship" a part of his brand narrative and, at least during the most heated moments of controversy over *Zealot*, a critical component of his scholarly persona. Of course, repeating a story over and over again as a means of representation does not necessarily make it real, though repetition may make it persuasive. That said, a hallmark of neoliberalism is that in brand narratives the differences between representation and reality are minimized. While some biblical scholars were (rightly) appraising the admittedly lackluster research "presented" as a part of *Zealot*'s story about Jesus, the point of discussing Reza Aslan, at least as far as we are concerned, has never been about engaging the research, the book, or his narrative about Jesus. It is, rather, about branding and identity: how our economic and cultural contexts have made "Reza Aslan," as brand, possible and desirable.

For the purposes of de-introducing the New Testament, as a means of defamiliarizing various aspects of the field that we often take for granted, we are more interested in what Aslan represents about constructions of scholarly identities than we are in his scholarship (how "good" or "bad" it is) or what kinds of contributions *Zealot* might make to conversations about the historical Jesus. To this end, we highlight Aslan as a potent example of how scholarly persona might work as a means of performing neoliberal subjectivity. It is not so much the content of his book that matters, then, but the narratives constructed around it concerning identity, method, and audience, that can help us identify issues and questions about the construction of a scholarly image in a neoliberal framework. Aslan, as such, is good to think with in this regard. For us, the three areas we have been considering in relation to constructions and performances of scholarly persona come together in representations of Aslan: identity politics and ethnic exegesis, methodological identitarianism, and scholarship for a public audience. Aslan capitalizes on his religious affiliation and social location by offering a story about his encounters with Jesus on his faith journey, which functions as a means to build a relationship with his readers as a "real person" and set him apart as distinct from scholars and others. While he minimizes attention to method in his narrative about Jesus, he admits that the "historical" way of understanding Jesus has both captivated him and challenged his faith, and it is this method with which he identifies most. And, finally, Aslan constructs the public in such a way as to presume that such readers desire another book about Jesus, written in narrative form so it is easy to understand, that proposes a "new" reading of Jesus' life "in context" without explaining much about how to understand the evidence involved in writing such a biography or the purpose of writing such a book in the first place. What matters most in neoliberal capitalist discourses is not who people actually are, what they say, or to whom they say it – what matters is that their brand engenders affection, loyalty, some measure of celebrity, and, most importantly, a consumer base that will enable the flow of capital.

Ultimately, Reza Aslan is a useful site from which we can raise questions about who are we as students of the New Testament, what are we doing, and for whom we do it. That there is a discipline called "New Testament studies" with "New Testament scholars" in it now is by no means "natural" – it originated in a specific time and place, and created the circumstances for its production of knowledge in the very act of naming and classifying and drawing boundaries in the first place. As the discipline is located in time and space, so too are its practitioners. New Testament scholarship, as a means of engaging biblical texts in particular ways, with particular goals, is a means, in the end, of engagement – with texts, to be sure, but mostly with ourselves. We are constructed through our relationships with the guild and each other, and yet we are also located in a broad economic and cultural framework of neoliberalism wherein performing relationships with the New Testament is, for better or for worse, a technology of the self and a part of branding culture.

We contend that, in so far as New Testament scholarship seeks to cultivate a different kind of relationship with the material than that of other epistemological spaces, and in so far as such scholarship is a mode of doing something with sacred texts, it is itself a means of scripturalizing, which, according to Vincent Wimbush, comprises a series of signifying practices pointing to articulations of selves, texts, and worlds, a "consistent focus on how societies and cultures continue to be formed and de-formed and re-formed and – on account of the power invested in them – how *texts* in particular are created and pressed into service to effect such things."[50] That is, texts do not do anything on their own, without people. As a signifying practice, New Testament scholarship is conducted by "real" readers who happen to be scholars, who inhabit and perform the role of "scholar" in many ways. If scholars express concern about readers, methods, and audiences as if those are objects unto themselves, that may actually be a mode of deflection from unsettled issues about who we are, what we are doing, and for whom we do it. De-introducing as an orientation and practice, then, is a way to unveil some of the ideological scaffolding surrounding common conceptions and presentations about, among other issues, scholarly image and identity in the study of the New Testament. To this end, we wonder whether it could be the case that neoliberal biblical scholarship enhances the individualistic perception, representation, and self-promotional inclinations of biblical scholars. We might ask what effects the collusion with the market, the drive toward "new" methods, the desire to be read by a mass public audience, and the seductions of celebrity have on our scholarly personae. We also find ourselves asking what it means to perform identity as a scholar in a culture that celebrates individualism and non-conformity whilst eliminating job security and the capacity for critical ideological and material intervention. These and other related questions are part of the denaturalization project we are proposing as it relates to the personae and performances of scholars.

Scholars are always products of specific historical and social contexts, and sometimes in ways of which they are not aware. This is by no means a new observation. We may not have a choice except to be hailed into being in a neoliberal late-capitalist moment. However, we might be able to choose how we negotiate this moment, how we intervene in it, how we make use of the New Testament and New Testament scholarship to do so, and how we might imagine something besides, and beyond, the neoliberal "there is no alternative." In technologically advanced neoliberal capitalism it is the case that "resistance" is built in to the structure as a means to hide the reality that the structure itself does not need to change. As the Frankfurt School social theorist Herbert Marcuse noted many years ago, a pervasive effect of advanced capitalist society is the widespread repression of possibilities for thinking critically about the system as such, while at the same time naturalizing the discourse that positions capitalism as the guarantor of infinite possibilities for self-expression, individuality, and freedom. What makes humans "one-dimensional," in Marcuse's terms, is their performance of practices that enable uncritical acceptance of and conformity to structural norms and behaviors.[51] The "one-dimensional man" participates in the loss of freedom at the same time that he (or she) touts the freedom of the market, even if unwittingly, by accepting its presence in every aspect of life. By contrast, a multidimensional discourse would be that which focuses on moving beyond the structural state of affairs. This would also be the case with our field, which is part of a much larger socio-economic landscape. When we consider how a New Testament scholar performs as a "scholar," it is worth taking such issues and questions into account – whether we, as scholars, wish to perform one-dimensionality, or multidimensionality. At stake is our capacity to imagine not just what the world would look like were we to arrange things a little differently, but what a different "we" and a different "world" altogether might entail.

Notes

1. See Andrew Kaczynski, "Is This the Most Embarrassing Interview Fox News Has Ever Done?" *BuzzFeed*, July 27, 2013. http://www.buzzfeed.com/ andrewkaczynski/is-this-the-most-embarrassing-interview-fox-news-has-ever-do (accessed November 30, 2014). For contrast, Aslan had also been interviewed by National Public Radio, both for *Weekend Edition* and by Terry Gross on *Fresh Air*, both of which focused not so much on his Islamic affiliations, but on his teenage conversion to Christianity and subsequent interest in scholarship on the historical Jesus that led to the publication of *Zealot*. See "Christ in Context: 'Zealot' Explores Life of Jesus," *National Public Radio*, July 15, 2013. http://www.npr.org/2013/07/15/198040928/christ-in-context-zealot-explores-the-life-of-jesus (accessed November 30, 2014). Still, even as these interviews might seem "different," they both focus on Aslan's narration of his authentic identity, his authority, and his appeal to a broad public audience, all of which we will discuss as a matter of branding bodies and advertising scholars(hip) below.
2. Reza Aslan, *Zealot: The Life and Times of Jesus of Nazareth* (New York: Random House, 2013), xviii.
3. Aslan, *Zealot*, xx.
4. Jeffrey Scholes, "Reza Aslan's Viral Fox News Video Reveals More than Christian Privilege," *Religion Dispatches*, August 19, 2013. http://religiondispatches.org/ reza-aslans-viral-fox-news-interview-reveals-more-than-just-christian-privilege/ (accessed November 30, 2014).
5. Elizabeth Castelli, "Reza Aslan – Historian?" *The Nation*, August 9, 2013. http:// www.thenation.com/article/175688/reza-aslan-historian# (accessed November 30, 2014).
6. Julie Bosman, "Odd Fox Interview Lifts Reza Aslan's Biography on Jesus," *New York Times*, July 29, 2013. http://www.nytimes.com/2013/07/30/business/media/ odd-fox-news-interview-lifts-reza-aslans-biography-on-jesus.html (accessed November 30, 2014).
7. Dale B. Martin, "Review of *Zealot: The Life and Times of Jesus of Nazareth*," *New York Times Book Review*, August 5, 2013. http://www.nytimes.com/2013/08/06/ books/reza-aslans-zealot-the-life-and-times-of-jesus-of-nazareth.html (accessed November 30, 2014).
8. Greg Carey, "Reza Aslan on Jesus: A Biblical Scholar Responds," *Huffington Post*, July 30, 2013. http://www.huffingtonpost.com/greg-carey/reza-aslan-on-jesus_b_3679466.html (accessed November 30, 2014).
9. For Evans, many of these errors concern claims Aslan makes about the social and historical setting of the Gospels that do not align with recent scholarly consensus born of textual and archaeological investigation. Craig A. Evans, "Reza Aslan Tells an Old Story about Jesus," *Christianity Today*, August 9, 2013. http://www. christianitytoday.com/ct/2013/august-web-only/zealot-reza-aslan-tells-same-old-story-about-jesus.html (accessed November 30, 2014).
10. Again, such responses have largely taken place online. See, for example, Micha'el Rosenberg, "Reza Aslan's Missed Opportunity," *Religion Dispatches*, August 8, 2013.

http://religiondispatches.org/reza-aslans-missed-opportunity/ (accessed November 30, 2014).

11. We would not be the first in our field to observe that biblical scholarship takes place in relationship to neoliberalism. See, for example, James Crossley's treatment in *Jesus in an Age of Neoliberalism: Quests, Ideology and Scholarship* (BibleWorld; Sheffield: Equinox, 2012). While we differ substantially from Crossley in terms of how, and to what ends, we might understand the intersection of biblical scholarship with identity and neoliberal discourses (a point on which we will elaborate below), we nonetheless understand his work to ask some important questions about the historical, economic, political, and cultural contexts in which New Testament scholarship is conducted.

12. Neoliberalism in this vein is often associated with economist Milton Friedman, who theorized how, under capitalism, society might benefit from governmental influence without bending to the fundamental threat it poses to individual freedom. See Friedman, *Capitalism and Freedom: Fortieth Anniversary Edition* (Chicago: University of Chicago Press, 2002).

13. David Harvey, *A Brief History of Neoliberalism* (New York: Oxford University Press, 2005), 2.

14. David Harvey, "The 'New' Imperialism: Accumulation by Dispossession," in *The New Imperial Challenge: Socialist Register 2004* (ed. L. Panitch and C. Leys; New York: Monthly Review Press, 2003), 64–87.

15. Jason Hickel and Arsalan Khan, "The Culture of Capitalism and the Crisis of Critique," *Anthropological Quarterly* 85.1 (2012): 203–228. See also Jim McGuigan, *Cool Capitalism* (London: Pluto Press, 2009).

16. Hickel and Khan, "Culture of Capitalism," 223.

17. Harvey, *Brief History of Neoliberalism*, 40.

18. John L. Comaroff and Jean Comaroff, *Ethnicity, Inc.* (Chicago Studies in Practices of Meaning; Chicago: University of Chicago Press, 2009), *passim*.

19. Comaroff and Comaroff, *Ethnicity, Inc.*, 140.

20. See "Welcome to KwaZulu-Natal," http://www.zulu.org.za (accessed November 30, 2014), which emphasizes Zulu service, food, culture, and nature. The "Zulu Kingdom" is but one example of the commodification of "ethnic" culture and identity under neoliberalism, particularly in poorer communities and nations who see the culture as a product and experience to sell, and thus a way to make a profit. See Comaroff and Comaroff, *Ethnicity, Inc.*, 6–21.

21. "I Love NY®," http://www.iloveny.com (accessed November 30, 2014).

22. "Texas®: It's Like A Whole Other Country," http://www.traveltex.com (accessed November 30, 2014).

23. Comaroff and Comaroff, *Ethnicity, Inc.*, 139.

24. As Harvey notes, neoliberalism "has the power to split off libertarianism, identity politics, multiculturalism, and eventually narcissistic consumerism from the social forces ranged in pursuit of social justice through the conquest of state power. It has long proved extremely difficult with the US left, for example, to forge the collective discipline required for political action to achieve social justice without offending the desire of political actors for individual freedom and for full

recognition and expression of particular identities. Neoliberalism did not create these distinctions, but it could easily exploit, if not foment, them" (*Brief History of Neoliberalism*, 41–42).

25. Angela Y. Davis, "Recognizing Racism in the Era of Neoliberalism," in *The Meaning of Freedom and Other Difficult Dialogues* (San Francisco: City Lights, 2009), 165–178.

26. Nancy Fraser, *Fortunes of Feminism: From State-Managed Capitalism to Neoliberal Crisis* (New York: Verso, 2013), 5.

27. Robert McChesney, "Noam Chomsky and the Struggle Against Neoliberalism," *Monthly Review* 50.11 (1999): 40–48.

28. See Noam Chomsky, *Profit Over People: Neoliberalism and the Global Order* (New York: Seven Stories Press, 1999).

29. Harvey, *Brief History of Neoliberalism*, 3.

30. For discussion, see Jodi Dean, *Democracy and Other Neoliberal Fantasies: Communicative Capitalism and Left Politics* (Durham, N.C.: Duke University Press, 2009).

31. Roopali Mukherjee and Sarah Banet-Weiser, eds., *Commodity Activism: Cultural Resistance in Neoliberal Times* (Critical Cultural Communication; New York: New York University Press, 2012).

32. Dean, *Democracy and Other Neoliberal Fantasies*, 34–37.

33. Specifically, McChesney concludes: "Left on their current course and driven by the needs of capital, digital technologies can be deployed in ways that are extraordinarily inimical to freedom, democracy, and anything remotely connected to the good life." See Robert McChesney, *Digital Disconnect: How Capitalism Is Turning the Internet Against Democracy* (New York: The New Press, 2013), 232.

34. See Bryant Simon, *Everything But the Coffee: Learning about America from Starbucks* (Berkeley: University of California Press, 2011).

35. Sarah Banet-Weiser, *Authentic™: The Politics of Ambivalence in a Brand Culture* (Critical Cultural Communication; New York: New York University Press, 2012), 5.

36. Banet-Weiser, *Authentic™*, 42.

37. On the branding of cultural institutions in highly affective, and effective, ways, see James B. Twitchell, *Branded Nation: The Marketing of Megachurch, College Inc., and Museumworld* (New York: Simon & Schuster, 2005). Higher education, in particular, has endured an ambivalent relationship to marketing, branding, and the market. See Derek Bok, *Universities in the Marketplace: The Commercialization of Higher Education* (Princeton: Princeton University Press, 2004).

38. The classic guide to personal branding and product management is Al Ries and Jack Trout, *Positioning: The Battle for Your Mind, 20th Anniversary Edition* (New York: McGraw-Hill, 2000). See also Al Ries with Laura Ries, *The 22 Immutable Laws of Branding: How to Build a Product or Service into a World-Class Brand* (San Francisco: HarperBusiness, 2002), which includes a section on internet and personal branding.

39. Banet-Weiser, *Authentic™*, 29.

40. Banet-Weiser, *Authentic™*, 32.

41. Fredric Jameson, *Postmodernism: or, The Cultural Logic of Late Capitalism* (Post-Contemporary Interventions; Durham, N.C.: Duke University Press, 1990).

42. Alice E. Marwick, *Status Update: Celebrity, Publicity, and Branding in the Social Media Age* (New Haven: Yale University Press, 2013), 12.

43. Michel Foucault, Luther H. Martin, Huck Gutman, and Patrick H. Hutton, *Technologies of the Self: A Seminar with Michel Foucault* (Amherst: University of Massachusetts Press, 1988), 19.

44. Marwick, *Status Update*, 12.

45. As of this writing, neither of the present authors uses an active Facebook profile, blog, Instagram account, or Twitter handle. One of us has a LinkedIn profile that lies largely dormant. We both participate in online shopping (the details of which we do not share publicly), and we have both contributed online essays for "popular" audiences to the Society of Biblical Literature's *Bible Odyssey* project (www.bibleodyssey.org). We are fully aware that our non-participation in some popular forms of social media does not mean that we are exempt from neoliberal subjectivity. We even concede that we might have failed at branding as we have discussed it herein. We also note that all of this might change by the time our readers access this note. We do think, however, that it is important to mention that the use of Web 2.0 technologies is not an innocent or neutral endeavor but is linked to the broad context of neoliberalism that we have been attempting to describe in this chapter.

46. The literature on this topic in the field is vast and multivalent. In our view, the seminal contribution is to be found in the essays collected in Fernando F. Segovia and Mary Ann Tolbert, eds., *Reading from This Place*, vol. 1: *Social Location and Biblical Interpretation in the United States* (Minneapolis: Fortress Press, 1995).

47. For an attempt to articulate "secularism" as a methodological tool in biblical scholarship, as well as a method in its own right, see R. Boer, ed., *Secularism and Biblical Studies* (BibleWorld; London: Equinox, 2010). For a critical appraisal of "secular biblical studies" as a method, see Todd Penner, "Is Boer among the Prophets? Transforming the Legacy of Marxian Critique," in *Secularism and Biblical Studies*, 67–81.

48. "Reza Aslan on Jesus, Faith, and Fox News," *Harvard Magazine*, September 27, 2013. http://harvardmagazine.com/2013/09/reza-aslan-zealot-discussion (accessed November 30, 2014).

49. Seth Zweifler, "For Professors, Online Presence Brings Promise (and Peril)," *The Chronicle of Higher Education*, April 21, 2014. http://chronicle.com/article/For-Professors-Online/145961/ (accessed November 30, 2014).

50. Vincent L. Wimbush, "Introduction: TEXTureS, Gestures, Power: Orientation to Radical Excavation," in *Theorizing Scriptures: New Critical Orientations to a Cultural Phenomenon* (ed. V. L. Wimbush; Signifying (on) Scriptures 1; New Brunswick: Rutgers University Press, 2008), 13.

51. Herbert Marcuse, *One-Dimensional Man: Studies in the Ideology of Advanced Industrial Society* (Boston: Beacon Press, 1964).

Back to the Future
Concluding Observations on History, Method, and Theory in New Testament Studies

"Think, McFly! Think!"

In the "classic" 1985 film *Back to the Future*, Marty McFly, played by the then-young Michael J. Fox, accidently finds himself transported back into the past. His friend, the somewhat crazed scientist Professor Emmett Brown, or "Doc," has constructed a prototype of a time-travel machine out of a DeLorean, powered by plutonium stolen from a Libyan terrorist group (both of which, of course, truly date this film). While testing the machine, Doc and Marty are found by the Libyans, who gun Doc down. Using the DeLorean to escape the Libyans, Marty inadvertently activates its time-travel capacity and ventures to the year 1955, where he in effect escapes his own life in 1985 as well. Marty finds himself reappearing in his parents' past, in the final weeks of their high-school days. His future parents, George and Lorraine, are on the verge of finally connecting and living out their future together as a couple, which would include getting married and giving birth to Marty at some point. As viewers already know from the opening scenes of the film, George and Lorraine's future together will not be one of normative American success and glory. Rather, George lives out a life of being weak and impotent, always the brunt of someone else's brutishness, signified most explicitly by a life-long bully rapping on his head while saying "Hello … hello … anybody home? Think, McFly! Think!" The family leads a drab and unexciting life. Lorraine is an alcoholic. There is

De-Introducing the New Testament: Texts, Worlds, Methods, Stories, First Edition.
Todd Penner and Davina C. Lopez.
© 2015 Todd Penner and Davina C. Lopez. Published 2015 by John Wiley & Sons, Ltd.

nothing that is visually appealing about their day-to-day existence: their occupations are dismal, the house is run-down, the lighting low. It is clearly subpar and depressing, evidence of dreams never realized – or dreams never had in the first place. Given these initial representations, it would not be difficult to wish for a different outcome of the past, that is, for a different present altogether.

Having successfully traveled 30 years into the past, and having figured out that he is in his parents' high-school world, Marty uses his knowledge of the future to inform his interactions with the people he meets in the past; he appears to assume that whatever is happening in his time has roots in this point to which he has traveled. For example, Marty confronts his would-be weak and feeble father, who simply cannot muster the courage to stand up to the bullies in his life nor summon a certain kind of confident masculine strength that would clearly make him more attractive by modern standards. Marty knows that his father's weaknesses will plague him for his entire adult life – that "Think, McFly! Think!" will become a humiliating refrain. A significant plot twist is that, in a turn on the Oedipal myth, Lorraine, Marty's mother, falls romantically for her own son, instead of for his father. This dramatic development, of course, raises the very real possibility that Marty's parents may never connect as is "necessary" for Marty to exist. Thus, his trip to the past has not only altered, but palpably jeopardized, his present. The rest of the story involves Marty trying to undo the damage caused by his own insertion and intervention into his parents' past. That past must play out as it "was intended" or "as it happened to begin with" in order for the present to be stabilized and for everything to go as it did, as "destined." The climax of the film visually represents the threat of the past not working out for the future, as Marty sees his own hand, along with the rest of his body, start to "disappear" at the moment when his parents' fateful connection – a kiss at a school dance – almost does not happen. As soon as his parents embrace, though, Marty returns to his solid, opaque self, he stands upright, and time marches on as required. In making sure the past happens as it once did, Marty ensures that he will, in fact, exist in the future.

While Marty does succeed in helping George and Lorraine regroup and get "back on track" so that they might become his parents, in the process he also changes the course of their futures (and his own). His interventions in the past cannot help but also alter that past, introducing trajectories that end up necessarily reshaping Marty's present upon his return. As a result of changes in George's character in the past, as nurtured by the friendship with his own son, the future fortunes of Marty's parents have shifted dramatically. George and Lorraine are now successful, upper-class, well-adjusted individuals, leading a colorful existence as an aging, happily married couple. They have a well-appointed home, work in fulfilling careers, and seem to be in good physical and emotional health. Everything has "worked out" for them. In this case, Marty's presence in, and alterations of, the past affected the present in a desirable way. And the added bonus is that Marty learns, upon his return, that Doc survived the Libyan attack, as he was wearing a bullet-proof vest on account of Marty telling him in the past about the future incident. That it easily could have turned out differently is a specter that haunts this film.

Back to the Future was the highest-grossing film of 1985, spawned a franchise, and has enjoyed a legacy of critical acclaim and pop-cultural appropriations. Aside from the celebrity star power of its cast and its combination of science fiction, humor, and romance, its enduring appeal lies in its alignment with a venerable story genre and tradition that nego-tiates broader questions raised by time-travel and the relationship bet-ween the past, present, and future. Such questions include whether we can travel through time, and if so, how might we do that; if we do go "back" to the past, how that affects the events of the present and future; what it would be like to visit the past with the knowledge of the present, which in the past is the future; whether the past, present, and future are causally related at all; and, importantly, what are the ethical implications of all this time travel in the first place.

As we think about our own work as biblical critics, *Back to the Future* offers a useful metaphorical framework for how we understand the poten-tially transformative nature of the historical enterprise – particularly, in our case, as it relates to the study of the New Testament, Christian origins, and early Christianity. We highlight two particular facets that are important for our concluding observations about the de-introducing project in which we have been engaged throughout this book. First, we contend that, in thinking about inhabiting the space of a critic who works with the past, one should consistently highlight the ethical nature of that task. That is, the present is where the past and the future intersect, and how we conceptualize these matters has consequences for human relationships. Desiring potentially more just and sustainable and humane futures and worlds always entails a revisiting of, and grappling with, our pasts, both recent and ancient. The ethical task of the New Testament scholar as biblical critic, in our estimation, is to dwell at this crossroads by carefully examining the past and its modern reception and interpretation, seeking to expose, if you will, the various human "hands" that have been at work and at play in the presentation and deployment of our pasts, as well as the hands that have been left out. In short, then, with an eye to the future, our de-introducing project will always first go back to the past.

Second, any engagement of the past, any visitation to a recent, earlier, or ancient phase of our present time, invariably has an impact on our own present and future, even as such interventions are shaped by the concerns and questions of the present, and even as the present and past may not be linked in as linear a manner as we might assume or hope. All too often, we proceed as if we are simply delineating and presenting the results of an obvious past that we trust is just "back there," a past that led us to where we are now in an uncomplicated manner, an ancient past that requires little if any human mediation or reflection. Even when we acknowledge that there are vast differences between the past and the present, we can be quite easily lulled into constructing a past that seems so much like our present. We should always be surprised when the conclusions of our studies of the ancient world so readily align with our own presuppositions. In our view, going back to the past as a means of engaging the present and future should not affirm what we already know, but should be a work of the imagination that has the capacity to confound us and lead into some defamiliarizing territory. As the very least, engaging the past, on whatever terms we do so, can be a work of transformation and revivification rather than a work of mere reification. And, as Marty McFly realizes shortly after he shows up in his parents' (and therefore his own) past, an immediate task before the biblical critic is how we might realize that we are agents in making and remaking the future, that is to say, that our involvement and intervention in our pasts helps us recreate the present and the future.

As New Testament scholars, we do not have the luxury of pretending that we are not a part of the project at hand, whether or not the project at hand involves the past. Given the nature and history of the Bible as a set of documents that has never been fully harnessed or controlled by one constituency – church, academy, or society – to interface with New Testament texts, their contexts, and histories of interpretation and deployment has always in some sense been to enter into contested territory. Contrary to how some might characterize the field, as New Testament scholars we have never quite been able to say that we are not invested somehow, on some level, in the work that we do. That is, we are not able to say that we do not possess the hands that create the project of biblical interpretation. We submit that it is not the genre of the texts, their deployments as sacred, or anything else we might label "intrinsic" to this material, but the obviously human and relational quality of studying the New Testament that makes our field so interesting and relevant. We might even say that there is no outside of ideological orientation, commitment, and investment. Similarly, we would suggest that biblical scholarship serves as a signifier that, in the end, no discipline is natural, neutral, or comes from nowhere. At the very least, a primary function of the biblical critic, in our view, is to constantly remind us that whatever the subject and object of our studies, what we are dealing with has human origins and human dimensions. That is, we are dealing in the realm of human endeavors, whether we are examining the categories and classificatory schemas we use in our work, the historical and social backgrounds or material culture we isolate and deploy to illuminate the New Testament and Christian origins, or even the rhetoric we use to construct "biblical scholar" subjectivity. With this in mind, below we will briefly explore the role of the critic more generally. We will then appraise the position of the critic, and historical criticism, in the study of the New Testament, Christian origins, and early Christianity. We will conclude with some further reflections on the habitation of the critic's space in terms of thinking about the present and the future of the discipline.

The Role of the Critic and the Critical Impulse

In our understanding, the scholar who adopts the role of a critic does so in order to expose, if you will, the humanity of ideas. Nowhere is this more the case, and nowhere is such criticism more necessary and misunderstood, than in the study of religion, and perhaps in the field of biblical studies in particular. To some of our readers it might seem strange, and to some it might seem obvious, but it bears noting that to the critic religion is fundamentally a human activity – it is that which is made by humans, for human consumption, with human consequences, as part of human experience. Yet religion has often been seen as that which is more than human, or somehow outside of human control. Such a characterization of religion is a product of what we would call an idealist framework. Methodologically speaking, an idealist framework reifies ideas in such a way that the human dimension all but disappears, and ideas become that which creates history. By contrast, a non-idealist framework, which is the basic framework to which we would say the study of the New Testament and early Christianity is historically indebted, in effect turns this narrative on its head. Seeing institutions and discourses like those associated with religion in a non-idealist way entails understanding that ideas are generated by humans in particular circumstances, and it is these human circumstances which make the ideas possible – not the other way around. As Ludwig Feuerbach (1804–1872) noted long ago, even our discourses about divinities are but reflections and projections of our own desires and circumstances. Therefore, the task of the critic (for Feuerbach, the philosopher) is to undress the theologian, to show that rather than originating beyond humanity, religion is really the means by which humans worship themselves through deploying the rhetoric that they are worshiping a god.[1] The tricky part about the role of the critic, especially when such a figure engages the history of religion, is that the critic is committed to examining those ideas and institutions that are constructed as

219

transcendent in a contingent and contextual manner. At some basic level, the controversies of historical research on the Bible can be summed up precisely in that way: when that which is held to be transcendent is made contingent, conflict invariably arises. The critic attempts to inhabit a space wherein such conflicts and tensions can be ummasked and interrogated.[2]

Now, we would want to push this consideration a bit further. For us, religion is simply one example within a larger system of transcendent ideas. In recognizing and exposing discourses wherein the contingent is made universal, the critic of religion may be construed as a "blasphemer" or "heretic" in much the same way as a critic of science (in all of its diverse manifestations) is considered "irrational" (or "religious"!). Functionally, those categories – blasphemy, heresy, and irrationality – serve to silence the critic and to regulate his or her analyses. Additionally, "criticism" is an oft-misunderstood descriptive category, as the critic is frequently, both in the popular imagination but also within the academy, considered to be "critical" in the pejorative sense. For example, perhaps some of our readers will be familiar with statements such as "All you do is criticize what I do and say and think!" To "criticize," as it is used in statements like that, means "to negate," or to shut down discourse, or to just not value something that others might consider worthwhile or normative. The critic, however, can be construed as a negative force only in so far as ideas are held up as idols, as sacrosanct conceptions that are to be accepted as the way things are, as that which is beyond question, beyond human scrutiny.

Bruno Latour's framing of issues related to the role and function of the critic and criticism in society is helpful for our orientation toward the project of de-introducing the New Testament. For Latour, religion and science occupy similar positions as institutions, discourses, practices, and categories that are thought to be transcendent and unassailable, or beyond defense and beyond criticism. He states: "[m]ore generally, the critical mind is one that shows the hands of humans at work everywhere, so as to slaughter the sanctity of religion, the belief in fetishes, the worship of transcendent heaven-sent icons, the strength of ideologies. The more the human hand can be seen as having worked on an image, the weaker is the image's claim to offer truth."[3] For Latour, the enduring role of the critic is to constantly expose the "lowly," human origins of that which is thought to exhibit "truth" beyond space and time – beyond merely human activity. Latour aptly utilizes this same principle in his discussion of science and objectivity, both of which are critical for the modern origins and legacy of biblical scholarship: revealing the hands at work in science serves to expose the mechanisms by which objectivity is produced and naturalized. Of course, such exposure is double-edged: "[t]he only way to defend science against the accusation of fabrication, to avoid the label of 'socially constructed,' is apparently to insist that no human hand has ever touched the image it has produced."[4] As the hands are revealed, so too are the revealers accused of iconoclasm, and the machinery that insists on the non-human involvement in objectivity and science redoubles its efforts to hide its own humanity. In some cases, the critic, as revealer and icon-smasher, can actually help to further the reification of the non-human origins of those images, despite intentions and efforts to the contrary. This might result in an obfuscation and confusion concerning the precise role of the hands at work, which Latour calls an "iconoclash." Whereas iconoclasm might be illustrated by the act of destroying images in the service of revealing their human origins, iconoclash denotes the moment when the critic is not clear about whether the act of revealing will be destructive or constructive, whether it will get rid of the idols or encourage the further reification of idolatry. Thus, the critic must make an ethical decision about the actions performed, regardless of whether the implications of such actions can be known. For the biblical critic, this would apply to decisions to engage in analyses and appraisals of the field. For example, when we aim to reveal the human hands involved in producing and naturalizing the discursive sites we have discussed in this book – texts, backgrounds, objects, and personae – we must also ask ourselves what the effects of such activity might be.

Latour would not be alone or entirely innovative in this type of analysis regarding the critic, however. Michel Foucault deploys almost the same configuration in his essay "Nietzsche, Genealogy, History," wherein he inhabits the space of a critic of historical study. He notes, "we want historians to confirm our belief that the present rests upon profound intentions and immutable necessities."[5] The idealist framework of history, Foucault argues, is like a demagogue, in so far as the latter's invocation of "truth, laws of essences, and eternal necessity" finds a correlation in the historian's appeal to "objectivity, the accuracy of facts, and the permanence of the past."[6] For Foucault, a non-idealist approach to history, which he, following Nietzsche, calls "genealogical," is an unmasking process whereby the critic exposes pluralities where singularities are narrated, and complex relations and webs of power where stories are told about "great men" alone.[7] And long before Foucault or Latour, Karl Kautsky (1854–1938) articulated a non-idealist, or materialist, conception of history that was profoundly concerned with the ethical stance of the historian as an interested observer of the phenomena of past epochs, while also acknowledging that ethical stances are themselves human constructions, and subject to change according to cultural and historical location.[8] Kautsky's contributions to history-writing, following Marx and Rousseau, maintain that it is impossible for the historian, as a human being located in space and time, to achieve impartiality or complete disinterestedness from the material under consideration.

Further, the only reason for the critic to study the past, in Kautsky's view, is an abiding interest in understanding, and transforming, the present and future.[9] Hence, in his study on Christian origins and early Christianity, Kautsky insists that the task of the materialist historian is to measure each era according to its own standards, rather than use the past to justify relations of power and privilege in the present. Moreover, the materialist historical critic is acutely aware that studying the past matters, for our conceptions of the past are deployable as "weapons" in creating a different future.[10] While an orientation to critical historical analysis such as the one Kautsky proposed proved useful to Marxist critics in particular, we would say that such considerations are traceable in the broader history of biblical scholarship as well, wherein the critic emerged as a figure who serves quite a different purpose than a priest or a theologian.

Much more could be said about the critic. For the moment, however, it is important to note that the critic inhabits a space where decisions are made, and one might therefore say that this space is where ethics takes place. That is, whether one refers to such a space as a discipline, a *habitus*, or a persona, and whether we are comforted or confronted by what a critic might say, the stance of the critic is an ethical stance, and, under the right circumstances, perhaps also prophetic. It would be a mistake to view the critic of religion, of science, or of history as someone who simply seeks to downplay, denigrate, or destroy belief in God, who denies the possibility of learning from observation, or who believes that events from the past are indescribable. The "truth" is that the critic is simply someone who underscores the fundamental human dimension of reality as construed through discursive practices. In so far as people are apt to conflate the sign with that which is signified, that is to say, to identify the human concept with ultimate reality – only in so far as that happens does the critic stand judged. But in this case he or she is guilty of nothing more than exposing the humanness of idols, the idolatry of others, and the relativity of "truth."

We should also note – and this is vital for the project we have outlined in this book – that the position of the critic relies upon, and is by no means antithetical to, two essential principles in the study of religion: empathetic identification and defamiliarization. The critic often undertakes the latter – defamiliarization, as we noted in the introduction to this book, is a mode of denaturalizing and humanizing those ideas understood to be familiar, natural, and trans-human. Such an undertaking, we would argue, is only possible in so far as the critic has developed a keen sense of empathy, or the capacity to identify with others. A critic is an architect of exposing the human hands at work behind that with which he or she has, at one level, identified, even if fictionally so. Using José Esteban Muñoz's classification, in so doing the critic "dis-identifies" with persuasive and pervasive cultural, social or ideological forces, or what we would call "hegemony." Disidentification comprises a different set of practices than those that binary, oppositional characterizations might engender. It is a rhetorical strategy through which the critic is able to situate him- or herself as both within and against the so-called "dominant" discourses, as well as participate in the reimagination of codes, tropes, and meanings toward different ends. As a dialectical process, disidentification "scrambles and reconstructs the encoded message of a cultural text in a fashion that both exposes the encoded message's universalizing and exclusionary machinations and recircuits its workings to account for, include, and empower minority identities and identifications."[11] Thus, disidentification takes a different trajectory than counter-identification in that it does not seek to simply reveal and "resist" dominant codes, but also to show their fundamental instability as such codes are reassembled in the service of non-dominant perspectives and positions. This is a crucial point, since the critic ultimately desires to transform cultural logics and societal forms from within a system rather than standing outside. The critic cannot, in fact, stand outside of what she or he seeks to criticize. Adding empathy to this configuration suggests, then, that the labor of the critic is ultimately a labor of love – that the act of exposing the "human hand" is fundamentally about resisting the de-humanization of the subject. Contrary to one popular assumption that the critic "hates" what is being criticized, the critic loves human activity, loves humanity, and loves that which he or she aims to critically engage.

Revisiting the Role of the New Testament Historical Critic

The role of the critic within New Testament scholarship is in some sense inseparable from the elaboration of historical criticism as the classical methodological orientation of the discipline. Biblical scholarship, as an historical enterprise, developed in large part to unmask the unassailable quality of biblical texts and traditions as maintained by church and state hierarchies. As historian Peter Charles Hoffer has noted, before biblical scholarship, and particularly before historical criticism, history and religion "shared a birthright," as "the priests of yore were the first historians."[12] That is, texts like the ones in the Bible were not only accepted as "history" – there was not necessarily a conception of history-writing that was significantly different from the composition of biblical and other "sacred" texts. Moreover, history, as defined by ecclesial power structures, was largely demarcated by dogmatic and doctrinal categories. The rise of historical criticism signified not only a thoroughgoing recognition that texts had original ancient contexts, but that they were of human origin. That is, historical criticism was "critical" in that it exposed the human hands at work in religion. The historical critic, then, emerged not necessarily as a figure who would control meaning, but as a figure who identified meaning-making as a human activity that adapts and changes according to historical, social, economic, and political circumstances. Such moderate to "radical" intellectuals, particularly during the late 19th and early 20th centuries, sought to carve out a space for the critical study of early Christian literature and history, the results of which would not be subject solely to the authority of dogmatic theology or ecclesial hierarchies.

We frequently find ourselves encountering and imagining the endeavors of earlier generations of New Testament scholars. These – admittedly, mostly European and male – critics initiated powerful trajectories of inquiry. Some of them – the moderate more than the radical – are held up still as cornerstones of modern scholarly and academic approaches to biblical texts and traditions. As part of our de-introducing project we have been most interested in the critical impetus and intuitions behind this work and its legacies rather than in the actual content. Identifying the traces of disciplinary genealogies in the process of lifting the curtain on the categories we use in the field should instruct us to see that not only do the categories we take for granted come from somewhere in space and time, but also that historical criticism, historically speaking, has not very likely been as monolithic, hegemonic, or un-critical as some have claimed. As we discussed in the Introduction, some New Testament scholars, particularly those who would identify more strongly with abstract theoretical trends in interpretation or those who would prefer to front identitarian concerns, often dismiss earlier historical critics of a bygone era, along with their historical impulses and contributions to scholarship. By charging historical criticism with outdated dilettante antiquarianism, and recommending that biblical scholars proceed in a more "ethical" manner, such scholars may in effect advocate a turn away from engaging the past altogether. We would argue that scholars ignore these earlier historical critics and the disciplinary histories of which they are a part at great cost to methodological innovation in the present.

In our reading of how the discipline of New Testament studies has come to be narrativized by detractors of historical criticism, that category, like "Marxism," has become something of a dirty and retrogressive concept and method. However, we also wonder if such characterizations function as a means of suppressing and forgetting the radical potential of what was once called the "higher" criticism. Historical criticism emerged as a way to ask critical and imaginative questions, rather than assimilate pat answers, about biblical texts. Further, a basic struggle of historical criticism involves asking who, in the end, "owns" the rights to biblical interpretation, and who can make meaning with biblical texts. At the base of historical criticism, as we see it, is the proposal that what we think texts mean and do for us is, as a result of changes in historical circumstances, necessarily different than what we think the ancients thought they meant and did. Meaning, then, is not natural, inevitable, and universal, nor does it develop in an unbroken line of tradition. In order to trace differences in meaning, one must first trace differences of humanity in variant time periods and cultures. This may entail paying some attention to the ancient world with "eyes wide open" – that is, with the understanding that all engagements with the past occur in, and are shaped by, the present. Again, we have no unmediated access to the New Testament or the ancient worlds that produced those texts. Of course, the reconstructions of what we like to call "the ancient world" have always been debatable, and in the history of historical criticism there have been as many proposals that have become passé as have become axiomatic. Ultimately, however, the premise that textual meaning is not fixed and stable and will change according to time and place depending upon who is doing the meaning-making is, from a methodological standpoint, not all that far removed from the multifaceted counter-narratives invoked as a challenge to the historical-critical status quo. And yet historical criticism has emerged, for some, as a signifier for all that is dusty and backward-looking about the discipline.

The very real question in New Testament studies as to whether, and how, one should learn the vast and varied history of the discipline is not at all settled. For some, we ought to abandon historical criticism altogether in favor of more presentist-oriented approaches, including those that front the identity of the reader and interpreter – since in this schema it is the reader who shapes the questions and concerns brought to the text, and even brings the text into being through the act of reading. We would agree that texts need people to do things with them in order for meaning to be generated, but in our estimation this is also already a methodological feature of historical-critical discourses. We also think it is important to talk about who we are in relation to the texts and our work, since no one comes to the New Testament as a *tabula rasa* or without being socially and temporally located. The politics of identity has emerged as a critical component of doing the work of New Testament scholarship. However, to focus on the identity of biblical scholars to the exclusion of other methodological issues in the discipline is to miss an important opportunity for critical disidentification. As Nancy Fraser has cogently put it, shifting from a focus on the politics of redistribution, or how we can work toward redistributing power and resources in the service of social transformation for all people and not just those with whom we resonate, toward a concentration on the politics of recognition, or the visibility of those who have been historically dominated, has lost a certain measure of credibility as our neoliberal capitalist crisis deepens.[13] Fraser's analysis of political organizing is easily applicable to biblical scholarship: focusing on identity politics and visibility within social hierarchies to the exclusion of broader issues and power configurations may not achieve the goal of transforming the conditions that created such abiding invisibility in the first place. Moreover, as we explored in Chapter 4, it is a hallmark of neoliberal subjectivity that so-called resistant or marginal identities are produced in a context where they are immediately taken up and resignified by the market as a guarantor of dialogue and freedom of expression. Thus, an ethical question that we might pose as we continue to contend with narratives of the field that position historical criticism as the oppressive "center" against which the "margins" push back is who benefits from such discourses, and on what terms. We might also ask whether such narratives about the history of historical criticism and biblical scholarship more widely actually serve to hide more than they reveal about hierarchies and power relationships.

With capitalism in view here, it is worth reiterating that a thoroughly neoliberal economic framework comprises the context in which our identity politics, and all of the work we do, are shaped and articulated. While we are searching for, or recovering, our scholarly voices in relation to what we call traditional historical criticism, and while attempting to narrate something authentic that we can call our own, with its own origins and *telos*, we submit that we often forget an important observation made by critical theory, and most explicitly by Herbert Marcuse: capitalism destroys traditions and particularities, erases memory, and puts a mass culture of self-interest in place, where identity is bought and sold in a marketplace – "branded," as we might say now, in our very late capitalist moment.[14] What does it mean, then, to construct and claim an authentic, and authentically resistant, identity in this context – when the very environment in which we do so leaves us so few options and choices beyond self-interest? In the end, when we narrate identity we are in effect narrating boundaries and limits that may or may not be helpful in terms of understanding the contours of power in the present, and we would do well to think about what we hope to accomplish in so doing. Further, when we attempt to map our own identity categories onto the ancient past, we might consider how such mapping projects contribute to the creation and maintenance of the past we desire to see, including the past within the discipline. In dismissing the history of biblical scholarship as "hegemonic" or otherwise refusing to engage how that disciplinary history has shaped our methodological and disciplinary present, it might be worth considering to what extent we are we in effect helping, as Marcuse would have it, to destroy particularities, erase memory, and foster a culture of self-interest in the name of "innovation."

Moreover, as we think it might be in the ancient world, so it is for the narratives we tell about the discipline: for every story there are multiple counter-stories. In the case of New Testament scholarship, we might also say that the stories and counter-stories about the field may not always be the ones we desire, but that does not necessarily render them irrelevant. It is the relationship(s) we wish to have with these stories, and what that desire says about us, that is worth discussing. To this end, we are not fully convinced by characterizations of the discipline's past as being one of monolithic traditionalism and value-neutral antiquarianism. That does not mean, of course, that there is nothing to criticize about that past, or that there is nothing "wrong" with biblical scholarship of previous eras. However, engaging dead biblical scholars is like engaging dead ancient worlds: such interactions reveal more about us than about them. Just because the questions of past biblical scholars are not our questions it does not therefore mean that their questions were bad or wrong or problematic in and of themselves. We hope that one effect of engaging in a process of de-introducing the New Testament will be to encourage more sustained reflection on how we characterize and continue to refine what it is that we do with our distant, and disciplinary, past as we seek to articulate, defend, and/or transform the stories of the present.

For the biblical critic, then, questions of ethics and audience must be raised in relation to our encounters with and negotiations of the past, as well as in relation to where we think we might go with studies of the New Testament in the future. Perhaps some in the field have not considered some of the questions we have raised in this book to the extent that they might have – not because the field has been unwelcoming, although that dynamic exists, but because for the most part the guild is set up so that scholars who identify with certain "methods" wind up preaching to specialized small choirs instead of posing larger questions related to discourse, power, and method as such. The tendency of the field has been to encourage the proliferation of methods and approaches in the name of "progress" and "difference" and "diversity." To return to Marcuse, it could be said that without critical engagement, we are always in danger of slipping into what he called "repressive tolerance," or the celebration of difference and tolerance to the point that tolerance itself becomes a means of repressing critical engagement and dissent. In the quest for visibility, voices, and acceptance we may in effect downplay our capacity for critical conversation across perceived divisions and boundaries. To move the field forward, we would argue that one potentially productive strategy lies in the need to openly engage in vigorous defamiliarizing, or de-introducing, conversations with people with whom we might not necessarily agree, including people we may have written off – not so we can debate who is more correct, but so we might discuss, as fully as possible, what is at stake in the claims that we make as biblical scholars, the horizon of our labor, and what we will do to move from describing (or narrating) the world to changing it.

It is our view, then, that part of the radical potential of de-introducing the New Testament lies in our refusal to give up on history, and historical criticism, as we continue to think through methodological questions and issues in the discipline. Thus, drawing on this historical-critical inspiration and imagination, and in the spirit of de-introducing the New Testament, we claim a certain responsibility to do history differently, rather than abandon history as a task not worth doing. In our reading of some of the detractors of historical criticism, it appears important to abandon the critical historical impulse altogether because the type of history written by earlier scholars was not done in the same way they would do it, or because there is a sense that paradigms need to be changed. As Edith Humphrey has argued, suggestions about paradigm shifts in biblical scholarship that front the concerns of contemporary interpreters because dominant forms of historical criticism are "oppressive" leave little room for those who are actually interested and invested in the distant past.[15] The critic, however, might say that we would do well to revisit the core issues in historical inquiry in light of changes in configurations of power over time. Rather than support a binary framework that pits history against identity, scholarship against experience, and value-neutrality against ideology, the critic might work to deepen methodological inquiry and expose counter-narratives and counter-historical methodologies that challenge and dismantle such oppositional characterizations. For our part, in this book we have attempted to reveal something of the historical dimensions and power relations inherent in major categories that the discipline has tended to take for granted.

We add a further note of caution, or perhaps encouragement, regarding the history of historical criticism. Failing to properly contextualize earlier scholarship enables the reification of stories about historical-critical discourse that characterize it as "objective," "unbiased," and "unchanging." Just as we encourage our students to become "biblically literate" by reading the actual texts instead of relying on interpretations to see "what the Bible says," we may also learn something from becoming more literate in the history of our own field, to see "what historical criticism says" rather than relying on second-hand narratives and interpretations, which is, sadly, common even among scholars who work within the tradition of historical criticism. As a point of contention, we would posit that one need not search that far in the "old" scholarly literature to see that earlier historical critics quite regularly deployed the rhetoric of change, movement, and subjectivity. There are many examples of earlier historical critics who use such rhetoric, and for our purposes here we choose just one from the American context. In his historical-critical appraisal of the efforts to wrest biblical scholarship away from what he saw as uncritical and controlling dogmatism in the religious institutions of the day, Orello Cone (1835–1905), writing in 1893, offered the following:

> For nothing is historically more evident than that religion, like science, art, institutions of society, government, and all other things finite and human, is constantly undergoing modifications in accordance with the changing knowledge, needs, and civilization which the development of human nature and the general progress of man bring about. Again, it is clear that religion cannot in its nature be fixed, and that absoluteness cannot be predicated of it.[16]

Cone goes on to describe the struggle within historical-critical biblical scholarship to distance itself, methodologically speaking, from theology, particularly dogmatics and doctrinal theology. For Cone, the assumption, taken over from dogmatics, that the New Testament represents a unity of theological and doctrinal perspective has served as an "impediment" to historical criticism, which may in fact reveal less consistency among early Christian texts than theologians might desire. The task of the historical critic, in his view, is to treat the texts as human productions and look at them anew: "[t]he historical and critical treatment of the Biblical writings proceeds upon the presumption that they are literature, and applies to them the canons of literary and historical criticism. It is indifferent to the relations which its results may hold to any doctrines or traditions however cherished and venerable. Its sole aim is to ascertain the facts."[17]

We might now contend that what the "facts" are is subject to much debate and controversy. We might also say that Cone's position on the "facts" is not without ideological dimensions and is conducted in an androcentric manner. However, the context in which Cone is making these claims is key to understanding their potential power as a critical-historical intervention. It is worth mentioning that Cone, an American and a Universalist minister, had studied in Germany and brought that historical-critical tradition back to the United States (at the time, there were very few graduate programs in biblical studies outside of the German context). Unlike their counterparts in Germany, though, scholars like Cone had to contend with such thoroughgoing issues as the fundamentalist/modernist debate, about which they were not shy in mentioning or expressing value-laden judgments – and suffering the consequences thereof! Cone was never tried for heresy, unlike more "famous" historical critics of the same time period such as Charles Augustus Briggs (1841–1913) or Henry Preserved Smith (1847–1927), who were also members of more theologically conservative Protestant denominations. Yet his rhetoric was quite similar. In fact, we are hard-pressed to find where Cone, and others like him, are promoting a "view from nowhere," are hiding their presuppositions, closing off and controlling meaning, or performing hegemonically.[18] To the contrary, we recognize therein a tension and methodological conundrum that has not gone away: namely, how historical critics can effectively conduct their work in as free a manner as possible without having to capitulate to already determined theological conclusions that affirm what is already thought to be the case about the New Testament and Christian origins.

In effect, by contextualizing earlier scholarship in its time period, rather than seeing such studies and figures as a series of fixed points in a linear history of ideas, we might be pushed further to reflect on how those contributions can enhance understandings of the field and the issues at stake within our own contexts, or to identify other issues that might be pressing and in need of attention in our rhetorical situation. The appropriation of ideas without proper attention to history, context, and purpose functions as a kind of proof-texting approach to doing scholarship, which results in a flattening of ideas and, importantly, serves to keep scholarship and texts contained. Our commitment to historical criticism is not to uncritically declare allegiance and defend it at all costs, but to challenge and transform our contemporary scholarly context on methodological grounds. De-introducing the New Testament, then, also includes de-introducing New Testament scholarship.

With a little effort in reading beyond contemporary stereotypes about gender, scientism, and historical and theological naivety, we can read Cone and others like him and see that his work may actually be fairly radical for its time – even as it might not appear to be all that radical now. But as an engagement strategy we suggest using previously radical work to ask ourselves where methodological radicality in the discipline exists now, and on what terms: in other words, we might inquire as to where exactly, among the plurality of approaches called "New Testament studies," is the work of the critic being performed, or we might ask how the role of the critic has changed over time, and to what ends. In our own context, simply to mimic older ideas, or to declare the conversation over or ended without engaging the history of the field, is to disembody those ideas and to take an idealist approach to history that militates against the efficacy of biblical studies in the first place and limits the imaginative and creative potential of historical-critical New Testament scholarship. In our view, rehearsing the history of scholarship in stereotypical ways constitutes a failure of the historical imagination. We have tended to keep replaying the old debates (do we have a stable text? can we get back to an original moment when Christianity began? and so on) on account of such failure. And because of this lack of imagination, we can see how Hector Avalos, for example, would conclude that the study and teaching of the Bible are completely irrelevant in the modern world, and thus should "end."[19] We can also see why Roland Boer concludes that the "problem" with biblical studies lies in what is popularly known as the "seminary model" of teaching and research, from which the Bible itself must be "rescued."[20] Further, we can see how Stephen Moore and Yvonne Sherwood would argue that "Theory" (with a capital T) is what will "save" biblical studies – from itself, or at least from biblical scholars.[21]

While we also are concerned about the direction of biblical scholarship, and we might resonate with such sentiments and conclusions as those mentioned above, we would also submit that there is no way out of these discursive battles, and no way to successfully destabilize the dichotomies that characterize the study of the New Testament, unless we revisit our "first principles" – including the legacies, afterlives, tasks, contours, and implications of historical criticism. Methodologically, failure to do so logically leads to two options in the study of the New Testament: (1) rearranging the data so as to squeeze out yet another nuance to a previously stated interpretive position, and (2) seeking and/or hoping for new discoveries from the ancient world, such as the "James ossuary" or the "metal codices" or the *Gospel of Jesus' Wife* that we in turn have to believe radically transform our understanding of the New Testament and Christian origins, much like the discoveries at Nag Hammadi or the ongoing publication of Qumran manuscripts or the Gospel of Judas are thought to do. Whether they are forgeries or bona fide ancient texts, our desire for such objects actually manufactures their importance and potential. Further, loading such transformative potential onto these objects essentially transfers responsibility from us to the objects – and further stabilizes the notion that there is nothing left to do in New Testament studies without new data. We would argue that the failure of historical imagination, in regard to both texts and histories of scholarship alike, amounts to a failure of the imagination for creative trajectories in the discipline as a whole.

Concluding De-Introductory Thoughts

At the conclusion of *Back to the Future*, when all ends well – better, even – in Marty McFly's present, Doc unexpectedly shows up at Marty's place, back in his DeLorean time-travel machine. He exclaims to Marty and his girlfriend that they need to come quickly to the future, because there are problems with Marty's children. Marty hops into the vehicle without any reservation. As the professor backs up, Marty is concerned that not enough room has been left for the car to reach its maximum speed to effect travel through time. And at that moment, the professor confesses: "Where we're going, we don't need roads." Just then, the car lifts off the ground, speeds off into the sky, and disappears into the future. We have to wait for the sequels to see how Marty addresses the problems with his future children, using, of course, the tools, proclivities, and knowledge from his altered present.

The historian of the New Testament constantly needs to construct a road map to and of the past. The question, however, is this: do we really need such constructions to make inroads into the ancient world? What would happen, for instance, if we did some off-roading? We have tried to do something akin to that in this book. In our de-introductory engagements with critical categories and narratives of New Testament scholarship, we have suggested that understanding, and yet still pushing beyond, the normative constructions and articulations of such categories helps us see the past differently and divergently. Obviously our treatment here has been partial and incomplete, as all treatments are. In what we have outlined, however, we have sought to argue that modern attempts to stabilize and control – and, in some sense, to dominate – the past inevitably produce rather sterile and unimaginative worlds in the present. Somewhat sobering, of course, is that these historical endeavors ultimately are a reproduction of ourselves, and a reification of our world and our relationships with and for each other. Focusing on singularity and stability comes at a cost, since there are always originating points that will of necessity be utilized to fix these coordinates. Who will fix these points? And on what basis will they do so? Social conflict, at all levels, arises not in small part from a difference in where coordinates are fixed and by whom. We could pick any of a host of current debates and "hot-button" issues: Immigration? Gun control? Healthcare? Voting reform? Reproductive rights? Marriage equality? All of these debates rest on particular coordinates that are thought to be fixed and firm. And, as there are evidently already multiple coordinates, it is all the more striking that we proceed in these discussions as if there are not.

In *De-Introducing the New Testament*, we have endeavored to think critically about our discipline by engaging with the questions, categories, and material conditions that shape the field and hail it into being as a mode of inquiry. We have attempted to appraise the stories we tell about the discipline that render its frameworks natural and, in many cases, invisible. And we are well aware that in the process we are telling a story of our own. We have asked questions about that which is ordinarily thought to be unassailable, including narratives that start out as resistant and shift to occupy a normative position. For us, this has been an exercise in the historical and ethical imagination. We have insisted that the study of the ancient world is best understood as way to articulate relationships with that world in the present, in the service of thinking about a different future. The New Testament, mediated by New Testament scholarship, comprises a series of spaces and moments in which we might think about who we are, what we are doing, and why we are doing it. We have, in some sense, gone back to the past in order to see the present and future differently.

However, we contend that going back to the past, especially in the service of either blaming or crediting the past for the present, has never been an innocent exercise, and asking "What would the ancients do?" will not give us any easy solutions to these societal contentions in the present. Perhaps it is not solutions we need, however, but bolder and more robust questions. In a twist on the Socratic maxim, we would suggest that the unexamined past is not worth living out in the present. By that we mean to suggest that we remake ourselves and our relationships with one another and with "our" New Testament in, and through, how we conceptualize, encounter, and "introduce" the past. It is precisely, we believe, in this way that both Nietzsche and then Foucault could refer to the labor of the historian as a *curative* practice. It is noteworthy that Latour, too, sees redemption in the practice of the critic:

> What if hands were actually indispensable to reaching truth, to producing objectivity, to fabricating divinities? What would happen if, when saying that some image is human-made, you were increasing instead of decreasing its claim to truth? That would be the closure of the critical mood, the end of anti-fetishism. We could say, contrary to the critical urge, that the more humans there are, the more human-work is shown: the better their grasp of reality, of sanctity, of worship. The more images, mediations, intermediaries, and icons are multiplied and overtly fabricated – explicitly and publicly constructed – the more respect we have for their capacities to welcome, gather, and recollect truth and sanctity...[22]

The critic does not expose the operations of the hands for the sake of mere provocation or de(con)struction. Rather, seeking to uncover the human labor of being in history and making and inventing history is ultimately a project of challenging ourselves in our own present. We cannot imagine a different and alternate and more humane future if we cannot conceptualize an alternate past. For only in engaging the ancient world anew, with a different map or with no map at all, do we begin to undo ourselves and our own idols and fetishes. And in so doing, we might become more fully human together, roads or no roads, but always by our own, completely visible, hands.

Notes

1. See Ludwig Feuerbach, *The Essence of Christianity* (trans. G. Eliot; Great Books in Philosophy; Amherst, N.Y.: Prometheus Books, 1989).
2. We are indebted in this line of thinking, and in other places throughout this concluding chapter, to Bruce Lincoln's work in methodology in the study of religion.

Indeed, Lincoln's theses on method and comparison, as well as his insistence that religious studies not give up on the historical enterprise, have inspired us to think more critically and expansively about the categories we use as well as the role of the critic broadly conceived. See, for example, *Gods and Demons, Priests and Scholars: Critical Explorations in the History of Religions* (Chicago: University of Chicago Press, 2012).

3. Bruno Latour, *On the Modern Cult of the Factish Gods* (Science and Cultural Theory; Durham, N.C.: Duke University Press, 2010), 71.

4. Latour, *Modern Cult of the Factish Gods*, 72.

5. Michel Foucault, "Nietzsche, Genealogy, History," in *Language, Counter-Memory, Practice: Selected Essays and Interviews* (ed. D. F. Bouchard; Ithaca, N.Y.: Cornell University Press, 1977), 139–164: 155.

6. Foucault, "Nietzsche, Genealogy, History," 158.

7. For fuller discussion of these and other related issues, see Todd Penner and Davina C. Lopez, "Of Mappings and Men (and Women): Reflections on Rhetorical Genealogies," in *Genealogies of Rhetorical Criticism: The Contributions of Hans Dieter Betz, George A. Kennedy, Wilhelm Wuellner, Elisabeth Schüssler Fiorenza, and Vernon Robbins* (ed. T. W. Martin; Minneapolis: Fortress Press, 2015), 245–69.

8. See Karl Kautsky, *Ethics and the Materialist Conception of History* (trans. J. B. Askew; Chicago: Charles H. Kerr & Co., 1918), especially 174–206.

9. Kautsky writes: "It is obviously quite impossible to maintain impartiality when one is interested in any way in the social contradictions and battles of his time, and at the same time sees these phenomena of the present as a repetition of the contradictions and battles of the past. The latter become mere precedents entailing the justification or the condemnation of the former; our judgment of the present depends on our judgment of the past. Can any one to whom his cause is dear stay impartial?" Kautsky, *Foundations of Christianity* (1908; trans. H. Mins; New York: Russell and Russell, 1953), xvi.

10. Kautsky, *Foundations of Christianity*, xx.

11. José Esteban Muñoz, *Disidentifications: Queers of Color and the Performance of Politics* (Cultural Studies of the Americas; Minneapolis: University of Minnesota Press, 1999), 31.

12. Peter Charles Hoffer, *Clio Among the Muses: Essays on History and the Humanities* (New York: New York University Press, 2014), 10.

13. Nancy Fraser, *Fortunes of Feminism: From State-Managed Capitalism to Neoliberal Crisis* (New York: Verso, 2013), 217–223.

14. For an elaboration of this argument see Herbert Marcuse, "Repressive Tolerance," (1965) in *The Essential Marcuse: Selected Writings of Philosopher and Social Critic Herbert Marcuse* (ed. A. Feenberg and W. Leiss; Boston: Beacon Press, 2007), 32–62.

15. See Edith M. Humphrey, "From Chess to Scruples: Changing Paradigms in Biblical Scholarship and the Games We Play," *Canadian Society of Biblical Studies/ Société Canadienne des Études Bibliques Bulletin* 73 (2013–2014): 1–25.

16. Orello Cone, *The Gospel and Its Earliest Interpretations: A Study of the Teaching of Jesus and Its Doctrinal Transformations in the New Testament* (New York: Knickerbocker Press and G. P. Putnam's Sons, 1893), 2.

17. Cone, *The Gospel and Its Earliest Interpretations*, 9.

18. For a more extensive discussion of the historical-critical legacy in the United States, see Davina C. Lopez and Todd Penner, *A House for All People: Engaging American Biblical Scholarship through Its Pasts* (Minneapolis: Fortress Press, forthcoming).

19. See Hector Avalos, *The End of Biblical Studies* (Amherst, N.Y.: Prometheus Books, 2007).

20. For an elaboration see Roland Boer, *Rescuing the Bible* (Blackwell Manifestos; Malden, Mass.: Blackwell Publishing, 2007).

21. See Stephen D. Moore and Yvonne Sherwood, *The Invention of the Biblical Scholar: A Critical Manifesto* (Minneapolis: Fortress Press, 2011).

22. Latour, *Modern Cult of the Factish Gods*, 72.

Index

De-Introducing the New Testament: Texts, Worlds, Methods, Stories, First Edition.
Todd Penner and Davina C. Lopez.
© 2015 Todd Penner and Davina C. Lopez. Published 2015 by John Wiley & Sons, Ltd.

Index